MIGRANT DEATHS IN THE ARIZONA DESERT

EDITED BY
RAQUEL RUBIO-GOLDSMITH
CELESTINO FERNÁNDEZ
JESSIE K. FINCH
ARACELI MASTERSON-ALGAR

MIGRANT DEATHS
IN THE
ARIZONA DESERT

La vida no vale nada

THE UNIVERSITY OF
ARIZONA PRESS
TUCSON

The University of Arizona Press
www.uapress.arizona.edu

Printed in the United States of America

21 20 19 18 17 16   6 5 4 3 2 1

ISBN-13: 978-0-8165-3252-0 (paper)

Cover photography and design by Leigh McDonald
Cover art: by Deborah McCullough, Social Justice Artist

The royalties for this book have been donated to the Binational Migration Institute.

Library of Congress Cataloging-in-Publication Data
Names: Rubio-Goldsmith, Raquel, editor. | Fernández, Celestino, editor. | Finch, Jessie K., editor. |
   Masterson-Algar, Araceli, editor.
Title: Migrant deaths in the Arizona desert : la vida no vale nada / edited by Raquel Rubio-Goldsmith,
   Celestino Fernández, Jessie K. Finch, and Araceli Masterson-Algar.
Description: Tucson : The University of Arizona Press, 2016. | Proceedings of a conference held in March
   2008. | Includes bibliographical references and index.
Identifiers: LCCN 2016007473 | ISBN 9780816532520 (pbk. : alk. paper)
Subjects: LCSH: Illegal aliens—Mortality—Arizona—Congresses. | Illegal aliens—Mortality—
   Mexico—Sonora (State)—Congresses. | United States—Emigration and immigration—Government
   policy—Congresses. | Immigration enforcement—Social aspects—Arizona—Congresses. | LCGFT:
   Conference papers and proceedings.
Classification: LCC JV6475 .M52 2016 | DDC 325.791—dc23 LC record available at http://lccn.loc.gov
   /2016007473

♾ This paper meets the requirements of ANSI/NISO Z39.48–1992 (Permanence of Paper).

*This book is dedicated with profound sadness and
deep respect to the thousands of men, women, and children
who have lost their lives while crossing the desert in
Arizona in search of a better life. May they rest in peace.
Recognizing that the deaths of migrants bring great
pain and suffering to their families, we dedicate
this volume to those left behind as well. May they
find peace and the fortitude to carry on.*

CONTENTS

The Cultural Presence of Death on the Arizona-Sonora
Border and Beyond   244
JAMES S. GRIFFITH

The Last Lords of the Border: A Hip-Hop Day of the Dead   254
JUAN FELIPE HERRERA

Conclusion: An Amen   261
ARACELI MASTERSON-ALGAR AND RAQUEL RUBIO-GOLDSMITH

ACKNOWLEDGMENTS

I N ADDITION TO THE THOUSANDS OF MEN, women, and children who have lost their lives while crossing the desert in Arizona in search of a better life, this book is dedicated, with much appreciation and affection, to Dr. Maribel Álvarez, associate professor of anthropology and associate research social scientist at the University of Arizona. A first-rate folklorist, Dr. Álvarez is a nationally recognized public scholar for her research and leadership in the discipline, including as executive director of the Southwest Folklife Alliance. Her collaboration in this project was instrumental at all levels: selection of the theme for the "No vale nada la vida" (Life has no worth) conference, identification of presenters, and acquisition of financial resources for both the conference and this book. We extend our gratitude thereof to the Ford Foundation, the College of Humanities, and the Southwest Center. It was also Dr. Álvarez who first suggested adding artists as presenters to the conference program. In addition, Dr. Álvarez serves as a trustee of the Library of Congress's American Folklife Center. In 2009–2010, she conducted research as a Fulbright fellow in Sonora, Mexico, on agricultural practices and regional foodways. She has documented the artistic practices of over twelve of the country's leading community arts organizations. She teaches courses on theories and methods of cultural analysis with special emphasis on objects and visual cultures.

This book, and the conference "No Vale Nada La Vida" (Life has no worth), would not have been possible without the support and assistance of many individuals and organizations, and we are deeply grateful for their involvement. Both the organizations and the individuals who assisted in some form along the way are listed here in alphabetical order.

University of Arizona programs that provided support of various types:

Binational Migration Institute
Center for Latin American Studies
Department of Mexican American Studies
School of Sociology
Southwest Center

Without the generous financial support of the following organizations, the conference and book would not have been possible:

Arizona Humanities Council
College of Humanities
El Patronato Pro Educación Mexicano
Ford Foundation
Little Chapel of All Nations
Office of Western Hemispheric Programs
University of Arizona Bookstores

The following University of Arizona faculty members assisted in some form:

Scott C. Carvajal, professor, College of Public Health
Colin M. Deeds, associate director, Center for Latin American Studies
Jill G. De Zapien, associate dean, Community Programs, College of Public Health
Jaime M. Fatás Cabeza, director, Spanish Translation and Interpretation Program
Anna M. Ochoa O'Leary, associate professor and head, Department of Mexican American Studies
Cecilia B. Rosales, associate professor, College of Public Health
Chuck M. Tatum, professor emeritus, Department of Spanish and Portuguese
Scott H. Whiteford, research professor emeritus, Center for Latin American Studies
Joseph C. Wilder, director, Southwest Studies Center

Thanks to the following former and current University of Arizona graduate students:

Consuelo I. Aguilar, Mexican American Studies (sadly, now deceased)
Francisco J. Baires, Anthropology
Luis Carlos Romero Davis, Mexican American Studies
Lorenzo Gamboa, Mexican American Studies
Daniel E. Martínez, Sociology
Robin Reineke, Anthropology
Prescott Vandervoet, Latin American Studies

Finally, we extend heartfelt gratitude to everyone who collaborated in this effort. To all, thank you.

MIGRANT DEATHS IN THE ARIZONA DESERT

INTRODUCTION

¿NO VALE NADA LA VIDA? (LA VIDA NO VALE NADA) (DOES LIFE HAVE NO WORTH? [LIFE HAS NO WORTH])

Cultural and Political Intersections of Migration
and Death at the U.S.-Mexico Border

RAQUEL RUBIO-GOLDSMITH, ARACELI MASTERSON-
ALGAR, JESSIE K. FINCH, AND CELESTINO FERNÁNDEZ

That uncomfortably hot night [June 8, 2002] Enrique Muñoz's phone rang with its first report of a deceased border crosser at 9 p.m., said Muñoz, the director of protection Tucson's Mexican Consulate. . . . By the time the weekend ended, at least 16 border crossers had expired, almost all of them from exposure to the overheated desert, and the deadliest summer of illegal border-crossings had begun." ("Searing Heat, Soaring Toll: Increasingly Crossers Aren't Likely to Survive," *Arizona Daily Star*, September 29, 2002)

MORE "DEADLIEST" summers followed the "deadliest" summer of 2002 announced in the news story above. Statistical data on migration has changed since 2002. So has the number of apprehensions along the border, with variability from year to year. Migrants have increasingly arrived from destinations in Latin America other than Mexico, and research shows that more women and children are now taking the journey to the North. The coverage of these deaths has also fluctuated. Its prevalence in the media for a period of time alerted the public to the issue, and scholars, writers, and filmmakers responded to the silence of death. *The Devil's Highway: A True Story*, by Luis Alberto Urrea, became a national best seller, and *Who Is Dayani Cristal?* was one of the most award-winning documentaries in 2013. Drawing attention as "extraordinary" events, deaths in our desert remain in fact a constant, and their "naturalization," we fear, is increasingly not news; less value, more silence, and justified impunity embalm "death by migration"—the dead of our desert. This volume grew from the conference "Death in the Arizona Desert: *La vida no vale nada*," held in the spring of 2008. Since then, and amid the increasing militarization of the border and growing socioeconomic disparities, our desert continues to render human remains, and with them also our questions remain. Who is responsible? What is a life worth? *¿No vale nada la vida?* (Does life have no worth?)

While embracing a variety of disciplines, each contribution to this volume follows its own methodology and expression in the search for answers to migrant deaths. These multiple approaches speak to the complexity of this tragedy as well as to the accompanying disaster: the plight of the missing. Scholars from the sciences and social sciences apply a variety of scientific and quantifiable methods that allow us to address the evidence surrounding migrant deaths. But academic rigor alone can hardly account for the immensity of this reality and its multifaceted effects on those closest to it and on those seeking answers. Thus, essays, poems, prayers, and ethical and spiritual reflections—in other words, the aesthetic—are, we argue, necessary expressions in the quest for new ways of seeing, listening, and pushing against the absence and silence that upholds impunity. From scholars, artists, folklorists, forensic experts, and social justice activists, our aim is to reveal hidden connections between cultural responses and policy effects, to deepen the conversation and move into action.

In a global context, immigration has been a long-standing historical phenomenon. The process of moving a short distance down the trail or traveling thousands of miles over mountains and across deserts and oceans has been a common human experience since people began to populate Earth. Human beings have migrated for a variety of reasons, including persecution, exploration, and adventure, but the primary reason for human migration has always been survival. From our ancient ancestors' need to find food and water sources to the current dilemma of finding sustainable employment and safe environments, migration has always been part of the human experience. Despite its recurrence and continuity, however, migration remains imbued in controversy and is generally understood as a "problem" if not a "hot" social and political topic.

The Americas have an extensive history of human movements. In the United States, early immigration is associated in the popular imagination with explorers and colonists arriving from Europe since the sixteenth century. However, *internal* migrations shape the region's history well before the European encounter. Furthermore, the Conquest, colonial periods, and national projects throughout the Americas relied on human bodies on the move. The removal and forced displacements of indigenous peoples became tied to those of millions of people arriving from Africa and Asia through the transatlantic and transpacific slave trades that would shape the global economy for centuries to come. In the United States specifically, the predominance of immigrants from Latin American and Asian countries in the late twentieth and early twenty-first centuries changed the trend of previous centuries when those labeled as "immigrants" were largely of European origin.

This book, however, is grounded in a very concrete location: the Sonoran Desert. Our locus of enunciation to address migrancy is the Mexico-U.S. border and the Mesilla Valley specifically. The voices that emerge from this volume are historically and spatially situated and address how a variety of scales—relationships between global dynamics and lived experiences at the local level—manifest through our limited access to those who never made it across our desert. Yet the migrants crossing our border are actors in a worldwide pattern of populations moving from the global south to more affluent national economies, most of them in the Northern Hemisphere. Hence, their reality is not isolated from other locations that have turned into doorsteps to death vis-à-vis global disparities that beg us to question the conversion of life into "cost" and of death into "value." Throughout the summer of 2015, thousands of migrants made it to the international press following their disappearance in the Mediterranean. Their corpses an ocean away lay alongside those found in the Sonora Desert. Whose lives have value? How are some human movements celebrated while others are punished? Deep inequalities speak through the celebratory movement of some—those termed *global citizens, entrepreneurs,* and *professionals*—and the criminalization and annihilation of those unable to cover the costs of "global entry." In his excellent book *Death and the Idea of Mexico* Claudio Lomnitz, one of the contributors to this volume, writes, "The premium on preserving the life of the citizen above all else has been the guiding principle not only of medicine, but also of the modern state."[1] What, then, is the role of the state in the migrant deaths that unify this volume?

Inseparable from U.S. history, migration has more often than not become "outside" of history and treated as "choice," "exception," or "problem" depending on the specific political and socioeconomic juncture. Thus, it has been condemned, encouraged, and often times promoted *and* criminalized simultaneously and in contradictory ways. Yet the increasing role of local governments in policies tied to migration and its actors is a major and particularly salient "new" trend since 9/11 fueled by events such as the recent economic downturn of 2008. For approximately the last 150 years, immigration in the United States had been exclusively a federal concern. During the past decade, however, because of inaction by Congress and overly zealous state and local elected officials, many states and municipalities have taken up the issue and enacted numerous laws and ordinances to govern migration, and specifically unauthorized immigration. In 2011, for example, sixteen hundred anti-immigration pieces of legislation were introduced at the state level; three hundred of these were passed and signed into law. Arizona has been at the forefront of this movement, enacting in 2001 one of the most punitive laws, SB1070 (copied by Alabama with HB56 in 2011). Without a doubt, from state laws to federal levels, human movement has been constrained to the confines of the "legal," and human lives have been reduced to its violation ("the illegals")—even when breaking immigration laws is a civil violation, not a crime. The language of legality ebbs and flows through political forces, often becoming an overwhelming tide, as evidenced when bodies began piling up in the Sonoran Desert. For at least the past thirty years, immigration to the United States has been mostly centered in the Southwest. Today, the desert of Arizona raises deadly concerns that permeate the daily experience of the region's citizens.

This book responds to the consternation and dismay of a growing number of people living in Southern Arizona in the face of the above reality. By the years 2000 and 2001, many involved in migration and human rights issues began calling for an end to increasing numbers of migrant deaths along the Sonora/Arizona border. The humane crises along the border made the national news in 2001 following the deaths of fourteen migrant workers in the desert in western Arizona (documented by Luis Alberto Urrea in the aforementioned *The Devil's Highway: A True Story*). Several new border rights community groups joined older organizations, and the demands for humane borders became in fact a call for the right to live. The summer of 2005 broke heat records, with daytime highs reaching well over 100 degrees and lows in the 80s.[2] But to many, it is remembered as the year when more human remains of undocumented border crossers were found in the Arizona-Sonora desert. The tie between migrating and dying became evident, and the outrage among immigrant rights advocates as well as religious leaders and academics echoed in daily news reports drawing attention to and calling for social action in response to migrant deaths.

Death by migration in general, but specifically along our homes in the Sonora-Arizona desert, raises a plethora of questions. Why are so many people dying *here* on our border? Who are they? Why do they come, and where from? Why do men, women, and children risk their lives in this way? How many die? What are the causes? Is someone responsible for the deaths? What of those who are never found or identified? What do their families know? When there are remains, how are they treated; are they given proper burial? *¿Qué velan las familias* (What remains do families mourn)? What in fact remains?

This volume reflects upon these questions, keeping its grounding on one specific location: the Arizona desert. Why and how has *this* physical space become the end of life and burial ground for so many people on their way to the United States? Most contributors to this volume live and work from this space, and for some of us this desert is our native land. We speak from this border as engaged academics but also as its people—as those who disrupt the narratives of the borderlands as "no-man's-land," empty territory to conquest, or a limbo that migrants cross. Thus, one of the premises of this project is that looking at migration patterns over time and with a focus on Sonora-Arizona borderlands is an analysis of the present but also an exploration into the continuities and persistent legacies of the past. Addressing this reality from the context of Europe, Paul Gilroy reminds us that "migrancy is not about social policy and discussions on diversity and political correctness, but about race."[3] The voices from the border, as Rubio-Goldsmith notes in her piece, speak "the markings of its history." Perhaps they are silenced because it is these markings (memories, remains) that, as she suggests, may "provide a clue into why it is this desert that was pinpointed for harsh closings of the U.S. Border." Those of us from the U.S. borderlands know that the dead bodies in the desert are not "nowhere." They happen on U.S. territory, sometimes less than fifteen minutes from our homes. We also know that dying in the Sonoran Desert is not a "natural circumstance," and we face, as Alex Nava beautifully lays out in his contribution to this volume, having to reconcile its "stunning, even at times, ecstatic experiences of beauty with the horror of history, the experiences of exile and poverty, of violence and war."

The goal of the conference in 2008 was to raise awareness of an already rising concern: the increase in migrant deaths and violence along the U.S. southern border. Nearly a decade later, to our dismay, this volume shares the same purpose. As both part and continuation of the conversations of 2008, it brings together scholars, artists, poets, and others to share the stories and facts about death on the border. But at the center of this volume are human remains, and too many questions remain. Can Gayatri Spivak's seminal inquiry "Can the Subaltern speak?" be asked about the dead?[4] Can they speak? How do we account to what is considered *nada* (nothing)? Who speaks for the dead and disappeared, and how? It seems that politicians, federal policies, and enforcement agencies have decided that these lives have no worth ("*la vida no vale nada*") (life has no worth). We disagree. Does being a poor immigrant relegate one's life less worthy? We think not.

The density of the absence of the dead and the disappeared runs in stark contrast with the lack of answers, and the air-conditioned spaces of our offices serve as *one more* reminder of our physical proximity and simultaneous distance from the lives attempting to cross the desert as we write. Yet this only accentuates our awareness of the ways in which the bundles of remains stored in the medical examiner's office and the silences of the missing are part of our history. We are part of the history of those remains, and accountability, including ours, is much overdue.

THEORETICAL FRAMEWORK: ACCOUNTABILITY, RESPONSE, AND THE UNQUIET SILENCE

This volume is a journey that works through the silences and absence of the dead and the missing. Yet it holds onto unquestionable truths; some traces speak the language of evidence. Studies clearly demonstrate that increased U.S. immigration enforcement has resulted in a twentyfold increase in desert immigrant deaths since 1990 (increasing from a yearly average of fifteen to over three hundred). In 2006, an examination of the records of the Pima County Medical Examiner concluded that people were dying here—in this desert—because of an enforcement strategy launched in 1994 by the U.S. Border Patrol and that extends to current immigration policy. This "lethal plan" is enforced by closing off urban points of entry (beginning with Operation Gatekeeper in El Paso and continuing to San Diego, Douglas, Nogales, etc.) and "funneling" migrants away from urban-accessible locations and into harsh geographic areas.

In the summer of 2007, for the first time in more than a decade of immigration debate, two divergent statistical measures converged: while the number of law enforcement apprehensions at the border showed a significant decrease, the number of deaths among migrants crossing the Arizona desert was the highest ever (the remains of over two hundred bodies were recovered in Pima County alone, excluding other counties such as Yuma, Santa Cruz, and Pinal, where remains of border crossers are also commonly found). With this, the underbelly of a deeply troubled policy is exposed. This is the truth that weaves through this volume: deaths in our desert are, as summed up by Robin Reineke, "preventable, predictable, and violent."

Armed with this knowledge, we seek further answers. Is there something inherent in the particular stretch of the Sonora-Arizona border that opens the door to this travesty on human life? That is to say, what can we learn about the political, social, and cultural life on this border that allowed immigration officials to think that they could bring death to our doors? Was the assumption that we, as inhabitants of this desert, would not notice them? Or was it presumed that we would not question them? Perhaps the underlying idea was that it would be easier to get away with these preventable deaths in our borderlands. Is it possible to find a place on our border where its residents, all of us, can demand an end to the implementation and enforcement of policies that kill?

This volume is a pilgrimage mapped onto that hope. Its voices join in the shared belief that the value we place on death is inseparable from that placed on the living. They also share the need to articulate feelings of helplessness and distress into acts toward "proper" burial, understood as the right to live, to be, and, it follows, to be remembered. The human remains that urge this project on are the presence of an absence. Their silence is a statement to persistent systems of power that are both global and local and where life has cost but no worth ("no vale nada la vida," "la vida no vale nada") (life has no worth). Human remains in the desert hold traces of life, of the life of those who died and of those who remember. They are traces of lives lived, of their personal hopes and actions. But these dead are, as Robin Reineke notes, "unquiet." Their voices join those of the "missing" and could, she argues, carve a space that potentially escapes the control of state narratives. They are markings to larger inquiries about the remains of a colonial history (Rubio-Goldsmith), of global trade from below (Martínez, Prescott, O'Leary, Reineke), of legal frameworks where "human rights" are too often a placeholder for "humans" who have no rights (Durán), and of deeply rooted systems of inequality working through ideologies of class, race, and gender that celebrate free trade, travel, and cosmopolitanism too often at the cost of human lives. As various contributors to this volume show, migrant bodies, turned bundles of absence, fill the arks of many. Javier Durán, for example, shows how "human trafficking and the economic value of migrant life has become increasingly profitable." In response to a context where the "high prof-its" of migrant crossers show a direct correlation to their increasing candidacy for death, each contribution in this volume is an effort to think *from* the lives lost in the desert while critically asking "what they are worth."

Speaking the "unquiet silence" requires many voices, and thus, this volume is a polyphonic effort. Some of us initiated research projects with the objective of providing immigration rights organizations factual evidence to buttress policy recommendations. Others worked the immensity of these deaths through atten-tion to the aesthetic as the means to render the countable and the uncountable (and unaccountable), the material evidence and its missing traces, the observ-able and its "markings" in memory and affect. Any search for truth must chal-lenge the "object" of research to maintain its "vitality." And in order to do this, Edward Said reminds us of the absolute need for the "realm of the aesthetic." In his words, "only the aesthetic rendered the meaning of experience as lived experience."[5] Thus, it is through the aesthetic—religious expression, song, word, and kitchen conversations—that we maintain the dead alive and ourselves— researchers, community members, activists—fully accountable.

To address impunity and injustice we must engage in the production of his-tory. But, as argued by Michel-Rolph Trouillot, "In history, power begins at the source."[6] Our sources are human remains and missing humans. In response to this "incomplete evidence," the work of Bruce Parks and his team in this volume reveals the possibilities of identifying human remains through new develop-ments in forensic medicine. Yet, questions remain. As researchers, advocates, and community members, we cannot speak for anyone, much less the dead. Con-tinuing with Trouillot, we must remain critically aware of the ways in which we inevitably partake in "generating silence while attempting its retrieval."[7] Stuart Hall also reminds us that in order to access the past—our dead—we must nec-essarily engage in its "retelling," a process that he argues is necessarily cultural.[8] Thus, any effort to unveil a truth demands, in Hall's words, "the most complex of cultural strategies."[9] And thus, in order to move away from the master nar-rative, the aim of this volume is to cross disciplines and challenge the bound-aries of the archive, opening spaces of enunciation, shifting, moving, crossing, and bridging matter with absence, fact with feeling.

During his Nobel lecture on December 8, 1982, Colombian author Gabriel García Márquez explained his reference to the *soledad* (solitude) of Latin America:

Poetas y mendigos, músicos y profetas, guerreros y malandrines, todas las cria-turas de aquella realidad desaforada hemos tenido que pedirle muy poco a la imaginación, porque el desafío mayor para nosotros ha sido la insuficiencia de los recursos convencionales para hacer creíble nuestra vida. Este es, amigos, el nudo de nuestra soledad. (Poets and beggars, musicians and prophets, warriors and rogues, all of us creatures of that immeasurable reality have not made large demands on the imagination, because our largest challenge is the insufficient conventional resources to make our lives credible. This is, friends, the knot of our solitude.)[10]

Through his speech, García Márquez claimed a place for writers—*inventores de fábulas* (inventors of tales)—to respond to this "solitude" with a "nueva y arrasadora utopia de la vida, donde nadie pueda decidir por otros hasta la forma de morir" (a new and raging utopia of life, where no one will decide how others live, including how they die). The contributors in this volume claim such a space, aware that academic rigor is not enough to respond to the *realidad descomunal* (colossus reality) of lives reduced to traces in the desert and of hopes reduced to survival. Thus, during the conference in 2008, musicians, painters, playwrights, and poets blanketed public sites. Through the arts and humanities they widened research possibilities and paved new grounds from which to theorize and "crunch" the data on the tragedies covering our beloved desert. Some of these contributions, such as that of Juan Felipe Herrera, the 2012 Poet Laureate of California and recently U.S. Poet Laureate, made it into this volume, but many others did not. Yet the plays, music, and visual art that could not fit its pages are nonetheless within them. And so are the altars, the crosses, the prayers, and each of the signs of collective "truths" that speak from the experience of loss.

OUTLINE OF THIS VOLUME:
PILGRIMAGE TO THE DEAD

With attention to the complex interrelation between evidence and its absence and between the physicality of human beings crossing the Sonoran Desert and the dense aporias and aura of mystery and suspicion surrounding their death or disappearance, this volume is in a way a pilgrimage. It holds to firm beliefs that rely on both evidence and on the belief that we can trace what is no longer there and open new venues to address the humanitarian crises on our border. Its five sections are named "stations" (*estaciones*), the term used to address each of the successive markings of the pilgrim's journey. These stations are linked together through the prayers gathered at weekly vigils led by Father Ricardo Elford for the dead and disappeared in the desert in Tucson's Barrio Viejo and specifically at the local shrine of *El Tiradito* (He who was thrown away). Its adobe structure, varnished with layers from the wax of many candles, holds wishes that span over a century. Its patron, Juan Oliveras, earned the status of "local saint" for nothing other than making mistakes. For loving the wrong person, he was left without proper burial—thus the name *El Tiradito* (He who was thrown away). Also known as the Wishing Shrine, this space earns its power not from past miracles but because it is what Raquel Rubio-Goldsmith addresses as a "memory with warnings." The prayers in these vigils are an expression of collective despair, resonant expressions against forgetting, and, above all, one more historical registry of violence in the borderlands. This volume calls for that kind of pilgrimage. It is a statement against the violence on our borderlands, against the price placed on human lives, and, we hope, one more marker in a long history of voices against impunity; a warning that, even if silenced, the histories of our communities endure.

Station 1, "The Markings of History," sets the tone for this volume. How can we speak of the dead and missing? How do their dim traces walk historical continuities? With attention to history, both authors in this section address the politics of the archive. How can we read the markings of histories with no archive? Claudio Lomnitz asks us to search for these "animas solas," people who die and whom we do not know but who "touch the social life and cultural expression across Mexico and the U.S." These deaths, he argues, are the object of a new political life working through unmarked graves that call for recognition but that simultaneously serve "as a pretext for misrecognition." This volume fights against the latter threat.

Self-defined as a "daughter of this border and student of its history," Raquel Rubio-Goldsmith speaks *from* La Mesilla, the terrain that grounds these graves and that demarks the Arizona-Sonora border. "Why this violence upon our peoples?" she asks. Rubio-Goldsmith questions migrant deaths as inseparable from a genealogy of two hundred years of borderlands history marked by complex ethnic relations and long standing conflicts over its resources. Her piece is a call to "remember." Through her work, the outcome of almost forty years of oral histories, "death by migration" reveals itself as part and parcel of the history of the borderlands, where U.S. sovereignty has worked through violence, injustice, and most of all, impunity. In response to the "code of silence" that is "prevalent in law enforcement agencies and well known in border communities," Rubio-Goldsmith turns to sources *beyond* the limits of the archive. Above all, this author suggests that the dead in the desert have "sparked memories" in the populations of the borderlands that can shed light on migrant deaths. Hence, she expands narrow definitions of *migrancy* as a journey from origin to destination to the experience of "dwelling in displacement" of borderlands communities as described by James Clifford.[11] Through the lens of *diaspora*, a term she does not use but that is implied, Rubio-Goldsmith links migrant deaths to the political struggles that define the U.S. borderlands "in historical contexts of displacement."[12] The deaths in the desert speak to ongoing continuities and persistent legacies of the past that challenge master narratives of U.S. national history.

At the starting point of our pilgrimage, Lomnitz and Rubio-Goldsmith open spaces to ask/read/trace the dead through the cultural practices of the living in a shared effort to address the absent while placing them as historical actors. They push the reader to turn history into a question, to move beyond narrow definitions of historical and scientific "evidence," and to trace the "missing archives" in the historical markings of memories audible in "trusted bars, kitchen tables, and back porches" (Rubio-Goldsmith).

Station 2, "Crossings," interrupts definitions of *migrancy* as tied to movement, calling attention to its very opposite: detention and death. The prayer transitioning to this stop in our pilgrimage speaks to the dreams, frustrations, and plans of migrants in shelters along the Arizona-Sonora border. These are locations of hope and failure, were movement and fixity flow into each other. Prescott Vandervoet and Anna O'Leary walk us through the narratives emanating from shelters in Altar and Nogales, respectively—spaces at the "intersection" of movement across the desert and "detention" by law enforcement. Through the work of these authors, the general label *migrant* proves to be inadequate to describe the diverse human experiences that make way across the Arizona desert. Both contributions highlight the correlation between migrants' increasing exposure to danger and higher economic profits. Thus, the lower the value of migrants' lives, the higher its "value." Women, more likely to die, cost more. The currency of the migrant—their "peso en la frente" (peso on the forehead), as O'Leary highlights in the title to her essay—can be cashed for millions. The voices in O'Leary's piece trace complex economies packed in the silence of the dead. The dried scraps of clothing that adhere to human remains find threads to the pockets of moneylenders, business owners, Mexican police, and officers in detention centers. In life, they sustain hundreds of "hotelitos" (small hotels) in borderland towns, assure the livelihoods of smugglers charging averages of $3,000, and keep cash flowing into Western Union stores (with wire transfers amounting to $28 billion in only two months in Nogales). Following from O'Leary, we add the lucrative business around "deportability," including the profits reaped from cheap labor with no rights. Furthermore, the commodification of "deportable" lives averages $200 per migrant per day and lines the pockets of corporate for-profit prison operators along our border.

In Station 3, "Found Remains, Missing Graves," Daniel Martínez creates the backdrop by highlighting two unquestionable "truths" tied to the dead and the missing: (1) the increase in migrant deaths in Southern Arizona was "a fore-seeable and preventable consequence of enforcement efforts of the 1990s," and (2) the deaths call "for greater attention to issues of structural inequality that force undocumented migration in the first place." Bruce Parks and Robin Reineke, following Martínez, offer two different venues to trace the realities surrounding the dead and the missing. Bruce Parks and his team apply their knowledge to the Pima County medical examiner's office. A native of Arizona and well aware of its social realities, Parks, together with his team, has worked to develop scientific techniques that increase the likelihood of identifying human remains. Their work traces the "living" through anthropologic examination of what remains. The silences of the migrants speak through levels of fluids, glucose, and electrolytes—the complexity of their stories finds its limits in the mummified, skeletal, and decomposed state of that which remains. Reineke, in an effort to reconstruct the story of those who are missing, traces the memories and experiences of those who knew them. The violence of the dead in the desert is inseparable from the violence of the disappeared, those who Reineke describes as "survivors of an absence of something." She effectively shows how the voices of the missing are traces into a regime of state terror that relies on sustaining an intimidated workforce in the interior of the United States; "deportability" therefore becomes the condition from which to generate a surplus out of the commodification of bodies, if necessary through detention and ultimately through disappearance and death. As Reineke explains, "those who cross the border are already missing persons in an international biopolitical system that appropriates them as exploitable bodies."

The prayer that transitions into this section addresses the desert landscape ("we pray for all the migrants who have died in the desert"). In the hope to comfort the dead, this prayer reaches out to the families that mourn them ("comfort their families who mourn") and inserts them in its rugged terrain. Like the contributions of this volume, this prayer does not shy away from speaking against violence and xenophobia ("turn hearts from violence and xenophobia"). The three essays in this section reveal multiple expressions of this violence, from the increase in expenditures for more refrigerators to house growing numbers of dead bodies (Parks) to the violence of "not knowing" if loved ones live. There is the violence of those mourning their dead and of others afraid to mourn their "disappeared" for fear that if they assumed they have died, they might be participating in their killing (Reineke drawing from the work of Rita Arditti), and, above all, the violence of U.S. policies that cash in deaths as tools of "dissuasion," as means to an end that they conceive more valuable than life (Martínez). These three contributions alert not only to the cost of life but to the expenses tied to its absence. Alive, missing, or dead migrant bodies cash profits.

In Station 4, "Metaphors," Alex Nava and Jane Zavisca turn to the traces of language. Nava reflects on the metaphor of the desert in the biblical corpus, and Zavisca analyzes the language of the press as a means into the ideological encodings underpinning public response to migrant deaths. She finds a complex gamut of metaphors that work to naturalize migrant deaths. The desert is portrayed as the agent of death, while migrants become animals, bush, and water, their journey north a "gamble," and their trajectories summoned as "flows." The border, like the desert, takes on human qualities, putting "plugs" on itself and "squeezing" immigrants into its interior. Alex Nava for his part rescues the desert from its metaphorical use in the biblical corpus and articulates it into the terrain where he was born and where he lives. His love for the beauty of this landscape becomes unsettled with the historical processes that speak through the bodies that are washing up onto his doorstep. How do we, he asks, inhabitants of this desert, reconcile its beauty and vitality with its tombs? Like Raquel Rubio-Goldsmith, Nava navigates the porous boundaries between history and memory, and while his argument is broad, there is no loosing site of the terrain of the borderlands and its actors.

Finally, Station 5, "Expressions from the Living Dead," turns again to the question of the "trace," and invites us to read, view, and listen to the cultural expressions—textual, visual, and sonic—that emanate from the reality of migrant deaths; that is, expressions from the absence of the source. Javier Durán notes the inviability of the *testimonio*, arguably the most politically engaged expression emanating from the Latin American literary tradition, to denounce migrant deaths. Once again, we can only engage in (re)presentations and (re)tellings. Durán picks up various threads present throughout this volume (biopolitics, the migrant as commodity, the significance of borderlands history) and, resorting to the tools of cultural analysis, extends our reflection to the Guatemala-Mexico border. Under this light, the militarization of the U.S. border and its deadly practices emerge as a "cultural export," part and parcel of the *dissemiNation*—to borrow Homi Bhabha's term—of social, political, and economic practices that are historically specific and tied to complex processes of production and consumption. In this piece, Durán reiterates the question by Carlos Monsiváis: "¿Adónde vas que más valgas migrante?" (Migrant, where are you heading to raise your cost?) This simple expression of concern, while personal, is in fact denouncing the ways in which the global economy is mapped through the commodification of the migrant's body.

Turning to the lyric and sonic, Celestino Fernández and Jessie K. Finch trace the language of migrancy through attention to music from traditions in both the U.S. and Mexico. Their focus on *corridos* (ballads) is one more invitation to "hear" the missing archive. Engaging in the tradition of the *corrido*, Fernández folds his personal history in the collective pasts and presents of the borderlands to enact his concern with migrant deaths. In composing his own *corrido*, Fernández enacts what Rubio-Goldsmith terms in her piece "memories with warnings"; voices absent from the archive but who made room for themselves through cultural expression tied to survival.

This is also James Griffith's search. His essay walks us into the violence of the borderlands through material expressions tied to the sacred. Here, the traces of the dead manifest through heavily sensorial experiences that are grounded locally: altars, crosses along the roads, living and dead saints, channelings, curations, and ultimately the veneration to Death itself through its materialization in La Santa Muerte (Holy Death). Delineating the tradition of the pilgrimage, Griffith's piece leads the way to the closing contribution of the volume, "The Last Lords of the Border: A Hip-Hop Day of the Dead," by Juan Felipe Herrera, where the sacred and the material, the traditional and the emergent converge in response to migrant deaths on the border—one more effort, the last one in this volume, to trace the dead and track the missing.

Writing from the sensorial immediacy following the various sessions at the conference and in an effort to digest the inedible, Juan Felipe Herrera introduces his piece as the outcome of "footprints baked upon layers of more caked footprints," "wiry tangles" and "charred branches of ink." His point of departure is three bits of information extracted from different sessions in the conference: *animas solas* (lone spirits), nine thousand children in the United States who have lost their parents to deportation, and the new freezer to store dead border bodies. It is clear, then, that as in each and every one of the contributions to this volume, Herrera's departure is cloaked in the absence of what "remains."

Through what he terms SPO-BOMO (Spoken Word Border Movement) Herrera recreates the mystic representation of the desert into the underworld of the Popol Vuh. In his piece, the two twins follow a ball of "remains"—bits of clothing, pieces of those dead in their journey to "North-Country." The piece rearticulates the "crossing" from a linear trajectory to cycles of death and rebirth. The twins return following each of their deaths, and each time they return, they perform. Their bodies are beheaded, frozen, ground, and dumped into the river, where they turn into fish and later into clowns. But because *every* vestige—every remain—holds the power of dancers to be, the twins ultimately win over the Lords. The "ball of remains" becomes the sun (thus, what served as evidence of death becomes a source of life), the Freezer cracks open, and the migrants head "home," which is both north and south. And the river flows, and this image returns us to El Tiradito (He who was thrown away) through the prayer that transitions into this station, the last stop of this volume. We let this prayer, the last one in our pilgrimage, mark the transition to its beginning:

> Flowing out of you and me,
> Flowing out into the desert,
> Setting all the captives free.
> Hope is flowing like a river . . .

NOTES

1. Lomnitz 2005, 16.
2. Even a low of eighty is somewhat deceiving because summer nights remain quite hot; that is, after dusk the temperature drops very slowly so that at midnight it can still be in the nineties, continuing its slow decline, reaching eighty degrees by around 5:00 a.m. and remaining there for only a few minutes, soon rising to ninety degrees by 9:00 a.m.
3. Gilroy 2005, 150.
4. Spivak 1999, 66.
5. Said 1983, 233.

6. Trouillot 1997, 26.
7. Ibid., 27.
8. Hall 1990, 224.
9. Ibid., 234.
10. García Márquez 1982.
11. Clifford 1994, 334.
12. Ibid., 308.

STATION 1

THE MARKINGS OF HISTORY

Envía tu Espíritu
Envía tu Espíritu
Envía tu Espíritu
Sea renovada la faz de la tierra
Sea renovada la faz de la tierra
(Send your spirit
Send your spirit
Send your spirit
Renew the face of the earth
Renew the face of the earth)

BORDER TRAFFIC AND UNMARKED GRAVES

Keynote Speech, March 13, 2008

CLAUDIO LOMNITZ

WANT TO BEGIN by thanking Raquel Rubio Goldsmith and Maribel for inviting me to this conference. It is a privilege for me to be here. I have read a fair amount about the things that have been happening along this border, but this is the first time that I am here, and I have much to learn about the condition of migrants and of immigration today. The invitation to speak is a privilege for me because it is an invitation to learn.

Given my lack of firsthand knowledge of what is happening here in the Arizona desert, my opening remarks are of necessity broad. They are reflections founded on sustained historical work in Mexico, this is true, but they are really only questions and impressions regarding the painful situation that we began hearing about last night and that we will be discussing today and tomorrow. I hope that the questions I bring prove to be helpful as a point of departure for our discussions. I'm afraid that the best that I can do is to share with you where my thinking is at the current juncture and then sit down to be educated by the work of the people who have been brought together for this important dialogue.

ANIMA SOLA (LONE SPIRIT)

The death of an individual is always an occasion in which social ties are made evident, in which they are at play. These ties are defined in many ways: they may be ties of friendship, of community or national belonging; they may be monetary ties linking an immigrant and a coyote; ties of solidarity based on identification between immigrants; ties of duty between a local official and a corpse; ties of solidarity between a landowner and an immigrant crossing her terrain; rivalries between documented and undocumented people.

I want to begin by thinking about the implications of dying in the desert from the viewpoint of community and national ties. Dying away from the village or town community of belonging is a phenomenon that has a deep history. The Portuguese, who were a maritime nation and part of the Spanish kingdom for about a century, were haunted by sailors who had never returned or been heard from again. *Saudades*, a nostalgia for home, came to be nationalized as Portugal's most characteristic sentiment, soulfully invoked in the fado, and written about by intellectuals interested in defining the character of their nation. As part of this configuration, Portuguese villagers built shrines to the so-called *animinhas*, or little souls, in the outskirts of their towns. Villagers worried about the lonesome and tormented souls that wandered about in hunger and thirst, forgotten by their relations, and perhaps also bringing suffering to the living who ignored them. In those shrines villagers made their offerings for the unnamed dead, who had died far away, forgotten or unrecognized by their families. The *saudades* (longings for home) of the sailor, then, are in fact only part of the national picture; the haunted village is the unnamed part. I believe that something like this phenomenon is occurring in Mexico and in the United States today.

Concern for the souls of unmourned dead, who were left to languish in Purgatory with no champions among the living—the concern, that is, for the *anima sola* (lone spirit)—was also a staple of Mexican village religion at least from the seventeenth century forward. In that context, people went missing not so much through maritime travel but rather because of internal migrations: people who had gone to work in mines or as muleteers, or simply as displaced vagrants, as *forasteros* (outsiders) who begged for work in the colony's towns and cities.

Today, we have a revival of this phenomenon on a massive scale and in a new international context. The deaths of thousands of migrants trying to cross into the United States through the desert is the tip of an iceberg of missing souls of women and men whose fates are uncertain or unknown to their families and to their communities because they have not written home or called or been heard from. Like the *animinhas* (little souls) of Portugal, it is likely that their souls will come to haunt social life in Mexico in ways that we still do not fully comprehend but that may yet become as pervasive as *saudades* (longings for home) have been in Portuguese popular and erudite national culture.

So, for instance, the number of assassinated women in Ciudad Juárez has kept mounting year after year, drowned at first in a sea of local denial and misrecognition. The phenomenon of women going missing has since been described as a common feature of our cities of migrants. It now haunts our understanding of who we are and of where we live.

There is something new about these forms of disappearance that I have difficulty thinking about. It was once the case, I believe, earlier in the twentieth century, that the cities that attracted migrants as laborers tended to be well policed. The connections between the great local industrialists, city governments, and policing in industrial towns such as Monterrey, in Mexico, or Medellín, in Colombia, or Rosario in Argentina—the "Manchesters" of their nations—were usually relatively tight, and the possibility of having hundreds of working women murdered and disappeared in a steady trickle was unthinkable.

There is, it seems to me, something new in contemporary modes of death and disappearance among urban immigrants within Mexico, and I would like to try to characterize it, very provisionally, before giving closer consideration to the situation of migrant deaths in the border crossing, because death and disappearance along the border is related to this phenomenon.

There are three qualities that seem striking about the current situation from the viewpoint of Mexican institutional and political history. The first is the intensity of a biopolitics in the current era, the second is its contrast with a relative underdevelopment of biopower, and the third is the disjuncture between open discussion of risk and death in the public sphere and the work of local policing and of local justice. I hope that I may be forgiven for moving so quickly into highfalutin terms such as *biopower* and *biopolitics*, but I only have fifteen minutes in which I can address you.

I say that there is an especial intensification of biopolitics in Mexico because democratic mobilization around public welfare is perhaps more intense than it has ever been—mobilization around health, education, and public safety, and also governmental discussion of these issues is the bread and butter of contemporary political life. In this context, the deaths in Ciudad Juárez—and in the desert—are today the subject of discussion in the media, the object of NGO organizing, and of countless state commissions and organizations. The discussion of disappearances of people and of their deaths has become, for this reason, something of a "crónica de una muerte anunciada" (chronicle of death foretold). The media and a set of governmental and nongovernmental institutions are ready to count bodies that they know will be showing up.

What I mean by a relative underdevelopment of biopower in the midst of this intense "biopolitics" is that the system of institutions that was designed by liberal governments to shape the ideal citizen—the schools, the hospitals, the courts, the modern penitentiaries and houses of reform—is today relatively corroded. Indeed, this corrosion is part of the reason why people leave towns and cities in the first place; and it is part of the institutional context of their deaths or disappearance. So we have an intense democratic biopolitics with a relatively weak institutional framework with which to actually provide the kind of attention that a welfare state once hoped and tried to provide to its citizens.

Finally, the third characteristic that I named pertains to the question of policing and of justice. These institutions of public safety and of dispensation of justice in Mexico still appear to be out of sync with the intense demands of public safety, security, and accountability that drench the daily news and that are pervasive in contemporary political life. As a result, we have a situation in which individuals can fall through the cracks of political institutions with relative ease and where these disappearances will become known: known perhaps to their families in a dreadful phone call or by e-mail; accessible to the public as statistics through the offices of local morgues, or thanks to the militant work of NGOs or of artists or indeed of governmental organizations. This is an especially disturbing aspect of contemporary unmarked deaths in Mexico: they are deaths alone, deaths severed from familial and community protection, but they are also deaths that are in many ways recovered in the intensity of contemporary biopolitics. These lonesome deaths are the object of a new political life.

BAD DEATHS AND SOCIAL RECOGNITION

In the colonial period, the fear of a sudden death, or more generally of a bad death, was so intense that religious life was to a large degree organized around religious sodalities that were designed to prevent this possibility. Working people pooled their meager resources to insure that their souls would receive proper care from members of their *cofradías* (brotherhood) upon their death. A good death was a death within the fold of religion, of family and community: surrounded by loved ones, having had time for confession of sins past, and having had time to arrange one's affairs, with the local church bells pleading for one's soul at the very instant of its separation from the body.

The deaths that are occurring here in the Arizona desert are distressing for so many reasons that I can hardly begin to enumerate them. One of these, though, is that the trek across the desert is so often predicated by an ideal of family unity and reproduction. Deaths in the desert in some regards represent a shattered unity in so far as they are the opposite of the ideal of the good death. Death in the Arizona desert is not the death of old Odysseus, back home in Ithaca, who grew old by his Penelope and his Telemachus, and who lived to be recognized upon his return by his nurse and by his expiring dog; it is, instead, like the death of so many of Portugal's unsung sailors, who died at sea, in another desert. There is some collective haunting that is bound to result from this. When Mexican artists say that the border is a scar that needs to be healed, they are in some ways displacing onto the border the wounds that are fracturing family reproduction across the entire nation. This displacement, which is so characteristic of public discussion of immigration in Mexico's media, may come back to haunt Mexican society in ways that we still do not comprehend.

THE WALL

Anti-immigrant groups sometimes hold up signs that read: "What part of the word 'illegal' don't you understand"? In fact, there are a number of connotations of that we don't understand—and it is not because we speak Spanish; not even the minutemen understand them.

The management of the border has been a biopolitical concern in the United States for close to a hundred years, as shown by Alexandra Stern's work on the history of eugenics and its connections to the institutional history of border crossing. Beyond early anxieties around the management of race, regulation of migratory processes manifests a desire to manage population movements in an international context similar to that I outlined for Mexico. That is, to manage the population in the United States when the institutional mechanisms for population management south of the border—biopower—are comparatively weak. This is a very difficult proposition that has already begun to lead the United States down the path to becoming a security state, concerned principally with risk management rather than with popular welfare. For such a state, deaths in border crossings are statistically measurable, and their publication and publicity may be a source of national embarrassment, but it is also a figure that can be used to infuse migrants with a sense of calculation of risk and so help contain migration in an institutional channel that is acceptable to the security state.

This strategy, however, presents many new problems that I know I will learn about in the discussions of today and tomorrow. One of these problems is that it turns the desert on the U.S. side of the border into a mass unmarked grave. As a result, residents in areas of border crossing become the point of human contact in a system that is trying to channel migration to institutional, rather than interpersonal, settings. There is, for this reason, a new kind of humanitarian crisis in certain regions of the United States, where local residents have become mourners of people who die and whom they do not know, like the old villagers making shrines for the *anima sola*. The humanitarian crisis on the U.S. side of the border pertains not only to the plight of the immigrants but is also manifested in the lives of local residents who become aids to the immigrants. They become the first people who do not understand the multiple parts of the word *illegal* even though they may be the prototypical upright and law-abiding citizen.

My point in these remarks is relatively simple. Each death in an unmarked grave is a call for recognition, though it can serve as a pretext for misrecognition. When a team of forensic doctors finds bones in an unmarked grave, they try to determine the date, context, and cause of death and to identify the individual who left these remains. When a local rancher picks up the remains or garbage that migrants strewed along their paths before expiring, he conjures up an image of the travail of the migrant and of her or his identity.

The people who die crossing this border are calling to be recognized. This call for recognition touches social life and cultural expressions across Mexico and the United States. It is much more than the border that needs healing. I look forward to beginning this work of recognition in our discussions today and tomorrow. Thank you.

REFLECTING UPON VIOLENCE, INJUSTICE, AND IMPUNITY IN SOUTHEASTERN ARIZONA

RAQUEL RUBIO-GOLDSMITH

We live without feeling the country beneath our feet,
Our words are inaudible from ten steps away.[1]

S UCH ARE THE WORDS AND FEELINGS that go through mind and heart each time I hear of another death in this desert. As a daughter of this border and student of its history, I ask the questions, why this violence upon our peoples? Why in this place? Why on the most vulnerable? As a historian, my first inclination is to turn to the past, to look more closely into our desert stories, stories that may help us understand the tragic times in which we live.

In order to do this, I turn to the work of many. Edward Spicer, an anthropologist studying Southwestern cultures, inspires generations of thinkers with his inerrant framework that exposes the violence resulting from continuing cycles of conquest.[2] Luis González y González implanted in my mind the greatness of microhistory;[3] his utter respect for the voices of all in San José de Gracía, in the Mexican state of Michoacán, teaches historians how to dig into the unknowns of master narratives. I gained courage to examine proposals from Walter Benjamin,[4] who reminds us that to articulate the historical past does not necessarily mean to tell it exactly as it was; rather, he poses, it entails appropriating a memory, as this memory provides a lightning rod at a moment of danger. I also call on James Scott's enduring trust in a universally held sense of justice and alertness to the multiple forms of "carefully calculated conformism."[5] I find guidance in the pathbreaking work by Alessandro Portelli and specifically in his insights on meaningful interpretations of oral history.[6] And of course, I am further encouraged by the outstanding work of many scholars who have opened the academic doors to the study of violence as an integral element in our understanding of inter-ethnic power relations in the reconstruction of the history of the West. With all the above works in mind, this paper turns to the memories of those called Mex-icans and/or Mexican Americans as they remember experiences of violence, injustice, and impunity in Southern Arizona. The analysis of interviews I have conducted with residents of Douglas, Arizona, since 1978 reveal continuities that shed light into the region's history. Combined with journalistic accounts and my own testimony, these interviews invite us to ask and reflect on how particular events of violence and injustice are remembered. How do these memories tran-scend the particular incident and inform other instances of injustice? What do they reveal about the ways in which impunity is understood and lived?

Can the past, the remembered past, respond to questions of the present? González y González, delving into the uses of history, recalls the words of José Miranda, Mexican historian, who stated,

> historical knowledge is not good to resolve the problems of the present; it does not immunize against the atrocities of the past; it teaches nothing; it avoids noth-ing; from a practical point of view, it is not worth a farthing [*un comino*].[7]

However, if on the one hand González y González recalls the uselessness of history, he also turns to the understanding of history as liberation in the works of Diderot, Voltaire, and other revolutionaries for whom the past was a teacher for the future. Particularly in prerevolutionary times, the past is called on to understand the workings of power. For those stumbling along the path of time and seeking ways to build a better world, the study of the past reveals continui-ties, disruptions, and possibilities. Living in the twentieth- and twenty-first-century United States, I join these efforts, looking into the past while sustain-ing a vision toward the future.

Filled with the hope that human beings can learn to create a world of jus-tice for all and as a firm believer in the rule of law and human rights, I turn in this chapter to the memories—lessons in the present—of a small community of *Mexicanos* on the Arizona-Sonora border. This journey is not without chal-lenges. If the study and writing of history has its rules, can the questions I ask of the past to a marginalized ethnoracial group in "the middle of nowhere" allow for an examination of the ways in which violence, injustice, and impunity are experienced and remembered? Positivistic, or, shall I say, scientific history demands a narrative based on official or at least hegemonic sources—an analysis of the archive. Yet the sources of this narrative are the memories and stories transmitted to me by persons all too familiar with the ways in which violence is lived—the ways in which they remember, I suggest, shed light into the silences of the past and are, in fact, a vivid trace. Portelli explains that oral history is not about facts necessarily, but rather about meaning. In agreement with his insight, my intention is to reflect on the stories. Their memories are part of my own, and my history is glued to their trace. Perhaps this essay should be two. One that carefully and diligently enumerates the long chain of acts of direct violence as well as the subsequent injustice and impunity born of such acts, and another that analyzes the memories of these acts as told by those who can't afford to forget. But they are all too tied. Thus, in this paper, I do a bit of both in an attempt to come closer to understanding violence, injustice, and impunity.

VIOLENCE, INJUSTICE, IMPUNITY

The terms *violence*, *injustice*, and *impunity* are difficult to visualize. Perhaps the former, *violence*, pushes more images to the fore than the other two. And yet all three are intimately intertwined. Without ignoring the evident specificities in defining these terms in time and place, in essence, human societies determine how violence is controlled, how justice is meted out, and the degree to which impunity is acceptable.

As an object of history, violence is too often regally enshrined in military and triumphal imperial histories. Meanwhile, structural violence, in its direct physical manifestations, in its complex social, cultural, and economic workings, and as experienced by so-called marginal or powerless groups, is often shunted. Historian Ned Blackhawke writes, "The narrative of American history . . . has failed to gauge the violence that remade much of the continent before U.S. expansion. Nor have American historians fully assessed the violent effects of such expansion on the many Indian (and I would add, Mexican) peoples caught within these continental changes."[8] The study of illegitimate violence visited upon peoples of Mexican descent living in the borderlands and in the United States, in spite of the pioneering historical studies by Rodolfo Acuña, is in its infancy.[9]

Injustice and justice, allow me to remind us, is, according to the social contract, to be meted out by the state. Citizens are not allowed to take justice into their own hands. The state, under the same social contract between the governed and the governing, is granted a monopoly over the use of violence. Injustice in the face of hidden or blatant state or vigilante violence is the usual consequence of illegal use of force. Injustice results when laws, practices, or both violate constitutional mandates. But one need not know the legal requisites to understand when an injustice is committed, and the sense of justice not received drives strong responses. On the border, inhabitants at times resist publically, but often resistance takes the form of narratives, some popular lessons and guides to the present, and others underground shouts of frustration. The positivist historical method is ill equipped to work these grounds.

Impunity, according to contemporary human rights scholars, is defined as the purposeful acts of government that protect "the powerful" from mandated consequences. In other words, some people get away with wrongdoing while others are denied justice when they are victimized. On the border, as part of a democratic republic based on the rule of law that declares equal treatment, the perception people hold of how justice is meted out is fundamental to a well-integrated and functioning citizenry. Injustice and impunity are enemies of what a democratic republic stands for. Therefore, I consider it important to know how justice, injustice, and impunity have fared for *Mexicanos* living in our border communities and how that may influence how recurring injustices are viewed. This essay calls on memories of a silenced group of voices to reflect on the present day and on what they might suggest about the ongoing humanitarian crisis on our border, the U.S.-Mexico border. Oral histories, testimonies, and lived experience all contribute to filling in the shadows of border history for those seen as "not American" or "not American enough."

LA MESILLA: DYING FIELD FOR MIGRANTS IN THE TWENTY-FIRST CENTURY

Space is not merely geographic contours. The land reflects human perceptions and meaning. We attach names to geographic configurations, establishing our views of what that land means to us. Geographer Joseph Nevins introduces his vision on the U.S.-Mexico border:

> While shaped to a significant degree by physical forces, geographic space is largely a social creation in terms of what is contained within it, how it is divided

up and bounded and how it is perceived and lived. It is thus a product of power relations and all the conflict—as well as cooperation—that they entail.[10]

La Mesilla, the specific region that demarks the Arizona-Sonora border, manifests through numerous markings its recent history. Road signs in English with distance measured in miles, high-reaching metal fences dividing urban spaces, checkpoints on highways, rivers, and mountains boasting names in Tohono O'odham and Spanish, all social constructions that in turn reveal the evident and the hidden power relations played out by the multiethnic, multiracial residents of these desert lands.

Border historian Oscar Martínez succinctly reviews the history of this demarcation, writing,

> The creation of the U.S.-Mexican Boundary is best understood as a long historical process that began in the sixteenth century when England, Spain and France competed for control of North America and that ended in the mid nineteenth century when the United States absorbed large portions of the Mexican northern frontier through annexation, warfare and purchase.[11]

Mexican territorial loss ended with "the final transfer of territory" through the signing of the Gadsden Treaty, which "occurred in 1854 when the United States purchased the Mesilla strip, consisting of present-day southwestern New Mexico and southern Arizona."[12] La Mesilla in Arizona covers the land south of the Gila River to the thirty-fifth parallel.

Not mentioned in the Gadsden Treaty is the Tohono O'odham nation, whose ancestral lands are divided by this boundary. This treaty does not confer U.S. citizenship on the members of said indigenous nation (nor does the Treaty of Guadalupe Hidalgo), though citizenship was conferred to Mexican residents who remained in La Mesilla after territories were transferred to the United States. The political identity bestowed by the nation-state to delimit rights and responsibilities does not respond to the clear and firm definitions most people might imagine. Borders between nation-states provoke constant redefinitions and reimagining of the various components of what it means to be a citizen of each country. For example, *Mexicanos*, persons of Mexican descent living in territories formally ascribed to Mexico, experience continuous depravations due to the renewed sense of the U.S defeat of an "inferior Mexico." That is to say, competing sovereignties in the bodies of border inhabitants are at the center of what Ana Alonso so aptly exposes:

> From a border perspective, sovereignty is not an attribute, but rather an ongoing and variable project of states and of groups which is more or less realized in practice. In addition, the state is not the only "sovereign body." Other territorially based sociopolitical bodies—from Indian nations to corporation communities . . . also compete for sovereignty both in relation to each other and to the state. Rights to resources, property, and territory are key stakes in these struggles, which are often legitimated by ethnocentric distinctions between "us" and "them," "here" and "there." Since the 19th century, U.S. nationalism had proclaimed the superiority of whites versus Indians, Asians, blacks and Mexicans, while the supporting ideology of Anglo-Saxonism has stressed the merit of pure race over hybrids. This ideology has located Anglos at the center and other groups—internal others—at the margins of the nation.[13]

If the state is the sole entity with the legitimacy to use violence and regulate its processes, it is reasonable that the memory of violence, injustice, and impunity are topics of repeated resonance for *Mexicanos* living on the border.

DOUGLAS, ARIZONA: WHY ORAL HISTORY

Written sources, with the exceptions of relevant court proceedings—such as the telling of the stories of the Camp Grant massacre in 1871, the Bisbee Deportation in 1917, and the killings at Miracle Valley in 1982—rarely include the voices of Apaches, *Mexicanos*, or African Americans. Following a similar pattern of voices silenced in public spaces, events such as the torture of three Mexican migrants by the Hannigan family outside of Douglas, Arizona, and the shooting death of Dario Miranda Valenzuela outside of Nogales, Arizona, are not unlike other incidents of abuse of state power. These events enter the encyclopedia of memories for *Mexicanos* living in border communities, and these stories are told and retold to remind others that peaceful-looking communities can deceive.

For the purposes of this essay, my interest is to unearth the memories of these incidents as a lens into history as lived by various relevant ethnic communities. How these events are remembered and why these stories are told are central questions into the larger U.S. history. Portelli affirms that "the first thing that makes oral history different . . . is that it tells us less about events than about their meaning."[14] I do not pretend to uncover all the meanings available through oral narratives remembering past incidents; rather, I intend to show that these events are engraved in the *Mexicano* memory of lives on this border. Furthermore, Portelli emphasizes that "what informants believe is indeed a historical fact (that is, the fact that they believe it) as much as what really happened."[15] Thus, in this paper, the historical events informed through the memories of Manuel Rubio, Saúl Quesada, Julio Vásquez, and Antonio Martínez and their wish to pass them onto others are understood as historical evidence. The purpose is not, thereof, to prove a specific "truth," but to offer a written rendition of their stories. In other words, and as historian Antonio Garcia de León writes of the indigenous history in Chiapas, "los muertos nunca mueren" (the dead never die);[16] they are kept alive when their stories are told and retold.

The oral histories included in this chapter are part of a corpus of interviews conducted over a forty-year period mostly in Douglas, Arizona. Douglas, a relatively new rural community in the region founded by the Phelps Dodge Company in 1901, is situated right on the border, directly across from Agua Prieta, Sonora. Douglas has a significantly different history than the long-settled city of Tucson, located sixty miles north of Nogales, Arizona, and which has been described by ethnohistorian Thomas Sheridan as the northern point of the cradle of Hispanic culture in Arizona.[17] Tucson is a true crucible of layering of conquests and cultures with at least four languages spoken within its boundaries (Tohono O'odham, Yoeme, Spanish, and most recently, English). Although Phelps Dodge shut down its Douglas smelter in 1987, the border town today does not differ that much from the unofficial copper company town originally heavily populated by "new" Mexican arrivals seeking refuge from revolutionary violence in Mexico during the first two decades of the twentieth century. Today, newly immigrated *Mexicanos*, with and without authorization, are a strong demographic presence. Douglas was an industrial town forming one point of the triangle of three communities, two in Arizona and one in Sonora, all sites owned by U.S., Canadian, and British copper companies. While there are differences between Douglas and Tucson, a larger city and a university town, both communities are considered "border communities." Both have defined whiteness as a condition for recognized citizenship, and thus, for residents of Mexican descent, legal status does not eliminate the social disparities in access to education, jobs, public resources, and social practices. The boundaries between *Mexicano* residents and white society are further defined through the interaction with border authorities, commonalities in both communities, and varying discretionary moments.

REMEMBERING: FIVE CASES OF IMPUNITY

Memories, individually told but forming part of a collective past, open a window into previously silenced histories. This essay covers five selected historical events of violence along the U.S.-Mexico border. None is an official memory recognized in the state's historiography, and yet all stand out in *Mexicano* memory. In some cases, the perpetrators were neither sought nor accused nor indicted. If ever indicted, juries and judges did not find them guilty in spite of strong and convincing evidence to the contrary.

I address two types of cases: three cases of state and vigilante activity (Camp Grant, the Bisbee Deportation, and Miracle Valley) and two cases where the perpetrators were accused of "individual" acts (the torture of three Mexican migrants by the Hannigans and the murder of Darío Miranda Valenzuela at the hands of a Border Patrol agent). All these cases (not unlike multiple other cases of border violence visited on people seen as inferior, "foreign," and, simply put, "not quite human") provide a backdrop and possible clue into why it is this desert that was pinpointed for harsh closings of the U.S. border.

CASE 1: CAMP GRANT MASSACRE

In an interview in 1980, Manuel Rubio remembers the Big Sycamore.[18] He passes on the story as it came from his cousin Sadie but adds his own experience of seeing a picture of a dead Apache, killed by a *Mexicano* in Douglas in 1927 or 1928:

> Fue allí donde esta ese árbol muy grande. El árbol más grande que he visto en Arizona. Le dicen "Big Sycamore." [It was there where that very big tree is. The biggest tree I've seen in Arizona. They call it "Big Sycamore."] It was my cousin Sadie who told me about Arivaipa Canyon. It is beautiful, a creek that always has water, and at that place there is a huge sycamore. Sadie, who lived in Mammoth, told me that it was not a good place to camp. But I went anyway. I wanted to see the place. Too many spirits. Some people, soldiers from Tucson, had killed a lot of Apaches there a long time ago. You know, when I was growing up, your

grandmother always told us how cruel the Apaches were in Chihuahua. Mexicans were always talking about it. I even saw it here in Douglas in about 1928 or 1927. There was a picture of a *Mexicano* who said an Apache had captured and killed his son, holding the head of an Apache by the hair . . . just the head. He said he had killed him for killing his son. But who knows if it was the same one that killed his kid. Nothing happened to the *Mexicano*. Sadie used to say nothing happened to the soldiers who killed the Apaches.

Even if this Camp Grant massacre memory has some factual mistakes, it is clearly a vivid memory with warnings, a story that provokes reflections on the horror of Apache deaths and acknowledges a certain impunity.

Numerous accounts of this tragic event exist. Citing Sheridan, feminist scholar Nicole Guidotti-Hernández outlines what she calls the common narrative.

Don Jesus Maria (Elias) and his friend William Oury masterminded an even larger assault upon the hated Araviapas (Apaches), who were camped under the protection of the U.S. military near Camp Grant on the San Pedro River. Known as the Camp Grant massacre, this expedition turned into a frenzy of violence in which more than one hundred Apaches, all but eight of whom were women and children, were slaughtered.[19]

In her seminal work on gender construction in northern Mexico, Alonso lays the foundations for Guidotti-Hernández's retelling of the killing of Apache women.[20] Guidotti-Hernández, reviewing violence in former Mexican lands, proceeds to unravel and retell the Camp Grant massacre, demonstrating the complexity of ethnic relations among the groups living in La Mesilla territories.[21] First, she points to marriages by Anglo males seeking fortunes to Mexican females, usually daughters of well-placed Mexican families. By this time, the definitions of maleness in Mexican *norteño* (northern) society had already been established to include clear roles, such as being good Indian fighters. The long-standing conflicts with indigenous groups over use of land and water resources provoked over two hundred years of hostilities. Settlers were part and parcel, first in the Spanish and later in Mexican strategies, joining forces with presidio military forces to fight the Indian attacks or simply Indian existence. At that time, to be a barbarian was synonymous to being an "Indian" and vice versa. Although some indigenous people were later described as peaceful and hardworking, such as the Tohono O'odham and Pima (canceling those occasions when Pimas had fought for their lands against the Spanish or Mexican onslaughts), those named

"Apaches" were categorized as savages and almost inhuman. During the late nineteenth century, Anglos arriving in Tucson and Arizona in general were well schooled in the idea that "barbarians" could not make proper use of natural resources and thus they, the "civilized peoples," had an obligation to do so regardless of what that meant or did to the so-called savage peoples. Similarly, the Tohono O'odham saw the Apaches as their clear enemy to the point that the word for *Apache* in the Tohono O'odham language is *enemy*.

Apache attacks on ranchers and settlers were a constant source of fear and anger in Tucson. The newspapers detailed Indian, or rather Apache, assaults, raids, and killings as well as the U.S. Army's announcements of cavalry raids, captures, and even treaties. But the fevers of fear resulted in citizens deciding that government action was not satisfactory or effective and that they had to take the situation into their own hands. So it was that a coalition of Anglos, Mexicans, and Tohono O'odham peoples decided to attack Apaches camped out near Camp Grant, where they were at the invitation of military authorities at the camp.

When word got out regarding the raid on Apaches, and that it was mostly women, children, and old men who were killed, people in other parts of the country voiced outrage. In Arizona, however, voices criticizing the killings were muted. The judicial system of the territory was brought into play. Indictments were announced. However, at the end of the trial, the jury deliberated for a mere twenty minutes before declaring the defendants not guilty; impunity.

Although the killing of Apaches could be rationalized based on stories of cruelty and killings committed by Apaches, Mr. Rubio's narrative above expressed a sense of wrongdoing and especially noted that the *Mexicano* who boasted killing the Apache who murdered his son could have been mistaken. Mr. Rubio's words point to the lack of accountability for the deaths, even of Apaches. Further, remembering Sadie's warning to stay out of Arivaipa confirms the longstanding knowledge of a horrible violence. The dead could not rest peacefully after their violent deaths, nor could their spirits rest. So it is best to warn others to stay away. These are stories that are not easily told, but when heard, they are never forgotten. Fortunately, Ian W. Record has now published the Apache memory of this tragedy in his book, *Big Sycamore Stands Alone*.[22]

CASE 2: BISBEE DEPORTATION OF 1917

These are the words of Julio Vásquez in a conversation with me at his home in Douglas, Arizona, in July 1979.

My father, he was a miner from Zacatecas [Mexico] and brought us here in 1912. I think it was because of the Mexican Revolution, but he worked for an American mine in Zacatecas, so he came here to get away from the Revolution. His brother and his family and my dad with his all came. My older brothers were born in Mexico, but I was born here in the U.S. Actually, I was born in Bisbee. That's where my father took his family. But he couldn't get a good job at the mine because he was Mexican. The Mexicans could only work the bad-paying jobs, and even then they only earned half of what the *Americanos* [Anglo-Americans] earned.

My father was one of the ones that was shipped out. They came to the house in the middle of the night, policemen or something, and took him. My mother never forgot that night. She said nothing like that had ever happened in Zacatecas. Miners were safe in their homes. The danger was outside at work; never at home. After that, my father could never get work in a mine. We ended up in Douglas. Years later, my brother and I got jobs at the smelter. No one ever wanted to talk about that terrible night. Later, when I started trying to organize a union at the smelter [Phelps Dodge], people would talk about how they couldn't join because they didn't want to be deported. I knew it was because of what happened in Bisbee. People were really afraid. Lots of people in Douglas knew people in Bisbee who were deported that night. They didn't want that to happen to them. Even when the deported miners came back, they were blackballed. That means your name is on a list and nobody will hire you. It took a long time for us to organize again. Some of us were involved in a lawsuit and complaints against the company [Phelps Dodge] because of the way they treated Mexicans. It didn't matter if you were a citizen or not.

Speaking of the "unspeakable," Mr. Vásquez pointed to the series of events historians have called the Bisbee Deportation. Not unlike other important moments of our labor history, this episode is often neglected and set aside from the Arizona historical narrative. However, in more recent times, especially since Chicano historians have thrust open the window into Chicano labor history, the Bisbee Deportation is leaving the shadows. In 1917, Bisbee, Arizona, was a booming mining town that had attracted workers from all over the world. Mexican miners fleeing revolutionary violence in Mexico, Eastern Europeans, Slavs, and even Finns found their way to the Arizona desert. Katherine Benton-Cohen, digging into company, union, and government sources, enriches her compelling narrative of this incident with numerous interviews as well.[23] She highlights the following threads from this rich and complicated event in history:

1. Working conditions in the Arizona mining industry provoked discontent among workers at a time when some unions were supposedly demanding radical changes. In Bisbee, a general strike began on June 26, 1917.

2. By 1917, Mexicans made up 13 percent of the mining labor force but accounted for more than a quarter of the deportees.

3. Walter Douglas, superintendent of Phelps Dodge operations in Bisbee, believed that a strike by miners would be a concern of national security because the First World War made copper production necessary for the protection of the nation.

4. On July 12, 1917, Harry Wheeler, sheriff of Cochise County, in cooperation with mine management, proceeded to deputize twenty-two hundred men in Bisbee and Douglas. It is said that the event even included the local Catholic priest, using an automobile paid for with donations from parishioners. It is even remembered that he had a machine gun mounted on the back of the car for this roundup of miners.

5. Over one thousand men were herded into twenty-three railroad boxcars and taken 180 miles out of town, crossing the Arizona/New Mexico state line. Some were detained for up to as long as three months in Columbus, New Mexico.[24]

In the roundup, Sheriff Harry Wheeler and the more than two thousand men he deputized invaded homes in the middle of the night, kidnapped working men, and hauled them off to the Warren ball park. There, they held them until the next day, when many were loaded into railroad boxcars and taken to the Chihuahuan Desert in New Mexico. For three months, most of them remained in a concentration camp in the desert waiting to be released. Little is known about whether the miners were fed or whether they had water in that summer heat. Upon release, they found themselves blackballed; that is to say, pariahs. Families were left without the possibility of a livelihood. These men and their families felt the effects of all-encompassing discrimination in everyday life—from where they were allowed to live, to where they could even hope to work, to even the schools of their children. They were subject to continual reminders of their secondary status in all sectors of society. That is what it was to be Mexican in southeastern Arizona; to be discriminated against by Euro-American ranchers hailing from the Midwest and Texas and by mine owners determined to maintain their privileged status.

Mining companies protected this raid system as a way of controlling labor demands. As described by Benton-Cohen, cooper companies used racist attitudes already ingrained in the newcomer from the Midwest and South to weave a net of oppression thread by thread.[25] Nativist beliefs roiled as a way to divide workers and resulted in onerous and dangerous working conditions and low wages for all, but even lower for Mexicans as a way to make "white" workers feel privileged. Why did this happen? And who was responsible?

The answer to the first question is complex. One thing is clear. In a so-called democratic nation guided by the rule of law, travesties occur that violate basic rights: the loss of liberty without due process and the loss of the right to make a living (the latter of which, although not an expressed right in the U.S. Constitution, is certainly a violation of the right to life). A person who cannot work cannot maintain life. Discrimination in the areas of housing, education, work, and political participation almost pales when seen in the context of the violations imposed by the Bisbee Deportation. Although not all the deported were Mexicans, proportionately, they were represented in higher numbers than white workers. The result of this series of events, however, clearly established Bisbee as what was called an "American camp." All residents knew Bisbee was for whites. To be nonwhite was to be aware of one's place and inferior status.

Can this be called state violence? That takes us to the question of who was responsible. Walter Douglas, superintendent of Phelps Dodge in Bisbee, was convinced that strike organizers (including members of International Workers of the World and Mexicans) were colluding with antiwar (World War I) groups or with German agents in Mexico who promised to return lost lands if Mexico supported Germany in the war. Copper—a necessary element in the war machine and mining—had to be protected. Any lapse would be dangerous for the national security of the United States. Douglas, working with Cochise law enforcement as he had always done, made sure that Harry Wheeler, the sheriff, was convinced of the international implications of the strike against Phelps Dodge. In July 1917, sixty-seven strikers in Jerome (located in northwestern Arizona) were deported. That same month, numerous men in Bisbee were also deported.

In spite of a Mediation Commission finally appointed by President Woodrow Wilson to investigate the deportation, no one was found guilty of any wrongdoing. Once again, violations, fear, and impunity shaded the life of all in southeastern Arizona. But clouds do not block out all of the sun. Throughout the following years, in spite of racialized social practices, there was continuous resistance. Taking a step forward and then suffering moments of retreat, the unspeakable was often remembered. If the Phelps Dodge Company and the sheriff were not guilty of any violations according to the law, the constant deprivations suffered by hundreds of women and children—the families of the blackballed workers—reaffirmed the impunity of the powerful in the Mesilla. With each unjust experience, the "unspeakable" was retold, recalling past impunity and braiding it with present lived injustices.

When the Depression of the 1930s resulted in the closing of mines and smelters, *Mexicanos* (and some citizens of Mexican descent) were "repatriated," that is, deported, but this time to Mexico. The relief programs put in place replicated inferior pay scales and second-class citizenship, explaining almost commonsensically that the "Mexican" standard of living was not as high as the "American" and, therefore, Mexicans, it was assumed, "could make do with less."[26] Here again, no one was held accountable. The violence to hungry families, described as receiving what was necessary for the Mexican life as opposed to the American standard of life, carves itself into community memory. The far-reaching power of the company allowed social workers, teachers, and other relief officials to discriminate against "Mexican" families. Knowing that company power and the sheriff's duties were essentially one and the same, Mexicans' fight for survival moved away from public spaces to the trusted bars, kitchen tables, and front porches.

Well into the twentieth century, Southern Arizona, bookending the Tohono O'odham Reservation with Cochise and Santa Cruz Counties on the east and Yuma on the west, remained that part of the border where racialized economic, political, social, and cultural groups lived in constant tension and contradictions. The racial attitudes of the Midwest and the South that focused on a black/white matrix combined with a Mexican racial hierarchy placing "Indians" at the bottom of the Euro-American white ladder. However, U.S. dominance over Indians, Mexicans, and blacks clearly ruled.

CASE 3: MIRACLE VALLEY KILLINGS, COCHISE COUNTY, OCTOBER 1982

Es como disco rayado. No castigaron a nadie. [It's the same old story. No one was punished.] Judd gets away with it again. That Court, the Grand Jury won't indict anyone. What's new? (Words of Antonio Martínez during a conversation with author in 1989)

Residents of Miracle Valley, located in southwestern Cochise County, not too many miles from the border, were caught in the middle of a shooting between members of the Christ Miracle Healing Center and deputies of the Cochise

County Sheriff's Department. Two members of the African American religious group were killed and two others were seriously injured (one with a severed spinal cord). Martínez, thinking aloud on a beating to his own son at the hands of the police, remembered,

> They killed them in their own home. Can you imagine, the police come to your house and end up shooting you in front of your own children? Nunca puedo olvidar esa noche que me tiraron al chamaco, el Tonito, en el porche. Cubierto en sangre. La jefa casi se vuelve loca. A la media noche un ruidero; salgo a ver que pasa y ahí está Tonito. Casi muerto. Los vecinos me dicen que fueron los policías. Con el Joe Borane, no hay descanso. Tanto que les digo a los chamacos: "No salgas," "Quédate quieto." Ni sé si fue el chief of police o el sheriff. Todos son . . . siqueira no me lo mataron como a los de Miracle Valley. [I can never forget that night in which they threw my kid, El Tonito, onto the porch. Covered in blood. My wife almost went mad. At midnight there were loud noises; I came out to see, and there he was, Tonito. Almost dead. The neighbors told me it was the police. With that Joe Borane, there is no rest. And I tell the kids all the time, "don't go out," "don't move." I am not sure if it was the chief of police or the sheriff. It is all of them . . . at least they didn't kill him like they did the ones in Miracle Valley.]

On October 24, 1982, the *Arizona Daily Star* published several stories covering the Miracle Valley encounter. Later, in 1992, it published a tenth anniversary story recalling the outrageous killing of two African American members of the church. Condensing the events in a chronology, one can better grasp the tenor of abusive state power over a group of isolated African Americans who had taken refuge from urban social problems in Chicago by moving to a far-off rural setting. Hoping to remove themselves from harassment and seeking the opportunity to practice their religious beliefs, it appears that they were unable to make Miracle Valley the peaceful, earthly paradise they so desired.

Quotes from the *Arizona Daily Star's* "Chronology," published in 1992, provide a glimpse into how the interaction between law enforcement in Cochise County and the group of people of color played out:

> Oct. 22: Stick- and bat-wielding church members force the retreat of deputies attempting to serve an arrest warrant on a church member. (It should be explained that the warrant was for a traffic violation.)

Oct. 23: Judd [Sheriff of Cochise County] sends two deputies backed by 35 other law officers into Miracle Valley with orders to make the arrest that had been foiled by church members the night before. The deputies are attacked by dozens of church members. The confrontation escalates and shooting breaks out. Two church members are killed, five deputies and two church members are hospitalized.

Oct. 30: Ten church members are indicted by a Cochise County grand jury on charges stemming from the shoot-out. Another nine members of the church are later added to the indictment also on charges related to the shooting incident. Other church members return to Chicago to bury their dead.

Nov. 11: The Rev. Jesse Jackson conducts a fact-finding visit to Miracle Valley and urges peace.

Nov. 15: A Cochise County judge removes himself from the case and orders it moved to Tucson.

May 1983: Church members announce they will not return to Miracle Valley from Chicago.

February 1984: Charges against the church members are dismissed by a Pima County Superior Court judge after Cochise County officials said they no longer could afford to pay the indigent defense costs associated with the case.

September 1984: A federal grand jury declines to indict either deputies or church members in the case.

End of case; continuing impunity. In spite of the fact that there was ample coverage of the Miracle Valley "War," it is not imprudent to ask how many people remember the events. Certainly they remain in the memory of the families of the church members who died. And certainly they remain as part of the background of Sheriff Judd and return when Sheriff Dever (who was one of the deputies named in the killing) is mentioned in conversations by people who continue to live under his jurisdiction. Antonio Martínez does not forget, and in his remembering of the Miracle Valley killings, he weaves the beating to his son at the hands of the police. Joe Borane, the sheriff, is the protagonist of both incidents.[27] Only the Martínez family and their neighbors learned about what happened to Tonito. Yet there is nothing that they could do besides retell the story. Who would want to taunt Joe Borane, chief of police? Furthermore, if they had called attention to the story, wouldn't he have zeroed in on many more young Mexican men in Douglas, accusing them of dealing drugs? Too many young *Mexicanos* had already been arrested, jailed, and punished on those grounds. Quesada, another neighbor, remembers that the chief of police became especially vicious after one of those youths composed a song denouncing Borane's consuming of cocaine. In Quesada's words,

> No me acuerdo el nombre [del chamaco] al que tanto jodía la policía. El chamaco, nada tonto escribió una canción, "Cocaine Joe," cantando como el Joe usaba cocaine. . . . Borane went after the kid, arrested and jailed him, and about two days later it was announced that the kid had committed suicide. ¿Como creer tanta mentira? But Borane got away with it. [I can't recall the name of the kid who messed with the police. The kid, smart kid, wrote a song, "Cocaine Joe," that told of how Joe used cocaine. . . . Borane went after the kid, arrested and jailed him, and about two days later it was announced that the kid had committed suicide. How can one believe so many lies? But Borane got away with it.]

Railroad workers assigned to the "car repair shop" labored ten-hour shifts of exacting and physically taxing exertion. Seeking relief during lunch hours, they often invented competitive games that showed off their highly developed skills. Play and performance also erupted, breaking the tensions of hard work and ill-willed bosses. Always ready to hear a joke, tell a story, and listen to a song, these men forged trusting friendships, friendships that carried into their social lives, including family celebrations, and helping each other out in times of woe and sadness. Manuel Rubio, Saul Quesada, and Antonio Martinez, working as car repairmen and as friends, easily exchanged "not convenient truths" on cool summer evenings, sipping lemonade or enjoying a cold beer, "chewing the rag," the stories would begin. Sometimes, in winter, taking shelter in a sunny corner of the "corral," their loud laughter would call attention to some outrageous memory. Remembering experiences as workers on the "Suffering Pacific," they brought the workplace to life for their families and friends. It was in such places that memories of violence, injustice, and impunity were retold for others. They told stories that had to be told, stories to remember and to teach the young, stories to build strength, and courage, and stories to warn.

CASE 4: HANNINGAN FAMILY, TORTURERS

Federal laws may proclaim equality, but local governance has played a different tune in Southern Arizona. State violence manifests itself not only in clear-cut state action but also through the impunity it provides to individual, private actions. Such was the case of the capture and torture of three Mexican migrants by the Hannigan family (a father and his two sons). According to media reports and later judicial proceedings, "they [the Hannigans: father, George, sons Patrick, 22 and Thomas, 17] stripped, stabbed, burned [the immigrants] with hot pokers and dragged [them] across the desert."[28] The ties between state violence and so-called individual actions become evident through the memories of Manuel Rubio who, during an interview in 1989, began recalling the events at Miracle Valley and ended with his memories of the violence caused by the Hannigan family.

Pues nos dicen que cambian las cosas, y pues, sí algunas están mejores. Pero lo que son las cortes y los policías, pues me parece que eso no cambia tanto. Desde chicos sabíamos que había que tener cuidado con los gringos. No ponerse en situaciones de pleito. Pero, qué quieres, a veces no queda otra. Hay gringos buenos, pero hay otros que nomas buscan humillarnos. Y no solo a los Mexicanos, sino también a los negritos. Yo me acuerdo de los que mataron en ese pueblito Miracle Valley. Hasta vino Jesse Jackson, pero de todas maneras el Dever y el Judd nunca pagaron por esas muertes. Y después, pues están los Hannigan. Los de la lechería. Nosotros siempre comprábamos esa leche, pero después de lo que les hicieron a los tres mojados, nunca más les compre su leche. Otros que hicieron lo que quisieron y salieron libres. (Well, they say that things change, and well, sure some things are better. But the courts and the police, well, it seems to me that those don't change much. Since we were kids we knew we had to watch ourselves with gringos. Not to put oneself in a dangerous position. But, what do you know, sometimes one must do so. There are good gringos, but there are others who only want to humiliate us. And not only Mexicans, but also blacks. I remember those that they killed in that little town, Miracle Valley. Even Jesse Jackson came, but even so, Dever and Judd were never held accountable for those deaths. Additionally, there are the Hannigans. The ones from the dairy. We always used to buy that milk, but after what they did to the three immigrants, I never bought their milk again. Another case of doing what they wanted, and they were set free).

Situated in the Sulphur Springs Valley on the border with Sonora, a few miles west of Douglas, the Hannigan Dairy had been a successful local dairy serving all of southeastern Arizona. Milk delivery trucks were familiar sights in Douglas and Bisbee, and people preferred local product to that brought from outside the area. Farm laborers from Sonora had been crossing through the area for at least thirty years. Some of them were hired by farmers and ranchers throughout the Sulphur Springs Valley—from the border to the north all the way to the towns of Wilcox, Double Adobe, McNeal, Elfrida, etc. Why the Hannigans attacked the immigrants is not clear from the records, although numerous nativist and racist comments stand out in testimony and public statements.

Pressured to conduct an investigation and to proceed with indictments, the first jury trial resulted in "not guilty" verdicts. Local protests supported by community groups in Tucson obliged federal officials to conduct their own investigation. Civil rights violations were cited and proceedings began. In the end, after years of judicial proceedings, father George Hannigan died, his son Patrick was found guilty, and Thomas was declared innocent.

For years, the incident was recalled with each perceived new violation from either vigilante-type actions against Mexican migrants (e.g., the case of the Bartlett ranchers and their rounding up and possible torture of passing Mexican migrants) or even the border patrol. Impunity by the justice system results in tearing the legal fabric that is an integral foundation of the rule of law.

CASE 5: THE MURDER OF DARÍO MIRANDA

Almost forgotten, like other *Mexicanos* killed by border authorities, after years, few recall the tragic event that Darío Miranda Valenzuela's family still suffers. Antonio Martínez and Manuel Rubio, in an interview in 1998, remembered.

> Lo mataron. Ese muchacho de Nogales. No es la primera vez que un Border Patrol mata a un muchacho Mexicano. Y nunca les hacen nada. Acuérdate como le entregaron el cuerpo a la mamá. Hasta tuvo que ir con el Obispo de Tucson para que le entregaran el cuerpo. Quesque no se lo podían dar para enterrarlo porque había una investigación . . . y cuando por fin se lo dieron estaba lleno de gusanos. Pobre mujer. Como de costumbre, hicieron la investigación y hasta hubo un juicio, pero como siempre, dijeron el juez y el "jury" que no era culpable el tal Elmer. (They killed him. Those young men from Nogales. It's not the first time that a

Border Patrol agent kill a Mexican man. And they never do anything to them. Remember how they turned the body over to the mother. She even had to go with the bishop of Tucson so they would release the body. Supposedly they could not release it because there was an investigation . . . and when they finally gave it to her, it was full of worms. Poor woman. As usual, they conducted an investigation, and there was even a trial, but as always, the judge and jury decided that Elmer was not guilty.)

A superficial review of court records and newspaper reports tell a story of abuse of power by border authorities, a story that is all too familiar to Mexican border residents. On June 13, 1992, (the day of St. Anthony), a Border Patrol agent assigned to the Tucson Sector, Thomas Watson, reported a fatal assault on a migrant, Darío Miranda Valenzuela. According to Watson, it took place in the hills just north of the border in Nogales, Arizona. Watson named Michael Elmer, a fellow agent, as the responsible party, and it was later clarified that two months before, Elmer had been party to the roundup of about thirty migrants. They were told to lie down, whereupon Elmer proceeded to shoot at their feet and over their heads.

This particular case provides a window into certain inner practices present in Border Patrol culture at that time. The "code of silence" prevalent in law enforcement agencies is well known in border communities. Agents never "tell" on each other and find ways to "cover up" such incidents. In this case, however, Thomas Watson decided he could not cover up a death. According to testimony from the criminal case, Watson waited almost twenty-four hours before reporting to his supervisor that a migrant had been shot and that he had helped the shooter, Michael Elmer, move the injured and bleeding person from the trail where he was shot at a spot under a tree. They had abandoned a dying man and not reported it.

As further revealed, Elmer had placed a "spare" personal gun at the side of the bleeding man so that if the body were found, he could argue self-defense. Darío Miranda Valenzuela was shot in the back. Testimony clarified that Valenzuela was running back toward Mexico when the Border Patrol agents saw the group. Shots were heard coming from the agents, and the migrant group turned and ran toward Nogales, Sonora.

Vigorous protests from immigrant rights groups, faith-based organizations, and many concerned citizens forced judicial proceedings. The county attorney of Santa Cruz County filed an indictment, which proceeded to trial. It is said that it was the first time an agent of the border patrol had been charged with murder in the killing of a Mexican at the border. The criminal trial that followed resulted in the jury verdict of "not guilty" in spite of incriminating forensic evidence buttressed with testimony of a pattern of Elmer's disregard for the agency's regulations.

Citing civil rights violations, the Department of Justice filed such a brief in federal court. This trial, decided by a jury, reaffirmed the strong anti-immigrant attitudes in Cochise, Pima, and Yuma Counties; actually, attitudes that are still alive and well throughout the state of Arizona. Elmer was found not guilty. Again, the death of a Mexican at the hands of a border authority is one more number in the files of a long history—and many memories—of impunity.

IT MUST END

Since the killing of Darío Miranda Valenzuela in 1992, the Arizona-Sonora border has seen the deaths of other migrants at the hands of Border Patrol agents. Just recently, Carlos Renaldo la Madrid was shot to death in the back as he climbed a ladder to jump over the border fence, hoping to land on the Mexican side. His family, with strong community support, has moved every legal venue trying to identify the killer, seek an indictment, and receive justice. None has been forthcoming.

As in each and every case "remembered" above, the authorities, the Border Patrol in this case, affirms that there is an ongoing investigation. Yet to many in our communities, this statement translates directly as impunity, or as the saying in Spanish says, *Puro atole con el dedo* (they're trying to deceive us; it's a cover-up).

The concept of "impunity" resonates with the legal results of direct physical violence suffered by hundreds of migrants in the Sonora/Arizona region. We can only continue our search for the profound meaning of so much suffering and death while remaining firm in our conviction that as residents and citizens of this deadly region, we must examine every dimension of this humanitarian tragedy. Profound sadness invades communities on both sides of the political division called *La Línea* (The Line), and it speaks through our memories and our intent to remember. As we continue to live these experiences, the retelling of past impunity sparks the demand for justice, unveils the continuities of our borderlands histories, weaved through violence, injustice, and impunity, and reminds us, above all, of the need to once again bring words into the silence of impunity.

NOTES

1. Mandelstam 2010.
2. Spicer 1981.
3. González y González 1973, 72.
4. Benjamin 1969.
5. Scott 1985.
6. Portelli 1997.
7. Gonzalez y Gonzalez 1989.
8. Blackhawke 2006.
9. Acuña 1988. Numerous Chicano scholars are recovering past violations. The work of F. Arturo Rosales (2000) is a prime example.
10. Nevins and Aizeki 2008.
11. Martínez 1996.
12. Ibid.
13. Alonso 2008, 231.
14. Portelli 1981, 96–107.
15. Portelli 1991.
16. de León 1985.
17. Sheridan 1986.
18. The Camp Grant massacre is sometimes remembered by Apaches as *Gashdla'a Chon O'aa*.
19. Guidotti-Hernández 2011.
20. Alonso 1995.
21. Guidotti-Hernández 2011.
22. Record 2008.
23. Benton-Cohen 2009.
24. Ibid.
25. Ibid.
26. Ibid.
27. "Joe" Borane, as he was known to residents of Douglas, Arizona, was a member of the Douglas Police Department for twenty years. During the last part

of his tenure he was chief of police with the added title of director of security (this last title varies from one source to another). In 1979, as chief of police he was accused of corruption. The issues were settled, and he resigned as chief. In 1980 he won election as Justice of the Peace of Pima County, a position he held until 1999, when he again was forced to resign. Numerous charges were brought against him by a grand jury, including conspiracy to commit money laundering and fraud. Although he was never a member of the Pima County sheriff's department, for many of the inhabitants of the region, the fact that he was a powerful police authority was never in doubt. See Samuel Dillon, "Small-Town Arizona Judge Amasses Fortune, and Indictment," *New York Times*, January 30, 2000, www.nytimes.com/. . ./small-town-arizona-judge -amasses-fortune-and-indictment/html.

28. Acuña 2002.

STATION 2

CROSSINGS

God of peace, we beseech your blessings upon our torn and tortured borderlands. We live in a time of hate, mistrust, fear, and violence. Bless us with your holy spirit, that we may follow your way and create a world where all may live and work together in peace.

RISK PERCEPTION AND INFORMAL BORDER CROSSING BETWEEN SONORA AND ARIZONA

PRESCOTT L. VANDERVOET

BACKGROUND

MEXICO AND THE UNITED STATES constitute the largest migration corridor in the world, with an estimated 10.3 million migrants passing between the two nations in 2005.[1] Migration across the U.S.-Mexico borderlands is as old as the respective nations, although the accepted directionality of south to north has not been the only way in which people have moved across the international boundary. Some of the first movements across an early incarnation of the border were from the United States to Mexico, as residents of the land assumed by the United States following the Treaty of Guadalupe Hidalgo moved south into Mexico to the area of La Mesilla, in present-day New Mexico.[2] Recently, communities with large American retiree populations have grown significantly in parts of Mexico such as Chapala, Los Cabos, and San Miguel de Allende.[3] Yet the vast majority of migration between the two nations during the last century has been work oriented and northbound. Along with this historical context of movement, the research outlined in this paper is also founded in the concepts of border control and surveillance, which has increased without precedence in last two decades along the United States' southern boundary.

Within this paradigm of border crossing and security, the study of migration risk between Mexico and the United States is important since migrants face dangers that are strongly linked to and even a direct outcome of enforcement on the U.S. side of the border. The effects of this enforcement manifest themselves not only in the way that people try to informally cross the border but also with respect to where along the border such crossings occur. Of similar importance is the seasonality of the border crossing, especially in relation to the binational Sonoran Desert region.

The purpose of this research is to cast light on the decision-making process of undocumented border crossers. Individuals intending to informally enter the United States will often base their decision on the availability of economic resources or the possibility of obtaining employment in the United States through the contact of a family member or a friend. Thus, while the precise conditions on the border may complicate the border crossing, they are often of secondary importance compared with the cost for the trip north across the border or the employment opportunities once there (direct push and pull factors).

Researchers have long studied the causality of Mexican migration to the United States and its effects on both sending and receiving communities as well as the way in which migrants negotiate the border-crossing experience, from origin to destination. An early analysis of the border-crossing experience was documented by Samora, while Conover detailed the journey from origin to destination. More recently, authors such as Massey, Durand, and Malone and Cornelius and Lewis have reviewed the migratory phenomenon over previous decades in light of increasing crossing pressures.[4]

BORDER MILITARIZATION

Beginning in the early 1990s, the United States government, under the auspices of the Immigration and Naturalization Service (INS) and its enforcement arm, the Border Patrol, began a series of reforms for policing the border. Until then, what had been a limited emphasis on "controlling" the border took center stage at both the local and national levels. Economic inputs to different agencies were administered in the forms of constructions along the border as well as increased enforcement through technology and agents on patrol.

A primary objective of the Border Patrol was to push migrants toward isolated areas along the border where they could be more easily apprehended.[5] At the same time, immigration policy makers hoped that the migratory flow would decrease as people desisted from crossing in these isolated parts of the border.[6] Interestingly, migrants were not discouraged from this new crossing scenario. It can also be argued that apprehension in an isolated, rural setting is logistically easier (when an adequate amount of law enforcement is present) than in urban settings. Yet within the enormous rural landscapes of the southwestern borderlands, detection and apprehension of unauthorized migrants continues to be a challenge for border immigration authorities.

Operation Hold the Line began in September 1993 with the deployment of four hundred Border Patrol agents with vehicles along a twenty-mile stretch of the border in the El Paso Sector. The intensification of vigilance along the border was a direct attempt at deterrence, which supposedly prevented potential border crossers from even trying to set foot in U.S. territory.

Similarly, Operation Gatekeeper in 1994 shared the same objectives for the Tijuana–San Diego corridor. The number of Border Patrol agents in the San Diego Sector increased from 980 in 1994 to over two thousand by June 1998. In fact, there were more Border Patrol agents in the San Diego Sector alone in 2002 than there were along the entire U.S.-Mexico border two decades earlier. Fencing along the border increased from nineteen to forty-five miles, and the number of INS port inspectors more than doubled.[7] As a result of these enforcement strategies, the now defunct INS became the fastest-growing federal government agency. During the 1990s its total budget more than tripled, with more INS agents authorized to carry a weapon than any other law enforcement agency in the United States.[8]

The massive increase in manpower and infrastructure along the border sought to increase the effectiveness of border control. Yet it can be argued that in light of governmental efforts to obtain operational control, the border has become an even more dangerous, violent, and uncontrolled space, especially for undocumented crossers. Studies suggest that additional agents may in fact increase the number of migrant deaths—at least in the short run.[9] Such research shows an increase in deaths vis-à-vis growing deployed agents along the border. However, as the San Diego case illustrates, the prolonged presence of large numbers of agents can change the direction of migrant flows, thus lowering the initial increase in deaths.

A report published by the Government Accountability Office (GAO) in August 2006 found that despite efforts of the Border Security Initiative (BSI),[10] deaths along the border have doubled since 1995. The report states that the number of deaths increased regardless of the number of people who entered into the United States by crossing the border illegally. Furthermore, the study shows that 75 percent of the deaths since 1995 occurred in the Arizona desert.

The GAO report finds that the most frequent cause of death along the border since 1995 is exposure, and in particular, heat-related exposure. Age groups most likely to die along the border remained the same during the time period under study, but female death rates doubled, suggesting that age as a determinate did not increase vulnerability whereas gender definitely did, although this may be a function of the increasing number of women migrants. This GAO report correlates with recent studies showing environmental heat exposure as a leading cause of death[11]—and also females being nearly three times more likely than men to die of exposure[12]—when controlling for other factors during undocumented border crossing.

WORK ON THE BORDER

There is a significant amount of research addressing the perspective of communities within Mexico where a high percentage of their population migrates to the United States seeking better employment opportunities. This investigative work spans three decades and has primarily been conducted by binational academic teams. Perhaps the best example of this is the Mexican Migration Project, which has conducted thousands of surveys in migrant-sending communities within Mexico since 1982.[13]

It is important to note that while there is a general lack of immigration research directly conducted along the border, one of the few large, quantitative-focused surveys addressing the issue of cross-boundary movement between Mexico and the United States was collected in the border region. The Encuesta sobre Migración en la Frontera Norte de México (EMIF; the migration survey in Mexico's northern border) has been in semiregular operation since 1993. EMIF surveys are conducted at sites within Mexican border cities such as regional bus stations, airports, train stations, international crossing gates, and Mexican customs inspection stations. Within these areas, surveys are conducted in locations where individuals will not tend to pass multiple times.[14] The EMIF focuses on four transitory populations along Mexico's northern border region:

1. Non-Americans originating from the south who are not residents of the border region or of the United States
2. Non-Americans who do not live in the Mexican border city of application but are transiting the Mexican border region
3. Non-Americans who are entering Mexico from the United States but are not residents in the Mexican border city of application
4. Persons turned over by the U.S. Border Patrol to Mexican immigration authorities

One of the most important priorities of the EMIF has been to provide information on the population of undocumented border crossers between Mexico and the United States. The survey responds to this call by specifically targeting people returned to Mexico by the U.S. Border Patrol and who either have crossed into, plan to cross into, have worked, or plan to work in the United States without documentation.

With respect to issues of risk associated with undocumented border crossing, the EMIF provides a unique source of data collected from people who have crossed the border informally. There is a vivid contrast of risk perception by those who have yet to attempt an undocumented border crossing with those who have been apprehended by U.S. immigration authorities and returned to Mexico.

En las encuestas realizadas a los emigrantes procedentes del sur, ellos tienen una percepción de lo que pudiera ocurrirles, y muchas veces, su imaginario personal y colectivo es muy optimista; en cambio, los expulsados de Estados Unidos regresan a territorio nacional después de haber vivido o sufrido la experiencia del cruce, contando con todo el bagaje de información sobre los hechos realmente sucedidos.

(The surveys conducted with emigrants coming from the south show that they have a perception of what might happen to them. Often, their personal and collective imaginings are very optimistic. In contrast, those forced out of the United States return to national territory after having lived and suffered the crossing experience, and thus carrying all the informational baggage related to what really happens.)[15]

According to EMIF data, the primary accidental risk associated with undocumented crossing, identified by returned migrants to Mexico, is that of falling while walking. This situation was identified by 54.9 percent of all surveyed un-documented border crossers. Other physical risks they identified were injured feet (14.3 percent, probably a result of blisters) and fainting and dizziness spells (10.1 percent, possibly a result of dehydration).[16]

STUDY SITE BACKGROUND

While the focus of this research was qualitative, a short survey instrument was used to collect quantitative, baseline data on research participants. This survey also served to introduce certain topics I wanted to discuss that were relevant to the research questions.

Using topics introduced by the survey, people were asked to expand on certain ideas. These open-ended questions gave participants the opportunity to express themselves more freely. This was important because it was apparent to me that a variety of questions from the survey limited the participants' ability to expand.

Snowball methodology was used for recruiting participants in my research. Most of this process occurred inside the Centro Comunitario de Atención al Migrante y Necesitado (CCAMyN).[17] This setting allowed for interaction with migrants in a secure place and with a somewhat relaxed ambiance. Perhaps one of the most important attributes of the shelter is that it is a space of refuge and safety from *coyotes* (smugglers) and *enganchadores* (recruiters)[18]—a constant source of consternation to many migrants in Altar, Sonora, especially in public spaces such as the plaza and city streets. I stayed at the shelter from opening time to closing. I worked closely with the staff there and was treated with respect by the patrons of the shelter. At the same time it was made clear to informants that my project was not an official part of the shelter, and had no connection to their stay at the CCAMyN.

The questionnaire was not introduced to anyone until at least one day after we had met, preferably at the CCAMyN. This was important for two reasons. First, it allowed the potential participants to become familiar with my presence and gave them the opportunity to observe me while I conducted other questionnaires. Second, it also allowed me to observe their behavior and ascertain their honesty as well as determine whether they were indeed interested in crossing the border to the United States. Frequently, coyotes and *enganchadores* pose as migrants in an effort to gain their confidence and make money by connecting them to other coyotes.

DEMOGRAPHIC INFORMATION OF THE STUDY

Of the people staying at the CCAMyN, 87 percent claim Mexican origin; the remaining 13 percent are almost entirely from Central America. One visitor from Peru represents the only (self-identifying) South American to the CCA-MyN during 2007.[19]

Of the Mexican population, some states stand out as primary sending regions, including Chiapas, Oaxaca, Sonora, Veracruz, and Puebla. Residents from each of these states accounted for at least 5 percent of the total CCAMyN population during 2007. Chiapas was by far the primary region of origin of CCAMyN patrons, accounting for nearly one quarter of the total population. It is important to remember that many Central Americans claim to be from Chiapas, Mexico (see note 19). The information that follows corresponds to the sample of my study where 70 percent of the participants were Mexican, of which 27 percent were from Chiapas. The remaining 30 percent were Central Americans, with Guatemala representing 12 percent of that total. Women represent a minority at the shelter, accounting for just 8 percent of guests.

RESEARCH METHODOLOGY AND RISK PERCEPTION BY MIGRANTS

Risks associated with undocumented border crossing explain perceptions of the border crossing that have serious effects on migrants' vulnerability. The focus of this study is to assess risk perception by those incurring the actual risks involved with crossing the border and to shed light on how people form an opinion in respect to such risks, in other words, how they educate themselves in respect to risk. Certain fundamental concepts to successful (or unsuccessful) border crossing, such as expected walking distances and climatic conditions, were also crucial to the research.

To tackle the issue of risk perception, participants were asked to list what they considered to be the three greatest dangers involved in undocumented crossing. At first the survey listed eight possible risks: heat, water, terrain, distance, venomous animals, Border Patrol, anti-immigrant groups, and an open option. After applying test surveys, "gangs" and "army" were added to the list. Gangs operate along the border in places remote or inhospitable enough to be considered "no-man's-land" by authorities from either side of the border. These groups frequently rob or assault migrants on their trek north. Some people suspect (not without reason) that some of these groups operate in conjunction with the guides who purposefully lead their group of migrants intentionally into the path of the gangs.

As for the army, during the research process, National Guard units from various states had been called to assist the Border Patrol with observation of the border.[20] The army, viewed as a group of people in camouflaged military and associated with warfare paraphernalia (automatic weaponry), was, for some migrants, more of a threat than the Border Patrol.

After three weeks of research, questioning was altered to elicit more open-ended responses from participants, giving them the chance to suggest their perceived risk without providing them with response options. Such open-ended questioning methodology required more effort on the part of the researcher to engage the participant in conversation, but it also proved more representative of the participants' personal feelings toward the issue.

RESULTS AND DISCUSSION

Figure 4.1 lists the potential dangers mentioned by people considering undocumented crossing.

The primary perceived risk associated with undocumented crossing is that of being bitten or stung by a venomous animal. This category is the combination of two different response categories, which include venomous animals and snakes. The terms *víbora* (snake) or *cascabel* (rattlesnake) were often mentioned specifically, but never in conjunction with the term *venomous animal*. Since no person who mentioned "snake" as a risk mentioned "venomous animal" as a separate response, the combination of the two terms was allowed. The usage of the different terms seemed to be an issue of semantics that ultimately referenced the same concept within the realm of risk posed to undocumented migrants while crossing the border.

Other perceived dangers, which accounted for 12 percent of total responses, included distance (3 percent), kidnapping (1 percent), anti-immigrant groups (2 percent), fatigue (4 percent), and disorientation (2 percent). Perhaps some of these categories can be grouped into the major themes cited in the graph.

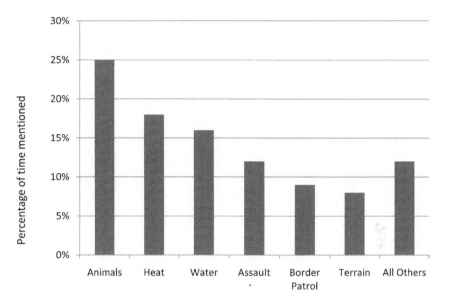

FIGURE 4.1. Perceived risks associated with undocumented crossing

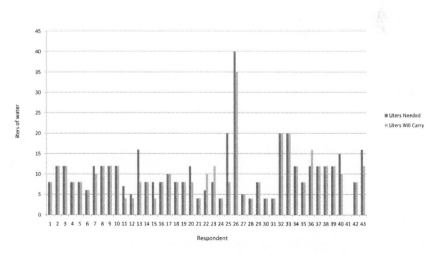

FIGURE 4.2. Necessity of water

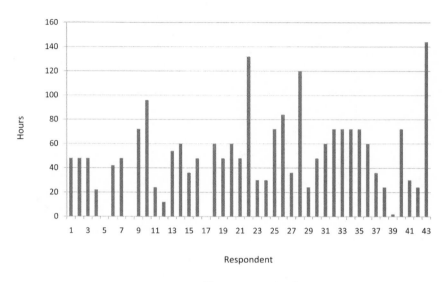

FIGURE 4.3. Time to cross border

For instance, kidnapping can be associated with assault; distance-fatigue-disorientation can be grouped with terrain or perhaps heat. Ultimately, there is some flexibility between different risk categories, but these groupings allow for a preliminary analysis of this particular facet of risk perception.

Data from the research suggests that, on average, people expect a need of just over 10.5 liters of water for a successful undocumented crossing of the border. This amount (equal to just over two gallons) approximates what most people carry when they cross. It is important to remember that many times guides will often restrict how much water each migrant can carry under the premise that too much weight can slow a person down during the journey across. Water is often sold by the gallon in Altar; many people will carry one gallon in each hand or tie them over their shoulder.

Data from the same participants suggests that despite the perception of needing over ten liters, on average, they would carry 9.76 liters. Only three of the forty-three participants stated that they would carry more water than that considered necessary to cross the border. Ten of the participants planned to carry less water than the amount they considered necessary to cross the border, while the remaining participants would carry precisely the amount they considered they would need.

Another interesting result of the investigation is immigrants' opinions on the time they will need to informally cross the border. On average, they expected to walk 54.75 hours to cross the border.[21] This number corresponds to anecdotal data of people spending three to four days walking either during the night or during the day (but not *all* day). The variety of responses is revealing, ranging from two to 144 hours. The most common response was forty-eight hours, which was mentioned eight times.

WHAT FACTORS PUSHED PEOPLE TO CROSS DURING THE SUMMER OF 2007?

Why do people decide to walk across of the harshest regions of all North America in the middle of the summer? This question was fundamental to the investigation in Altar. In addition to inquiring about what people considered to be the greatest risks to the crossing, the research aimed to better understand immigrants' reasons for crossing the border during the summer months.

By and large, the primary motivation for a person to cross the border is economic necessity. Extensive research and many of the responses garnered by this investigation reiterated such findings.

The following are quotes from immigrants concerning their reasons for crossing.

No pude esperar más, por la falta de dinero. (I couldn't wait any longer, because of the lack of money.) (Participant 26)

México ya está muy mal. Hemos intentado cruzar cinco veces en el último mes. (Mexico is in a really bad state. We've tried to cross five times in the last month.) (Participant 36)

Decidí venir en esta temporada porque hay más trabajo (I decided to come in this season because there is more work.) (Participant 11)

Mi primo me dijo, "vente, aquí hay chamba," (My cousin told me "come on, there is work here.") (Participant 38)

The urging or support from a family member or friend, as a complement to possibly improving one's economic outlook, also factored into many people's decisions to try to cross the border. Participant 38 combines both economic incentive and familial support as motives to cross the border during the summer. Thus, the decision to cross, while based in economic necessity, is solidified with the insistence from the participant's cousin.

While one may suppose that the decision to migrate to the United States is a result of much mental deliberation and planning, this is not always the case. As shown by participant 38, the decision occurred once he received the word from his cousin. Thus, the cousin sparked the realization of the migration project. The "instantaneous" decision to migrate was not uncommon.

A young woman from Nicaragua who was traveling with her mother, cousin, and another Nicaraguan described a similar circumstance: "Este fue un viaje que salió de repente. No sabíamos del calor" (This was a trip that happened all of a sudden. We didn't know about the heat; participant 25).

Another participant (15) mentioned that the decision of when to migrate was a function of being able to save enough money for the trip. Rather than reflecting on what would be the best time to cross, immigrants exhibit a mentality of "the sooner, the better." "Al juntar el dinero, salimos del pueblo" (Upon getting the money together, we left town; participant 15).

These decisions illustrate a disregard for temporally defined risks associated with undocumented border crossing, and while such an attitude is inferred by participant 15, others were quite straightforward about the perception, or lack thereof, of certain seasonally defined risks. They felt that what lay ahead depended on individual psychological and physical strength. For example, one man, upon being asked whether there were risks (heat and climate related) associated with crossing, gave the following response: "No hay, depende del valor de uno. Sabes a lo que dispones" (There aren't any [risks], it depends upon one's valor. You know what you're capable of; participant 33).

On the other hand, some participants mentioned that during the summer months, they felt that crossing the border would be easier because there would be fewer border crossers and because the Border Patrol would be suffering from the effects of the heat.

Es más fácil cruzar en el verano porque hay menos personas [cruzando]. (It is easier to cross in the summer because there are fewer people [crossing].) (Participant 4)

Pensé que hubieron menos personas cruzando, asi que no seríamos tan obvios para la migra. (I thought that there would be fewer people crossing, so that way we wouldn't be so obvious to the Border Patrol.) (Participant 13)

Fue lo más conveniente, venir durante el verano. También, por el calor pienso que los migras no están tan atentos. Les afecta más [el calor]. (It was the most convenient, to come during the summer. Also, because of the heat I think that the Border Patrol agents aren't as attentive. It [the heat] affects them more.) (Participant 22)

El frío es más peligroso que el calor. (The cold is more dangerous than the heat.) (Participant 7)

While the decision to cross the border during the summer was made purposefully by each of these participants, the logic behind each decision varies. Participant 4 considered the large influx of migrants to the border in late winter and spring to be detrimental to one's chances at a successful crossing. He felt that when fewer people were crossing, a person (like himself) had a better chance at getting a good guide and a safer route across the border. This reiterates anecdotal information that surfaced throughout the research. During the high season for crossing, there are so many people trying to cross that guides organize people into groups that literally have to wait in line for the opportunity to use a predetermined route across the border. This wait can take days or even weeks. Priority is given to groups with stronger networks (personal or financial).

Participant 13 felt that as fewer people migrate during the summer, there would be less overall traffic across the isolated border region, and thus, it would be easier to avoid detection by the Border Patrol. During the high season, groups of up to one hundred people attempt to cross the border under the guidance of up to ten guides. As one can imagine, such a large number of people is more likely to be detected by immigration enforcement officials who patrol the region. Nonetheless, if this were true, it seems illogical for the guides to attempt to cross so many people. Participant 13 is alluding to the possibility of other (unassociated) migrants who are crossing the border, inhibiting one's crossing chances, as they may draw the attention of Border Patrol to a certain crossing corridor or area.

As suggested by anecdotal evidence, Border Patrol agents consistently focus their attention on apprehending large groups of undocumented crossers, even driving past individuals who are sitting on the side of the road wanting to be apprehended. Had participant 13 been knowledgeable of the geography and route north from the border, he would have preferred to have crossed during the high season, when he could potentially use the large number of border crossers as a screen for his own individual crossing attempt.

Participant 22 exhibits a very unique logic for deciding to cross during the summer months. He obviously was aware of the prohibitory effect that the summer temperatures have on one's physical capabilities. He reasoned that Border Patrol agents would be detrimentally affected by the summer heat and thus less attentive or able to make apprehensions. Ultimately, he felt that the heat would affect the Border Patrol agents more than the migrants (himself in particular) attempting to cross the border and thus could be used to one's advantage in avoiding apprehension.

Finally, as illustrated by participant 7, heat-related risk is not always considered to be the most dangerous climatic condition that a migrant can face. In this particular case, the person felt that crossing during the winter would jeopardize one's health more than attempting a summer crossing. Without a doubt, wintertime crossings are very dangerous, and hypothermia-related deaths have been documented by the Pima County Medical Examiner's Office. The urban border cities of Agua Prieta and Nogales, Sonora, are located at close to four thousand feet above sea level and are surrounded by hills and mountains, which are often used by undocumented entrants to reach pickup locations along major roads north of the border. These hilly regions can reach nine thousand feet in elevation and consistently drop below 20 degrees Fahrenheit at night during the winter months.

These wide-ranging attitudes illustrate that migrants perceive many different potential border-crossing situations and conditions that may ease or inhibit the undocumented crossing. This research did not attempt to understand how such opinions were formed (i.e., previous personal border-crossing experience or second-hand information passed on by others), thought such information would assist in understanding why the individuals cited envision the border crossing in such ways.

CONCLUSION

This research demonstrates the evident disparity between the manner in which migrants perceive the risks associated with undocumented border crossing and that which has been defined as danger or dangerous by authorities and academics. For the people who participated in this study, neither the heat nor distances (conditions that many times are linked to migrant death during undocumented crossing endeavors) are identified as outstanding risks involved with the crossing. Rather, the perceived risks of possibly being bitten by venomous animals, such as snakes, are more common.

With respect to heat, the qualitative part of the research shows a large variety of opinions concerning how it may or may not affect one's potential success or failure while crossing the border. Unfortunately, heat does not always figure into the decision-making process of the migrant when they plan their journey toward and across the border. Many people commented on the danger that heat may cause to a person walking in the desert, but heat is also described as an advantage to the migrant in his or her attempts at informal crossing.

The size of this study does not lend itself to detailed statistical analysis, but the demographic tendencies of the sample do correspond to seasonal and annual trends of visitors at the CCAMyN. There is a need for continued research of this sort to better understand the notions held my migrants of the undocumented border-crossing experience. If agencies and organizations continue to aim to inform migrants of the dangers involved with crossing the U.S.-Mexico border, especially that shared by the states of Arizona and Sonora, such warnings should take into account and build on the perceptions held by migrants regarding the crossing experience.

NOTES

1. World Bank 2008, 5.
2. Rippy 1921, 726.
3. Dixon, Murray, and Gelatt 2006.
4. Samora 1971; Conover 1987; Massey, Durand, and Malone 2002; Cornelius and Lewis 2007.
5. Orrenius 2004, 281
6. Rubio-Goldsmith 2006, 5.
7. Nevins 2002, 4
8. Andreas 2003, 4.
9. Eschbach et al. 1999.
10. The BSI was implemented in June 1998, by the INS as a response to growing concern about migrant safety. The primary objective of the BSI was to reduce injuries among migrants and to prevent further migrant deaths in the Southwest border region. Some BSI initiatives included the construction to rescue beacons in decidedly perilous border-crossing areas as well as the staffing of certain Border Patrol sectors with Border Patrol Search, Trauma, and Rescue (BORSTAR) teams. While the Border Patrol did not initiate the BSI, they

viewed it as complementary to their ongoing law enforcement and border-security activities.

11. Sapkota et al. 2006.

12. Rubio-Goldsmith et al. 2006, 44.

13. Durand and Massey 2004.

14. STPS 2002, 24.

15. Cortes Larrinaga 2004, 157.

16. Ibid.

17. The CCAMyN is a free shelter in Altar, Sonora, supported by community members and the local Catholic parish.

18. *Coyote* is a general term for individuals who may perform a variety of roles related to the undocumented migration experience. In general they may act as a leader or organizer for a group of migrants. An *engachador* is more specifically a person who recruits migrants to connect them with guides or coyotes.

19. Many non-Mexicans will identify as being Mexican so as to avoid harassment by Mexican authorities regarding their legal status within the country. Such identification will also aid if detained by Border Patrol as they may hope to only be returned to the Mexican northern border rather than their country of origin.

20. McCombs 2007.

21. It is important to note that this sum represents time walking and not total traveling time. Almost all the people who participated in the study clarified that there is a difference between walking at day and walking at night, and this number takes that difference into account.

"CON EL PESO EN LA FRENTE"

A Gendered Look at the Human and Economic Costs of Migration on the U.S.-Mexico Border

ANNA OCHOA O'LEARY

MARCELA'S STORY: "CON UN PESO EN LA FRENTE"

THIS PAPER BEGINS WITH A STORY. In March 2007, I sat in a stark office space provided by the managers of the migrant shelter, Albergue San Juan Bosco, in Nogales, Sonora. I was nearing the end of a year-long study titled "Women at the Intersection: Immigration Enforcement and Transnational Migration on the U.S.-Mexico Border." The aim of the study was to systematically document migrant women's encounters with immigration enforcement authorities. On this night, the hazards inherent in the migration process had once again surfaced with an outbreak of armed violence in Arizona, allegedly between rival bands of human smugglers. Five undocumented immigrants were killed in these incidents, two of whom were women.[1] It was in the context of this event that Marcela's story unfolded.

Marcela had migrated from the Mexican state of Hidalgo hoping to reach Texas, where she had family. Tragically, she had been abandoned in the desert after she fell, and her injury prevented her from keeping up with the rest of the migrant group as they were briskly led by their coyote through the desert. She had wandered in the desert for three days after being abandoned before being picked up by a Border Patrol agent and repatriated to Mexico.[2] This evening, upon reflecting on her ordeal, she recalled the coldness with which her *paisanos* (fellow countrymen) agreed to leave her behind, and the callousness with which the coyote considered her, and ultimately, her misfortune. After all, she observed indignantly, to coyotes, migrants represent nothing more than a cash commodity: "¡Así nos ven, con un peso en la frente!" (That is how they see us, with a peso on our forehead!").[3] Marcela's cynical remarks were understandable in light of the news article that day that highlighted the risks to which migrants are subjected. Indeed, the business of human smuggling has been further complicated by post-9/11 border-enforcement measures and the incrementally more perilous strategies involving unauthorized entry into the United States. The dangers and the corresponding price of safety are most certainly correlated to the increased obstacles to historical circularity of migration and the parallel increase in U.S. dependency on migration to meet its need for labor.

In this paper, the transnationalized economy of reaching and crossing the U.S.-Mexico border will be discussed in light of migrant women's experiences. Based on research on the U.S.-Mexico border in 2006–2007, stories shared by migrant women help illustrate what I have dubbed elsewhere as the "ABCs" of migration costs: those related to assembling, *bajadores* (border bandits), and coyotes (human smugglers).[4] All add up to a formidable financial burden disproportionately shouldered by the most economically destitute, like Marcela, for an opportunity to work in the United States.

Human migration across international boundaries is a global phenomenon, with economic implications for migrants and for their sending and destination countries. Heckman notes that because human smuggling is a clandestine activity, it does not lend itself well to scientific inquiry.[5] Moreover, smuggling has increasingly become dominated by powerful mafias that go to great lengths to assure that their identity is hidden. As such, accurate information about the amount paid to coyotes is illusive.[6] For this chapter, some information on the costs of migration has been gleaned from a range of sources on human smuggling to help gauge the rise in the cost of migration in the most active migration corridor in the U.S. border region. However, primary data is drawn from testimonies of women gathered over twelve months of research on the U.S.-Mexico border. The data gathered in this research offers additional information about the cumulative costs of migrating, of which only part is the price paid to human smugglers. In this respect the research presented here is one of many attempts to address the gap in our knowledge about this elusive phenomenon as part of the overall experience of crossing borders surreptitiously.[7]

THE COSTS OF MIGRATION AND BORDER ENFORCEMENT ON THE ARIZONA-SONORA BORDER

The implementation of the Border Patrol Strategic Plan 1994 and Beyond National Strategy introduced measures to make it more difficult to enter the United States using traditional crossing areas.[8] The plan thus included the building of triple walls in highly urbanized areas along the U.S.-Mexico border where migrants were likely to find needed resources for crossing into the United States (such as shelter, food, and social support). The building of the wall in a well-trafficked corridor in El Paso, Texas, and in another well-trafficked corridor in San Diego, California, sent migrants attempting to cross into the United States toward the desert areas in between these two major urban centers. The Sonoran Desert area is one of the most isolated and thus more dangerous areas of the passage north.[9] Because of the intense immigration activity in this area, the migrant shelter in Nogales, Sonora, was selected for the study. This city of approximately two hundred thousand inhabitants[10] straddles the U.S.-Mexico border and lies fifty-five miles south of Tucson, Arizona, and within the area created by the 1994 Border Patrol Strategy.[11] By 2006, Nogales was approaching its peak of migration traffic north to the United States and back again via repatriation or removal from the United States.[12] As much as 48 percent of all migrants moving to or through Nogales were estimated to be women.[13]

Until the implementation of Operation Streamline in Tucson, Arizona, in 2008,[14] it was customary to simply remove most unauthorized migrants by repatriating them through the port of entry in Nogales, Arizona. Under this "voluntary" removal policy, most Mexican nationals apprehended near the border were fingerprinted and returned to Mexico without criminal charges. In practice, voluntary removal works to relieve immigration officials from having to incarcerate hundreds of migrants apprehended daily. However, in so doing, migrants are often apprehended and released more than one time,[15] and this accounts for inflated apprehension figures reported by the U.S. Border Patrol. Nogales, therefore, resembles a highly congested "intersection" where the process of transnational movement north and south is disrupted by the daily grind of border enforcement.[16] In keeping with the "intersection" analogy,[17] migrants at the shelter where the study was conducted can be seen as temporarily immobilized in a bottleneck of sorts: unable to move forward in their migration journey because of border-enforcement measures and unable or unwilling to return to their communities of origin.

THE RESEARCH: SITE AND METHODS

Approximately three kilometers south of the U.S.-Mexico border, Albergue (shelter) San Juan Bosco houses repatriated migrants who find themselves without a support system in the area upon their release from the custody of U.S. immigration enforcement authorities. Like other migrant shelters that have sprouted along the U.S.-Mexico line, Albergue San Juan Bosco is a nongovernmental organization that accommodates both male and female migrants and provides the opportunity to interview migrant women who had been repatriated.[18]

In 2006–2007, when the research was conducted,[19] migrants who had been repatriated or deported and who found their way to the shelter in Nogales typically stayed only one to two days before returning to their communities of origin or attempting to reenter the United States. Because of this, a rapid appraisal (RA) method was chosen for the research. RA emerged initially from development research,[20] but it has increasingly been used in the design and assessment of public health interventions.[21] In RA, interviewees are active participants in the interview process, and a semistructured topic guide is used as a checklist of issues that are pertinent to the study. For the research, it was expected that not all topics would be discussed with all interviewees and that in fact each interview might depart from the basic questions to pursue interesting, unexpected, or new information. The emergence of data was enhanced by observation and secondary information (triangulation), and in this way RA helps capture detailed information on the issues that are of greatest importance to both the individual interviewee and the interviewer. As such, each experience also becomes situated within broader contexts, such as the social economic situations that ultimately informed decisions about migrating and crossing into the United States. In this way, the all too common border-crossing ordeals that culminated in apprehension by immigration enforcement agents were situated within the broader border-security policies and practices. This helped document the circular pattern of migrant entry-exit-reentry that has come to characterize this particular context, one in which stepped-up border enforcement is both cause and effect of intensified efforts to cross when as more families are separated.[22] At the same time, the need to satisfy the demand for labor in the United States has triggered its systems to facilitate border crossing. These include social networks,[23] employer/employee relationships,[24] and the logistical and organizational mechanisms of the human smuggling industry, including bribery and corruption of U.S. Border Patrol agents and other U.S. law enforcement officers.[25]

Between February 2006 and June 2007, 129 women were interviewed at the shelter using a semistructured interview guide (the majority of these interviews were tape-recorded), through informal conversations, and by sharing activities such as eating or assisting with shelter tasks. Interviewing the women was often challenging because of the limited time that I had to solicit their voluntary cooperation and establish a measure of trust. However, I found most if not all of them were willing to talk to me about their border-crossing experiences. The shelter opens its doors at 7:00 p.m. every evening, and during a span of about three hours, migrants register, eat, wash, and bed down for the night. Few stayed beyond one night. A few respondents were reluctant to be tape-recorded, in which case I (or my research assistant) wrote notes during the interview and attempted to capture as many quotes as possible. Beginning in September 2006, I visited the shelter every two weeks, which provided for the systematic quality of data collection that was a goal of the research. With more visits to the shelter, I fell into the shelter's rhythm and gained rapport with the managers and volunteers. Being of Mexican heritage, while not a guarantee that I was a person to be trusted, was, I believe, also helpful in projecting myself as trustworthy (*de confianza*) and supportive among shelter guests.

THE COSTS OF NORTHBOUND TRAVEL

The distance and mode of travel are some of the most important factors for appreciating the material cost of migration. For those coming from Mexico, expenses begin with the initial financial outlay for the journey northward to the border. However, more than the absolute dollar cost of such an undertaking is the proportional cost to migrants based on their socioeconomic status. Table 5.1 shows that between 2005 and 2010, the southern states of Mexico had the largest percentage of emigrants, most of whom were destined for the United States. These are also the states that tend to be the most impoverished (table 5.2). The distribution of the sample of women interviewed in 2006–2007 indicates that

TABLE 5.1. Top ten sending states by percentage of emigrants 2005–2010

STATE	EMIGRANTS (%)
Oaxaca	83.9
Guerrero	78.1
Puebla	75.4
Guanajuato	71.9
San Luis Potosí	70.5
Michoacán	70.1
Morelos	69.4
Hidalgo	69.2
Chiapas	69.0
Veracruz	68.1

SOURCE Instituto Nacional de Estadística y Geografía, "Censo de Población y Vivienda 2010," http://www3.inegi.org.mx/sistemas /tabuladosbasicos/default.aspx?c=27303&s=est.

TABLE 5.2. Mexican states by percent of population living in extreme poverty

STATE	POPULATION LIVING IN EXTREME POVERTY (%)
Chiapas	38.3
Guerrero	31.8
Oaxaca	29.2
Veracruz	18.8
Puebla	17.0
San Luis Potosí	15.3
Campeche	13.8
Tabasco	13.6

TABLE 5.2. *(continued)*

STATE	POPULATION LIVING IN EXTREME POVERTY (%)
Michoacán	13.5
Hidalgo	13.5
Yucatán	11.7
Zacatecas	10.8
Durango	10.5
Tlaxcala	9.9
México	8.6
Guanajuato	8.4
Nayarit	8.3
Querétaro	7.4
Morelos	6.9
Chihuahua	6.6
Quintana Roo	6.4
Tamaulipas	5.5
Sinaloa	5.5
Jalisco	5.3
Sonora	5.1
Baja California Sur	4.6
Aguascalientes	3.8
Baja California	3.4
Coahuila	2.9
Colima	2.5
Distrito Federal	2.2
Nuevo León	1.8

SOURCE Consejo Nacional de Evaluación de la Política de Desarrollo Social, "Medición de la pobreza: Anexo estadístico de pobreza en México: Anexo estadístico 2012," http://www .coneval.gob.mx/Medicion/MP/Paginas/Anexo-estad%C3 %ADstico-pobreza-2012.aspx.

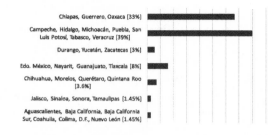

FIGURE 5.1. Distribution of sample (N = 125) of Mexican-origin interviewees by state of origin and percentage living in extreme poverty in sending states

the overwhelming majority of them were from these extremely impoverished states in Mexico (fig. 5.1).

Although the cost of this bus fare varies by point of origin, it is first important to factor distance into the initial financial outlay: more is paid by those who are coming from farther away. In general, the proportional cost in transportation fares will be more for resource-disadvantaged populations, and because most of these will be coming from farther distances (from mostly southern states in Mexico), more is needed for food, water, and shelter. These initial financial investments may be lost if the traveler is apprehended. Finally, it is also important to consider that while entry into the United States is an uncomplicated matter for those able to obtain visas—usually by providing a combination of documents that prove some proof of economic stability (e.g., wage receipts for the last six months, business tax receipts, retirement income receipts) and material holdings (e.g., property tax receipts, bank accounts, utility receipts)—providing such required documents is nearly impossible for resource-depleted migrants whose movement is largely driven by their poverty in their communities of origin in the first place. Not surprisingly, for many migrants who cannot provide such documents, most of the subsequent informal costs associated with migration (banditry, bribes, and smuggling fees) are related to avoiding apprehension for entering the United States "without inspection," that is, in a place other than an official port of entry.

With growing economic disparities between the United States and Mexico (in part aggravated by the North American Free Trade Agreement [NAFTA] signed in 1994) and the hardening of border-security measures that began in 1994 with the Border Patrol National Strategy, the cost of crossing into the

United States without authorization has spiraled upward. With increased security measures implemented largely in reaction to the September 11 attacks on the World Trade Center in 2001 and the U.S. war against terror, avoiding apprehension has become even more time consuming, more complicated, and therefore more expensive. I have argued elsewhere that as human smugglers become increasingly influenced and controlled by lucrative smuggling economies, they are more likely to succumb to the trend of commodifying and dehumanizing migrants, and this paves the way for their abuse.[26] Allegiance to powerful smuggling rings in essence works to devalue the commitment to human relationships and ultimately foments distrust and suffering and ultimately imperils lives.

The initial costs associated with avoiding apprehension must also be multiplied by the number of times the border crossing is attempted. In making the decision to repeat the attempt to cross, migrants weigh the price of failure. With no change in the economic conditions that prompted their migration to begin with, there are few options except to try again. If they do not succeed in crossing, the initial financial outlay is not only lost, but in addition, families in sending communities may need to come up with additional funds to pay for the bus fare home, losing in the process any hope for economic relief that employment in the United States would have provided.

LOANS AND INTEREST

To finance the initial migration journey, many migrants borrow the money and may put up their meager properties as collateral. On March 24, 2007, I interviewed Concepción at the shelter. She reflected on the futility of her efforts and the ultimate outcome of her investment:

> El dinero, que con aquel sacrificio que ahorra uno para pagar el camión, para terminar donde mismo.
> (The money, that with which such sacrifice one saved to pay for the bus, to end up none the better.)

The other women who were with Concepción that night described in more detail the moneylending process: The loans came from moneylenders, landowners, or business owners. They charge a high interest rate and/or take properties as collateral to offset the risk of borrowers disappearing. Reina, another migrant woman, was on her way to the United States to join her husband when she was apprehended. Her husband had worked in the United States for four years. She borrowed 1,000 pesos (about US$100) and would be accumulating debt of 200 pesos (about US$20) a month in interest. This financial burden weighs heavily on the decision to return home after being apprehended. For example, two women from a group of three, Ana and Rosalinda, all from Veracruz, had decided to stay in Nogales to look for work to pay for the bus fare home. However, for the third woman from this group, Agustina, there was no going back. She would not return because she borrowed money from a woman who had her sign a contract saying that if she did not pay the 1,500 pesos she borrowed her parents will lose their land. She was worried because she would have to stay in Nogales long enough to save that money to send home and pay the lender and then work more to pay for her return. She explained that there are people who are well off who make these deals with people who are willing to cross, and many lose their land, which is the only thing they have, if they cannot make it across the border. She said that these rich people make them sign a legal document, and as a result, they legally lose their land. Agustina, who was twenty-four years old and had two children who lived with their father, was hoping to help support her mother with money because although her mother had a husband, she was elderly, and she was responsible for the care of her younger brothers.

> Ella tiene marido, pero él ya no puede trabajar. . . . Tengo hermanos que están chiquitos. . . . Cuando estaba chiquita mi papá empezó a tomar, y pues yo nunca pude ir a la escuela.
> (She [her mother] has a husband but he cannot work. . . . I have brothers who are little. . . . When I was little, my father began drinking, and well, I was not able to go to school.)

Agustina had previously lived in the United States and worked in the fields. She had been living with a man who had a drug-abuse problem. He promised her that if they returned to Mexico, he would stop, but he did not. So she left him, and she was returning to the United States to look for work. Since she had attempted to cross twice and had been both times repatriated, she had decided not to try again. Like so many other women, their smugglers had lied to them about how long it would take to cross into the United States and how long they would have to walk. Her cousin who accompanied her on this night explained,

> Nos dijeron que iba a ser una noche . . . nos faltaba agua . . . estábamos deses-peradas porque era mucha subida y bajada. . . . A veces se ve un bordito y se ve la barranca . . . muy feo.
>
> (They said that it would only be one night . . . we needed water . . . we were des-perate because it was a lot of up and down hill climbing. . . . At times, you can see the unevenness and you can see the gorge . . . very ugly.)

> Anoche estábamos como dos horas con el frío, y todavía caminamos otra vez como dos horas. . . . Nos dejaron caminar todo el día, ya como a la una de la tarde, ¿no? Y ya es cuando nos agarraron a la una de la tarde.
>
> (Last night we were two hours in the cold, and we still walked another two hours. . . . We walked the whole day and around one in the afternoon, yes? And that is when they caught us at one in the afternoon.)

The magnitude of the costs due to the "bottleneck" created by apprehension and repeat crossing cannot be comprehended fully without considering the numbers of apprehensions in the Tucson Border Patrol Sector alone. Beginning in 1997, the Tucson Sector became the busiest of the southwestern sectors. According to a Department of Homeland Security website,[27] the Tucson Border Patrol Sector, which includes Nogales, led all other sectors with 439,090 investigations in 2005. Arizona has also had the most voluntary departures when all field offices were considered, a total of 395,597 out of a total 887,115 reported by all field offices for 2003. Of those migrants who are removed or deported, it is estimated that over one third would reenter the United States without authorization.[28] As a deterrent to repeat unauthorized reentry without inspection, progressively longer prison terms—based on the number of times they have been charged with this violation—are imposed on those who are reapprehended.[29] The high recidivism attests to the economic imperatives that outweigh the risk of serving longer prison terms if reapprehended. In Arizona, about thirty-one thousand individuals, the vast majority of whom are Mexican nationals, were imprisoned in 2004. Even without the implementation of Operation Streamline in 2008, this prison population has been growing.[30]

THEFT AND COST OF SUPPLIES

The loss of personal valuables is necessarily added to the cost of the initial migration journey. Through the course of the research, it was not uncommon to field complaints from migrants who stated they had been robbed by Mexican police or while in the custody of the U.S. Border Patrol. While interviewing Lydia and Lucila in February 2008, Lydia complained that she lost seventy pesos in detention, a little over the average fifty-five pesos minimum daily wage in Mexico). She suspected that when forced to relinquish their possessions when under custody at the U.S. Border Patrol station, the money had been stolen. They, too, had taken out loans to make the trip.

Returning briefly to the case of Rosalinda from Veracruz who had already borrowed money to make the trip, on that March night that I interviewed her, she was upset because she was repatriated to Mexico with no money. Rosalinda says that she lost everything when they were apprehended because she had given her backpack to a young man who was helping her with it, and when they were stopped, he took off with it. She had her money and ID in there.

SUPPLIES

Because for many, food and supplies are precious and hard-earned commodities, they were shocked at having to throw away all of their food supplies carried in their backpacks after being apprehended by the Border Patrol. One migrant woman interviewed on February 10, 2007, was particularly emotive when she explained, "Cuando llegaron [las autoridades] nos tiraron todo, todo, todo . . . agua, todo lo tiraron, luego nos llevaron en el carro" (When they [the authorities] came, they threw away everything, everything, everything . . . water, everything was thrown away, then they took us away). For resource-depleted migrants, food was a harmless necessity, and the practice of throwing away food was wasteful and made no sense. Their regrets were aggravated once they were in detention for many hours and hunger set in, especially in light of the fact that they had been for many hours or even days trekking through the desert. Their want of food while in custody of agents was a frequent complaint. Agents would distribute some crackers and juice, but this was hardly enough. For those who would eventually reattempt to enter (and perhaps as a Border Patrol strategy to discourage a subsequent attempt), the loss of supplies also meant that they would have to repurchase them. The neglect or inability to do so could lead to potentially deadly consequences.

LODGING

An important characteristic of the Nogales landscape is the proliferation of small hotels, *hotelitos* that cater to transnational migrants. On any day, one may observe shuttle vans from Hermosillo, the capital of Sonora and two hours south of Nogales, drive up to any *hotelito* and drop off groups of passengers with all the telltale signs of destitute migrants en route: backpacks, caps, sneakers, jackets, an aura of extraneousness. They are hurried into the *hotelito* while the wary-eyed doorman scowls at onlookers with cameras that may be paying too much attention to the activity. *Hotelitos* serve as interim safe houses for migrants while the necessary arrangements with coyotes are made. Understandably, such establishments guard their privacy. In this way, *hotelitos* embody the force of transnational movement that runs counter to the forces that attempt to impede it. As if standing in defiance of the security systems designed to impede migration, the colorful and brazen *hotelitos* that adorn the city's streets are Nogales' best-known "secrets," catering to illicit activity (human smuggling is also against the law in Mexico), often within yards of the wall that separates them from the United States and often within sight of officials who undoubtedly know of their purpose. Not staying at a *hotelito* exposes migrants at risk of physical abuse by bandits and extortion by corrupt police.

STRATEGIES TAKEN TO AVOID COSTS

For some, like Lila from Guatemala (interviewed in February 2007), certain precautions were taken to avoid additional costs associated with apprehension. It appeared that there were others who were also from Guatemala in Lila's group. Because they were from Guatemala, the guide had instructed them to say that they were Mexican if they were caught; otherwise, they would be deported to Guatemala, and it would only cost them more money to try to get back to attempt again to reenter the United States. For Lila, this advice and a stroke of good luck ensured that she would not suffer a major economic setback.

Así gastar menos, porque si a mí me van a detener va ser un buen rato porque...a mí me deportaron una vez, y así son los reglamentos. . . . De plano me van a dar unos seis meses, un año, qué se yo. . . . Por mi está bien [ser deportada hasta Guatemala] pero no me deportaron hasta allá, pero aún me tiraron aquí no más y sin dinero y sin nada . . . lejos de mi familia, no puedo hablarles, no tengo dinero para decirle a mi mama [en Guatemala] que estoy bien, no tengo para escribirle, ni cómo llamar a California más decirle que estoy bien, que donde estoy para que le puedan avisar a mi mamá, la verdad no sé qué hacer. Mi hermana está en Bakersfield con mis niños. Pero no tengo dinero para comprar una tarjeta para llamarles para decirles que estoy bien.

(This way, you spend less, because if they detain me, it will be for a good while because they deported me once, and those are the rules. . . . For sure they will give me six months or a year, but I don't know. . . . That's fine by me [to be deported to Guatemala] but they didn't deport me all the way there, but still they threw me here without any money and with nothing . . . far away from my family, I can't call them, I don't have money to let my mother [in Guatemala] know that I'm fine, I don't have anything to write her with, nor can I call to California to say I am fine, or where I am so that they can let my mother know. The truth is I don't know what I will do. My sister is in Bakersfield with my children. But I don't have money to buy a [phone] card to call them and let them know I'm OK.)

While the shelter provides a safe refuge for migrants, another alternative is to immediately reattempt to cross the border without waiting or without resting. This decision involves boarding a shuttle immediately upon repatriation for

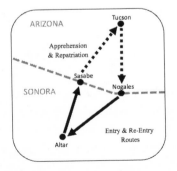

FIGURE 5.2. U.S.-Mexico border showing the circular pattern of migrant entry and exit and reentry in the Arizona-Sonora migrant corridor

the two-hour trip west to Altar, Sonora, the proverbial *antesala* (waiting room) for migrants going north. This pattern of entry-exit-reentry then assumes the aforementioned circularity depicted in figure 5.2, one that may be repeated several times until migrants either succeed or give up and return home.

THE COSTS OF BORDER BANDITRY: *LOS BAJADORES* (THE BANDITS)

Adding to the cost of migration are those associated with the almost certain assault from *bajadores*, the bandits who take advantage of the remote migration routes to rob migrants. The name *bajadores* comes from *bajar*, the Spanish verb that means to "pull down," and refers to the tactics these bandits use of forcing victims to pull down their pants at knifepoint or gunpoint in order to keep them prostrate and to facilitate a body search for valuables. During the interviews, other words used to refer to the bandits surfaced, such as *cholos* (gangsters) and *pandillas* (gangs). For example, Florencia and her husband borrowed money from her brother to go to the United States to work. They still had their land, but she did not know how they would pay the money back.[31] Their second attempt at crossing had dissuaded them from trying again. The couple had contracted a coyote to help them cross into the United States, although she did not know the details of this agreement. Of the robbery by bandits, she said,

> Nos robaron. . . . Nos quitaron el dinero, los Cholos, vimos a tres. Veníamos como ocho, y a uno le quitaron $1,500, a otro $800, a otro $300, nosotros le dimos $1,500, y ya no hay nada porque nos quitaron todo. . . . Si no traes nada, te van a pegar.
> El camión nos cobró caro, $3,500 a Hermosillo, salimos de Oaxaca en autobús, 20 dólares de Altar, Sonora.

> (They robbed us. . . . They took our money, the *cholos*, we saw three. We came with eight others, and from one of them, they took $1500 [pesos], and another $800 (pesos), and another $300 (pesos), we gave him $1500 [pesos], and now we don't have anything because they took everything. . . . If you don't have anything, they beat you.
> The bus charged us $3,500 [pesos] to Hermosillo; we left Oaxaca in the bus, $20 [dollars] from Altar, Sonora.)

Gladis, another migrant woman, explained that their journey to the North began with a group of eighteen other migrants. Gladis was traveling with her husband and an uncle, and they were robbed by *bajadores*. When their group encountered the bandits, there was already a group of about fifty migrants ahead of them who were being robbed. This large group of migrants were searched extensively for any valuables or hidden money. Because there were so many ahead of them, Gladis's group of eighteen was let off with a cursory demand for cash. She handed over her fifty pesos and considered herself fortunate. Her group had been spared the humiliation that comes with having to strip and be physically searched.

COYOTES

The term *coyote* is one of the most common terms to refer to a human smuggler in the U.S-Mexico border region. A discussion with almost any border denizen will refer to commonalities between coyotes and human smugglers in that they are both sly and masters in the art of camouflage. Human coyotes will often "disappear" when migrants are caught, much like how the four-footed desert creature blends into the environment. If perchance they are apprehended with their group, unless they are identified by any individual, they very much blend into the group of migrants, frustrating officials' efforts to isolate them for prosecution under Arizona's harsh antihuman trafficking statute. Some refer to the coyote as a coordinator or head of the human smuggling ring, which is hierarchical in structure. They are unlike the guides that lead migrants through the desert and are subjected to the same risks. As smuggling "coordinators,"[32] coyotes organize the step-by-step migration process and outsource certain smuggling actions, such as guiding across a border or transporting smuggled migrants to their final destination. However, consistent with the analogy to their four-footed counterpart, these, too, are individuals who are rarely caught.

The label *pollero* (from the Spanish, *pollo* [chicken]), also has its analogous reference. In this analogy, migrants are much like chicks, and a guide who is responsible for keeping group members together on the trek through the desert is like a mother hen. Throughout the interviews, and indeed throughout the border region, *coyotes*, *polleros*, and *guías* (a more neutral word and Spanish for "guide") are often used interchangeably, and whenever anyone raised a question about whether there was a distinction between them, it was more likely to make for a lively conversation than to agree on a definition.

TRACKING THE COSTS OF SMUGGLING

A variety of published sources, in addition to the information provided by the research here, can be used to argue that increased border-enforcement measures have contributed to the upward spiraling costs of migration.[33] As Lee states,

> Fees have gone up as the United States has cracked down on its borders after the Sept. 11, 2001 attacks. The cost to cross the Mexican border has increased about 50 percent, in part because improved surveillance technology has made the trip more difficult.[34]

For those contracting coyotes in the late 1980s, migrants reported paying as little as $50–$200 for each.[35] Petros reports that in 1996, the cost of smuggling migrants to the United States from Mexico was $150.[36] Later, Spener reports that the price of crossing the Texas border at the Rio Grande and reaching Houston or Dallas was rising, from $500 to $700 per person to $1,000.[37] At that time, migrants reported that $1,000 was not too much to pay. More recently, the reported amounts paid to human smugglers vary widely but are consistently higher. A 2004 study of 538 cases from papers, reports, journals, newspapers, magazines, and conferences worldwide reports that migrants to the United States from Latin America are paying an average of US$2,984.[38] This average amount paid is consistent with the approximately $3,000 reported by Lee and the Associated Press.[39] Migrant women sheltered at the Kino Border Initiative in Nogales, Sonora, between January and April 2010 reported to shelter administrators having paid the following amounts: twenty-three reported $1,000; ten reported $1,600–$2,000; thirty-eight reported $2,100–$3,000; fourteen reported having paid $3,100–$4,000; and one reported having paid more than $4,000.[40]

Without a doubt, the costs of smuggling are a significant part of world trade. An Associated Press article reports that a truck loaded with ten "illegal immigrants" is worth about $25,000 to a human smuggling organization.[41] Using court records, the reported figure was the "upfront costs to the immigrants," which are reported typically to run about $2,500 a person. The report from the Arizona Financial Crimes Task Force estimates that payments to a single collector of smuggling fees can reach $70,000 per day. An analysis done in February 2006 showed that in a two-month period, about $28 million in wire transfers were sent from the United States to 201 Western Union stores in Sonora, Mexico—transfers suspected to be tied to human smuggling.[42]

My study suggests that the range in the cost of migration is related to smuggling route and therefore the smuggling mode. This is also an important dimension that needs to be factored into the assessment of migration costs.[43] The mode of travel is more than transportation and may require assistance, specialized knowledge, infrastructure, or equipment. For example, my interviews of women for this study revealed various modes of crossing: some climbed over the border fence, some entered the United States through underground tunnels, some crossed packed in vehicles, and others crossed through the port of entry in cars with borrowed documents (*papeles chuecos*).[44] This latter mode was the most expensive, costing nearly $3,000 per person. Mari, a migrant woman from Yucatan, contemplated asking her grown daughter to raise the money so that she could cross. Ultimately, she decided it would place too much of a burden on her daughter and her family, and she returned home.

Entering through the port of entry either on foot or in a vehicle with *papeles chuecos* is by far the safest, especially if the person crossing is a child or an elderly individual. In doing so, they avoid the dangerous crossing on foot through the desert or the risks associated with climbing the thirty-foot wall and falling to the other side. While entering with *papeles chuecos* is the safest, it bears the greatest punishment if the migrant is caught. Those in possession of such documents who are caught may be charged with identity theft and face severe penalties that are added to charges of unauthorized entry. The least expensive and therefore most common mode of crossing among resource-disadvantaged migrants is to walk two to four days through the desert. For example, Azucena and her husband agreed to pay $750 to cross the desert in this fashion, according to my field notes dated May 3, 2006.

García Castro's research shows that the variance in fees may also vary based on the degree of familiarity between migrants and certain coyotes, *coyotes comunitarios* (community coyotes).[45] This nuanced understanding of coyotes has also been documented by García Castro and by Sanchez.[46] Having interviewed admitted smugglers (including some women coyotes), these authors qualitatively challenge notions of the coyote as ruthless criminals solely motivated by economic gain.[47] Instead, the activity is also largely social. These authors provide a rare glimpse into the social commitments between coyotes and family members, and, consistent with many of the supportive values that work to keep families together, the job of coyotes is shown to be also driven by their desire to remain in good standing with members within one's social network. Based on the coyotes' familiarity with their clients—as family members, as former clients, as friends or relatives of former clients—coyotes "comunitarios" ("community" smugglers) may offer discounted rates and in this way they help reduce not only the cost of crossing but also the risks associated with crossing as they may be more likely to feel social pressure to ensure the safety of those they are helping cross (which many times includes children). Offering "guaranteed smuggling services" is one way of dealing with the possible client's assessment of the risk involved, and due to the illegal nature of the activity, building trust is only possible through word of mouth among the migrants.[48] For example, an interview with Rosita, further detailed below, reveals that her father borrowed the money and arranged for the coyote to help her, her husband, and their young child cross into the United States. In addition, because the coyote was a friend of the family, they were only charged $1,100, and because she would be bringing her baby, he would arrange for the shortest route possible. Similar accounts dot the literature on border crossing and provide a nuanced understanding of the social context of human smuggling that is inherently varied and that factors into the costs of migrating.[49] As a business activity, there is a high premium on a coyote's good reputation.[50] However, as I have argued elsewhere, maintaining a good reputation is subverted by the lure of greater profits and excessive demands made on those charged with escorting migrants through the desert.[51] Moreover, with a reputation comes a risk of being identified by authorities. This encourages the elaborate use of client recruitment by middlemen who also operate clandestinely, are themselves partially or imperfectly informed about the whole operation, and results in greater risk for migrants.[52]

ADDING THE COSTS OF STAGE MIGRATION

The costs of migration necessarily include those expended over time and are related to "stage migration" of entire families. *Stage migration* is a term defined by Hondagneu-Sotelo and refers to the piecemeal reunification of families that begins with the initial migration of an adult and continues with the subsequent migration of spouses and each child over a period of time.[53] Rosita, one of the women interviewed in February 2007, exemplifies the process that looks like an installment payment plan for assuring that families might eventually be together. Rosita's parents left their children in Paracho, Michoacán, ten years ago when they migrated to the United States. At that time, Rosita was nine, the oldest of four. The children were left with Rosita's grandmother and aunts, and Rosita helped raise her raise her younger siblings, the youngest of which was a little over one year old. Over the years, Rosita's parents had arranged for the children to journey to the United States and be united with their parents. Rosita was the last of the siblings to make the journey.

In the last few months, Rosita's father had called them and urged them to make the journey because there was much work in Oregon. Rosita's father worked in the agricultural sector, routinely working the potato harvest. Not surprisingly, Rosita and her husband's decision to follow her parents to the United States was based on economic need. She stated, "A veces ni de comer teníamos" (At times we didn't have anything to eat).

In another example of stage migration, in February 2007, two women and a minor, Alva (nine), Lydia (twenty-two), and Lucila (eighteen) had arrived at the shelter. The three were not related but rather were *amigas* (friends) that came from a village in Santo Domingo, Oaxaca. They were also friends to the child's mother and had been charged with helping little Alva cross the border so she could join her mother in Atlanta. Alva was a petite, wide-eyed little girl. She seemed attentive and happy and only shyly smiled and answered an occasional question when asked. She had not seen her mother since she was three years old. Her older brother, age fifteen, had been able to cross.

CONCLUSION: GENDERED IMPLICATIONS OF UPWARD SPIRALING COSTS OF MIGRATING

On July 19, 2008, an article in *El Imparcial*, Sonora's state newspaper, again brought my attention to the problem of human smuggling.[54] My thoughts turned to Marcela and that night in February 2007, when I met her. The article, "Alertan sobre secuestros entre 'coyotes' in Arizona" (Alert regarding abductions by "coyotes" in Arizona), reported that for smugglers, each undocumented migrant represented US$2,000–$3,000. The article went on to report that the violent competition for migrants had reached a new high, with confrontations between bands of "coyotes" while abducting migrants from other bands. In 2007, the Phoenix, Arizona, police department had registered 356 cases of persons held hostage in drop houses by coyotes awaiting payment.[55] Thus, it seemed that Marcela's appraisal of the coyotes rang true: for coyotes, migrants were only regarded for the price they brought: migrants displayed the proverbial *peso on their forehead*. The article further reported that smugglers were fully armed and increasingly neglected the safety of innocent victims. If families did not send the money for the release of their family member, they were badly beaten. Accompanying this article were unsettling pictures of about twenty despondent migrants, unclothed save for their underwear, sitting on the floor of the safe house in Phoenix. The removal of their clothing, presumably to prevent anyone from escaping, also dehumanized them.

The rising costs of migrating and the associated violence as the stakes are raised have particularly grave implications for women migrants.[56] Castro Luque and her colleagues have documented a dramatic increase of 32 percent in the number of women migrating through Nogales, Sonora (from 4.9 in 1994 to 37.1 in 1998).[57] It has been argued that this dramatic rise in female migration is related to the neoliberal structural adjustment policies introduced by NAFTA in 1994, such as those that have resulted in the feminization of poverty in many other developing countries.[58] Gendered migration patterns, those in which the movement of unaccompanied men is followed by that of wives and other family members, are also undergoing change.[59] These studies suggest that more recent female migration patterns are less likely to follow a "stages" approach to migration, where women migrate after the initial stage that begins with their husband's migration, and more likely to resemble patterns established by their unaccompanied male counterparts.[60] My study here suggests that an overwhelming majority of women are increasingly traveling "alone" as *madres solteras* (single mothers). It can also be assumed that with the increased feminization of poverty in disadvantaged parts of the world and with families strained economically, women may be less able to count on more reliable, and therefore more expensive, modes of crossing. This increases their vulnerability to assault and banditry. In the interviews, there were several accounts suggesting that women and children were differentially treated based on the perceived liability that slower moving individuals would pose for the guides.[61]

For example, Yesenía, a migrant woman from Chihuahua, recounted how before arriving in El Sásabe, Sonora, they were exchanged twice among bands of smugglers. After the second exchange, the coyote seemed reluctant to guide them through the desert because they were accompanied by children, and he tried to dissuade them by asking the women whether they knew how long they would be walking.

¿Sí saben cuanto van a caminar? . . . Van a ser tres noches, quizás cuatro porque vienen niños. (You do know how much you are going to walk? . . . It will be three nights, maybe four because you are coming with children.)

They replied that they were determined, but after all was said and done, they were ultimately left behind. She felt that their group was left behind because it was smaller in number and in it were women and children. Margarita, in her interview, mentioned that the last *pollero* (smuggler) they hired told her that he would charge her more to get them across because they were women.

Scholars have consistently pointed out that rising costs of migrating and smuggling have increased with increased border enforcement.[62] The intensification in one process (enforcement) provokes a challenging response by the second process (migrating).[63] With costs mounting, financially weaker segments of society will increasingly become marginalized and made more vulnerable. Worldwide, being female and poor increases the likelihood of being discriminated against, and differentiated access to mobility and labor markets based on gender can only mean increased dependency and subjugation. The increase in the migration of women coupled with increases in migration costs can only predict greater risks for women especially as border-enforcement measures intensify.

NOTES

1. Quinn and McCombs 2007.
2. O'Leary 2008.
3. Field note entry, March 2007.
4. O'Leary 2009a.
5. Heckman 2007.
6. Petros 2005.
7. The policy report by Petros (2005) is a rare attempt to systematically collect and analyze the costs of human smuggling worldwide.

8. This strategy involved the intensification of border closures known as Operation Hold the Line (1993), Operation Gatekeeper (1994), and Operation Safeguard (1995). See Nevins (2002).

9. Cornelius 2001; Rubio-Goldsmith et al. 2006.

10. According to the city's web page, http://www.municipiodenogales.org/mapas_Nogales.htm, in 2005, Nogales, Sonora, had 189,756 inhabitants.

11. Rubio-Goldsmith et al. 2006.

12. Castro Luque, Olea Miranda, and Zepeda Bracamonte 2006.

13. Castro Luque, Olea Miranda, and Zepeda Bracamonte 2006; Monteverde García 2004. This figure is consistent with the percentage of female migrants in Latin America and North America (Zlotnik 2003).

14. Up until 2008, many undocumented migrants who were apprehended in Arizona were "voluntarily" removed from the United States at the Nogales, Arizona, port of entry. However, in 2008, there were changes in the voluntary removal policy in the U.S. Border Patrol Tucson Sector with the implementation of Operation Streamline. This policy change, a modified version of a pilot operation implemented in the Border Patrol's Del Rio, Texas, Sector in 2005, essentially selects certain undocumented immigrants who have been arrested for immediate prosecution for illegal entry. Because of Operation Streamline, a percentage of arrested migrants now face punishment of up to 180 days in jail, and formal deportation procedures are initiated once they complete their jail sentence. In Arizona, the program began with the prosecution of forty arrestees a day and has added to this number, with a goal of reaching one hundred per day by September 2008.

15. However, if and when found guilty of this charge, migrants serve sentences, after which they are deported. The vast majority of the detainees in Arizona, roughly between 75 and 90 percent, are serving sentences for illegal reentry after removal.

16. Cunningham and Heyman 2004.

17. O'Leary 2008, 2009c.

18. Albergue Plan Retorno, a governmental organization discontinued in the spring of 2007, sheltered only men, and Albergue Menores Repatriados typically only shelters unaccompanied minors under the age of eighteen, although on occasion, women may also be sheltered there.

19. Support for the initial pilot study for this research was provided in early 2006 by a Social and Behavioral Science Research Institute (SBSRI) Small Grant

at the University of Arizona. The research subsequently was made possible by a Fulbright grant awarded for 2006–2007.

20. Carruthers and Chambers 1981.

21. Robert Chambers might be the scholar most commonly associated with pioneering "rapid rural appraisal" techniques. Beebe (2001) provides a comprehensive history of the adoption of the method in a wide range of disciplines. Often known by different names, *rapid assessment* remains consistent with the early procedures advanced by Chambers and others.

22. O'Leary 2009c.

23. Fussell 2004.

24. Granberry and Marcelli 2007.

25. Erfani 2009; Blankstein and Kay, 2015; Garske 2013; Hernández 2015.

26. O'Leary 2012.

27. U.S. Department of Homeland Security 2007, table 36.

28. This figure is taken from a June 9, 2005, article in the *Arizona Daily Star*, Tucson, Arizona.

29. Alvarado 2004.

30. Ibid.

31. Field notes, May 4, 2007.

32. Heckman 2007, 5.

33. Petros 2005.

34. Lee 2006, 1.

35. Conover 1987.

36. Petros 2005.

37. Spener 1999.

38. Petros 2005.

39. Lee 2006.

40. Kino Border Initiative 2010.

41. Associated Press 2008.

42. Ibid.

43. Petros 2005.

44. Literally, *papeles chuecos* means "crooked papers"—documents known to be used wrongfully.

45. García Castro 2007.

46. Sanchez 2014.

47. Izcara Palacios 2014.

48. Heckman 2007, 4.

49. Petros 2005.
50. García Castro 2007; Petros 2005.
51. O'Leary 2012.
52. Heckmann 2007.
53. Hondagneu-Sotelo 1994.
54. *El Imparcial* 2008.
55. Generally, smuggling fees are due when immigrants arrive at a drop house, a place where those who just crossed the border are temporarily housed. Once the migrant has arrived, the drop house operator will telephone the migrant's sponsor, usually a family member who has agreed to come up with the smuggling fee, with instructions on how to pay. Once the money is received, the migrant is let go or taken to his or her final destination.
56. Ruiz 2009.
57. Castro Luque, Olea Miranda, and Zepeda Bracamonte 2006.
58. Marchand and Runyan 2000; Sadasivam 1997.
59. Cerruti and Massey 2001; Donato 1993.
60. Hondagneu-Sotelo 1994.
61. O'Leary 2008.
62. Erfani 2009; Heckmann 2007.
63. O'Leary 2009c.

STATION 3

FOUND REMAINS,
MISSING GRAVES

O God, we pray for all the migrants who have died in the desert . . .
bless them with eternal life and comfort their families who mourn.
Turn hearts from violence and xenophobia, so that reconciliation
and peace may reign on the border. Amen.

MIGRANT DEATHS IN THE SONORA DESERT

Evidence of Unsuccessful Border Militarization Efforts from Southern Arizona

DANIEL E. MARTÍNEZ

INTRODUCTION

A S I SAT WRITING AN EARLY DRAFT this chapter in the comfort of my air-conditioned office at the University of Arizona, I was well aware that hundreds of undocumented migrants were, on that very same day, attempting to cross the Arizona-Sonora border in an effort to improve the circumstances of their day-to-day lives. Temperatures in the Sonoran Desert of Southern Arizona regularly exceed one hundred degrees Fahrenheit during the summer months, something that U.S. immigration officials were well aware of when crafting the 1994 prevention-through-deterrence strategy that had ultimately funneled undocumented migration into the region by the early 2000s. Needless to say, the aim of this effort was to make clandestine crossings through Southern Arizona a risky and dangerous endeavor. For many of these border crossers, undocumented migration was a fairly new experience, one that could be described as an act of resistance and resiliency—a last-ditch effort to seek employment and offset the dire economic situations plaguing their hometowns stemming from failed free-trade policies that led to agricultural displacement and underemployment. For others this may have been one of a dozen crossing attempts they had made throughout their lifetimes, but now they were attempting the journey through a new area. The migration process was likely very familiar—something that had been engrained in them from a young age. Migration across the U.S.-Mexico border is as much a part of these individuals' local culture as the *santo patrón* (patron saint) or *fiestas* (holidays) of their *pueblo* (town), for in many communities of Mexico people have made the trek *al norte* (to the North—the United States) for generations in search of a better life for themselves and their families.

Surely many of the undocumented migrants of which I speak successfully reached their desired destinations. Others were likely apprehended and found themselves in what migrants describe as *la perrera* (the dog cage), or the back of a U.S. Border Patrol vehicle, on their way to a processing center and then back to Mexico shortly after signing a voluntary return. Yet others were perhaps processed through Operation Streamline, convicted of illegal entry or illegal re-entry, and spent several months in a detention facility before being formally deported to their country of origin. However, a few were probably not as lucky and paid the ultimate price in the desert while attempting the journey north—death. Sadly, the latter scenario has played out frequently in Southern Arizona, and the rate of migrant death has risen exponentially in the area over the past two decades. Since the beginning of fiscal year 2000, more than twenty-four hundred migrants have died while attempting a clandestine crossing through Southern Arizona—and this only includes the deaths that have come to the attention of U.S. authorities. The reality is that there is no definitive or exhaustive count of migrant deaths that have occurred in the region or in any other region. Nevertheless, several studies have empirically demonstrated that the increase in migrant deaths in Southern Arizona has been a direct consequence of the way the United States has chosen to address the issue of undocumented migration—through increased border enforcement.[1] My aim here is not to minimize migrants' individual agency in the undocumented migration process, nor is it my intention to place the responsibility of these deaths entirely on the migrants who choose to cross. Rather, my goals are to (1) briefly highlight how undocumented migration is a social process that extends beyond the individual-level decision to make the trek across the U.S.-Mexico border, and (2) draw further attention to one of the many consequences of increased border enforcements by specifically focusing on the case of migrant death in Southern Arizona. Perhaps most important, I contend, as other scholars have, that these deaths were foreseeable and thus largely preventable.

If we are to understand why the migrant death rate has increased in Southern Arizona, we must have a baseline understanding of why and how people migrate as well as how these factors vary according to the immediate circumstances people face in their country of origin. Because people migrate for different reasons, it is important to emphasize the diversity among migrants and the variations in histories of migration found throughout regions of Mexico. In other words, structural conditions, local context, and individual experience matter even among a group that is often erroneously seen as a homogenous demographic category.[2] I then provide a brief history of recent Southwest border-enforcement policies to illustrate how undocumented migration shifted away from urban crossing points into more remote areas. We must be conscious of how all of these factors interrelate and not only contribute to the perpetuation of migration but also how they are directly tied to the increase in undocumented migrant death rates in Southern Arizona.

Throughout this chapter, I draw on data from two sources: the first wave of the Migrant Border Crossing Study (MBCS, N = 415) and undocumented border crosser (UBC) death records from the Pima County Office of the Medical Examiner (PCOME) located in Tucson, Arizona. The MBCS consists of surveys with a random sample of Mexican UBCs who had attempted a border crossing along the Arizona-Sonora border, were apprehended by any U.S. authority, and repatriated to Nogales, Sonora, Mexico. All surveys were completed at a migrant shelter in Nogales, Sonora, between October 2007 and July 2009. Here I draw on the migration history of an MBCS respondent, Miguel, to help contextualize the circumstances and conditions of migrants' crossing experiences through Southern Arizona. On the other hand, PCOME records help illustrate the relationship between UBC deaths in Southern Arizona and border militarization efforts that began in the 1990s. In addition, data from PCOME records are used to highlight what we know about UBCs who have died while attempting to cross the border through the region. I conclude by addressing some of the other less-understood consequences of border militarization efforts beyond migrant death that are currently unfolding along the U.S.-Mexico border.

MECHANISMS OF MIGRATION

The existing literature describes the reasons people migrate as ranging from global or national-level pressures to household or individual-level decisions. In the broadest sense, theories surrounding the reasons people migrate can be

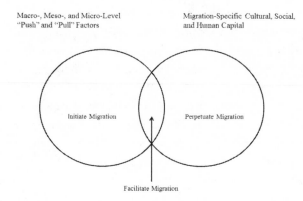

FIGURE 6.1. Overlapping mechanisms that initiate, facilitate, and perpetuate migration

described as dynamic and complex overlapping mechanisms that initiate, facilitate, and perpetuate migration (see fig. 6.1).[3]

Much of the literature discussing mechanisms that initiate migration focuses on various *push* and *pull* factors.[4] In the most parsimonious sense, *push* factors consist of circumstances that lead people to leave their communities of origin, while *pull* factors include circumstances that attract people to receiving communities. Push and pull factors can operate independently of one another, or they may be interdependent. Moreover, push and pull factors may act on multiple levels (e.g., global, national, regional, community, household, or individual).[5] Examples of push factors include unemployment, underemployment, or natural disasters in communities of origin, while pull factors include a structurally embedded demand for immigrant labor,[6] educational opportunities, or family reunification in receiving communities.[7] These push and pull factors are often the result of structural, political, and economic processes beyond the control of the individual. The following vignette describes the experience of an undocumented Mexican migrant I had interviewed as part of the first wave of the MBCS in Nogales, Sonora. Miguel's story helps contextualize and humanize the ways in which these factors come together and culminate in an undocumented crossing through Southern Arizona.

I interviewed Miguel three days after he had been deported from the United States. He was a forty-year-old male from the relatively impoverished southern Mexican state of Chiapas and had just nine years of formal education. Miguel informed me that he had been working as a security guard in Mexico earning about $480 per month but found himself unemployed for nearly six months before his most recent undocumented crossing attempt. Being the sole economic provider for a household of five other people, including his common-law wife and a teenage child, he felt mounting pressure to secure steady, decent employment. But there were few job prospects Chiapas, which has one of the lowest levels of human development in Mexico. In April 2009, Miguel decided to attempt to return to Phoenix, Arizona, where he had actually lived and worked in 2007. He wanted to go back to Arizona, work for a few years as he had done in the past, and eventually return to Chiapas.

Miguel left his hometown with a small group of friends and traveled four days by bus from Chiapas to Altar, Sonora, where they met a coyote (human smuggler) who agreed to guide Miguel across the border and up to Phoenix for $1,500. Miguel, the coyote, and a group of eleven other migrants then went to the town of El Sásabe, Sonora, where they began the journey across the border. Before long, Miguel had run out of water and was forced to drink from small stagnant puddles along the way. After walking for two days, Miguel, who was slightly older than the typical undocumented Mexican migrant, became exhausted, fell ill, and was no longer able to keep pace with the rest of the group. The coyote decided to leave him near a highway and advised him to wait there for the Border Patrol. Eventually the Border Patrol passed by and apprehended Miguel.

I asked Miguel to describe his emotional state when he turned himself in. He stated, "Better—I felt more certain that I wasn't going to die in the desert." But his relief began to turn to sadness and frustration once the reality of his situation set in. "As I began to recover physically I kept thinking about the plans I had and how all of my plans had fallen apart," he said. After being processed by Border Patrol, Miguel was tried through Operation Streamline, convicted of "illegal entry," and formally deported to Mexico. If Miguel is ever caught crossing again, he could be charged with "illegal entry," which is a felony, and he could face up to two years behind bars. Despite the difficulty and legal consequences of his most recent failed crossing attempt, when asked if he planned on crossing the border again, Miguel responded, "Yes, tomorrow or the day after. In Chiapas there is very little work, and they don't pay well. I have already seen life on the other side of the border, and I want to do it."[8]

As Miguel's story illustrates, push and pull factors can operate simultaneously at the macro-, meso-, or individual levels. However, the mechanisms that facilitate migration; that is, how one goes about the *process* of migrating, tend to be heavily influenced by social network ties as well as people's previous migration experience.[9] The facilitation of the migration process includes the preparation that goes into leaving one's community of origin, the actual migration experience itself—such as knowing where to cross and how to find a reliable coyote—and resettling into a receiving community, including securing housing and employment. In Miguel's case, he had ties to family members and friends in Arizona that could serve as a sort of social support system until he got back on his feet in the United States. He was also able to draw on the knowledge he had acquired through his six prior border-crossing attempts and the seven years of experience he had living and working in the United States to prepare logistically and mentally for his journey. These factors surely helped assuage some of the uncertainty or perceived risks Miguel had about the migration process—including his most recent failed attempt.

While the mechanisms that initiate migration flows tend to be generalizable to most migrants, documented and undocumented alike, access to legitimate means of migrating (i.e., securing employment-based and family-sponsored immigrant visas) vary significantly according to factors such as socioeconomic status and social equity in the United States. For example, high-skill workers or highly educated individuals are much more likely to have access to visas allowing them to migrate legally than do low-skill workers, people with lower educational attainment, or those of lower socioeconomic status.[10] Miguel's limited human and financial capital made it nearly impossible for him to secure an employment-based immigrant visa. In a similar vein, immediate family members of U.S. citizens have better chances of getting family-sponsored immigrant visas compared to family members of noncitizens.[11] Even if a person is eligible for such a visa, which Miguel was not, the backlog is so long that in some cases, the person may end up waiting over a decade to be able to migrate legally.[12]

A comprehensive overview of the U.S. Immigration and Nationality Act (INA) is beyond the scope of this chapter. Nevertheless, the INA clearly notes that prior immigration violations on a person's record can make accessing legal immigration channels an extremely difficult prospect. For instance, individuals with a prior deportation (i.e., formal removal), such as Miguel, are ineligible, in many cases for between five and twenty years, from applying for reentry to the United States. In some cases, people can request reentry following a removal, but they are required to apply for an I-212 waiver, pay a fee, and demonstrate high levels of social equity in the United States. More often than not, the immediate economic and social needs of people in situations such as Miguel's make pursuing legal immigration channels virtually impossible, and they are, therefore, forced to migrate in an undocumented manner.

The root causes of undocumented migration are social and economic in nature, and therefore the solution to stemming undocumented migration lies in addressing these root causes, not in increased border enforcement. The enforcement of immigration policies that do not account for this reality creates and perpetuates the precarious situations currently associated with the undocumented migration process (e.g., an underground economy of human smuggling and migrant deaths). Although U.S. officials have pointed to recent decreases in Border Patrol apprehension statistics in certain regions of the border as evidence of ebbing migratory flows and, therefore, proof of the success of border-enforcement policies, these decreases are more likely a consequence of the 2007–2009 economic recession in the United States and demographic transitions in Mexico. Furthermore, although it appears that unauthorized migration from Mexico has waned in recent years, U.S. Border Patrol apprehension statistics clearly illustrate that hundreds of thousands of migrants continue to cross the U.S.-Mexico border in an undocumented manner (see table 6.2). Moreover, throughout U.S. history, migration, as well as the de facto enforcement of immigration policies, has fluctuated with economic conditions, including the demand for low-wage labor in the United States.[13] It is perhaps premature to cite recent decreases in apprehensions as evidence of the success of border-enforcement policies or indicative of future migration. People have migrated across the U.S.-Mexico border for over a century and will continue to do so despite border-enforcement efforts. As Miguel's case illustrates, if there is a social or economic need to migrate, people will (and do) find a way to do so.

THE DIVERSITY OF UNDOCUMENTED BORDER CROSSERS

Non-Mexicans, especially Central Americans, are beginning to immigrate to the United States without proper documentation at increasing rates. For example, according to U.S. Customs and Border Protection, only 14 percent of the 327,577 undocumented migrants apprehended by the U.S. Border Patrol in fiscal year 2011 were "Other than Mexican" (the majority of which were from Central America). By 2014 this share had increased to nearly 53 percent. Much of this recent influx has been driven by the out-migration of unaccompanied minors and family units from the Northern Triangle of Central American (i.e., Honduras, Guatemala, and El Salvador) attempting to flee violence in the region. However, Mexican nationals continue to account for the majority of undocumented migrants residing in the country. In fact, according to the Pew Research Center, Mexican nationals accounted for 52 percent of 11.7 million unauthorized migrants residing in the United States as of 2012.[14] And as will be noted, Mexican nationals make up the largest country-of-origin category among undocumented border crossers who have perished in Southern Arizona. Therefore, this chapter will focus primarily on undocumented Mexican migrants, but Mexican undocumented border crossers are not a homogenous group. Migrants from Mexico come from various areas of the country with different histories of migration, ethnic and linguistic backgrounds, and socioeconomic statuses. Many of these differences vary by region of the country. Mexico's Consejo Nacional de Población (CONAPO) (National Population Council), divides Mexico into four main sending regions: *Northern, Traditional, Central,* and *Southern/Southeastern.* Table 6.1 illustrates the regions and states of Mexico as defined by CONAPO.

TABLE 6.1. Migrant-sending regions of Mexico

REGION/CITY
Northern
Baja California
Baja California Sur
Chihuahua
Coahuila
Nuevo León
Sinaloa
Sonora
Tamaulipas
Traditional (West Central)
Aguascalientes
Colima

TABLE 6.1. *(continued)*

REGION/CITY

Durango

Guanajuato

Jalisco

Michoacán

Nayarit

San Luis Potosí

Zacatecas

Central

Distrito Federal

Hidalgo

México

Morelos

Puebla

Querétaro

Tlaxcala

South/Southeastern

Campeche

Chiapas

Guerrero

Oaxaca

Quintana Roo

Tabasco

Veracruz

Yucatán

SOURCE Consejo Nacional de Población.

The Northern region includes Sinaloa, Baja California Sur, and the six Mexican states that share a border with the United States, including the state of Sonora where Miguel had last tried crossing when I spoke with him. These states have a unique relationship with the United States because of their proximity to the border. This relationship consists of a deep sociohistorical connection as well as a great deal of cultural exchange between the southwestern United States and these Mexican states. In addition, social institutions such as kinship networks and friendship groups have spanned this political boundary for generations. The Northern region tends to have some of the highest levels of economic development in all of Mexico,[15] attracting migrants from areas throughout the country. However, despite the higher level of economic development and higher wage rates in these areas, the proximity to the U.S. border has made many people well aware of the relatively higher wages and greater economic opportunities that are available on the other side of the border.

The Traditional region has a history and culture of migration that dates to at least 1917, when cohorts of migrants began working in the United States to fill the demand for labor during World War I.[16] However, the Great Depression and anti-immigrant sentiment during the 1930s resulted in the repatriation of thousands of Mexicans to their communities of origin.[17] The demand for low-wage labor in the United States increased once again during World War II. As a result, the U.S. government implemented the Bracero Program (1942–64) and contracted tens of thousands of workers from communities in this region to fill the labor shortage in the agricultural industry throughout the country.[18] A unique, socially embedded culture of migration further developed in the region during this time period. Many migrants had created and fostered relationships with employers in the United States and continued to migrate seasonally despite the termination of the program in 1964. These persistent journeys continued to contribute to a "culture of migration" in many communities in this area of Mexico. Thus, many people in this region have grown up hearing stories of migration from their relatives and, in some cases, anticipate or are expected to migrate to the United States sometime in their lives—something that has been considered as a rite of passage into adulthood. To this day, people from the Traditional region continue to migrate to the United States in high numbers. On average, people from these areas tend to have higher levels of what immigration scholars describe as migration-specific social capital (i.e., social ties to kin and friends in receiving communities)[19] and longer community histories of migration[20] that aid in the migration process and continue to perpetuate migration despite increased enforcement efforts.

The South/Southeastern region truly illustrates the diversity of migrants from Mexico, as individuals from these areas tend to come from agricultural backgrounds and are more likely to come from indigenous communities when compared with people from other parts of the country. In general, these communities have a relatively recent history of migration when compared with other regions of Mexico.[21] Consequences of free-trade policies, such as the 1994 North American Free Trade Agreement (NAFTA), have resulted in the displacement of agricultural workers in this region, as they were no longer able to bring their surplus goods to market and compete with imported agricultural products from abroad. The inability to compete with such imports has led to agricultural displacement and in turn has forced many campesinos (impoverished agricultural workers) to migrate to urban areas within Mexico and to the United States. By migrating abroad in search of new opportunities, such individuals are playing an active role in the determination of their futures and are demonstrating resiliency and resistance when faced with overwhelming economic circumstances. Campesinos from this area are, for all intents and purposes, economic refugees attempting to economically and culturally survive the consequences of detrimental free-trade policies that have affected them and their communities since the implementation of NAFTA in 1994.

Ultimately, undocumented migrants from Mexico come from distinct socioeconomic, linguistic, and cultural backgrounds. Further, areas such as the Northern and Traditional regions have a longer history of migration when compared with other areas of the country. The economic and cultural diversity of Mexico can help shed light on the reasons why people continue to migrate despite an increase in border militarization. Given the long history of migration in the United States, sociohistoric connections between the two countries, and the economic displacement many Mexicans have experienced because of NAFTA, it is not surprising that people continue to migrate despite an increase in border-enforcement efforts, the 2007–2009 economic recession, and ever-changing U.S. immigration policies.

RECENT BORDER-ENFORCEMENT EFFORTS: PREVENTION THROUGH DETERRENCE

Throughout U.S. history, the enforcement of immigration policies has fluctuated according to economic conditions in the country.[22] For the most part, immigration enforcement has been lax when there has been a demand for low-wage workers in the United States and more strictly enforced when economic conditions in the country have been bleak. The enforcement of immigration policies has also varied significantly with the political climate and public opinion; however, these factors are also undoubtedly tied to the economic situation in the country at the time.

Prior studies have noted that there was a systematic shift away from interior or worksite enforcement of immigration policies to the southwestern border during the 1990s.[23] Following the recommendations of a study conducted by Sandia National Laboratories, the U.S. government opted to adopt a prevention-through-deterrence approach to undocumented immigration enforcement.[24] Rather than simply continuing to apprehend and repatriate people to their countries of origin, U.S. officials believed that they could deter would-be undocumented migrants from emigrating in the first place by heavily enforcing traditional points of crossing such as El Paso, Texas (1993 Operation Hold the Line), San Diego, California (1994 Operation Gatekeeper), Nogales, Arizona (1995 and 1997 Operation Safeguard), and parts of South Texas (1997 Operation Rio Grande). Between 1993 and 1999 the southwestern border underwent an unprecedented increase in border militarization. Corrugated steel walls replaced chain-link fencing in cities such as San Diego, El Paso, and Nogales. In addition, the number of Border Patrol and Customs and Border Protection agents increased across the entire border at exponential rates, and millions of dollars were spent on new technology, vehicles, floodlights, and vehicle barriers throughout the San Diego, Tucson, and El Paso Sectors.[25]

Early on, these border-enforcement efforts were deemed successful, as there were substantial decreases in Border Patrol apprehensions in the El Paso and San Diego Sectors.[26] However, what officials failed to realize was that "success" in one area of the border simply meant failure in another as people shifted their routes into more desolate areas such as Southern Arizona.[27] For instance, during the early 1990s, roughly one in every eighteen Border Patrol apprehensions occurred in the Tucson Sector. Since 2000, on average, approximately one in every three Border Patrol apprehensions has occurred in this sector.[28] Table 6.2 illustrates the proportion of total U.S. Border Patrol apprehensions to apprehensions is the Tucson Sector between fiscal years 1990 and 2014.

Clearly, border-enforcement efforts have forced migrants such as Miguel to cross into more remote and dangerous areas such as Southern Arizona, thus increasing the likelihood of death. Had Miguel attempted a crossing in the early 1990s, it is probable that he would have done so near San Diego or El Paso,

TABLE 6.2. Comparison of total U.S. Border Patrol (USBP) and Tucson sector apprehensions, fiscal year 1990–2014

FISCAL YEAR	TOTAL USBP	TUCSON SECTOR	APPREHENSION RATIO (TOTAL : TUCSON)
1990	1,103,353	53,061	20.8
1991	1,132,933	59,728	19.0
1992	1,199,560	71,036	16.9
1993	1,263,490	92,639	13.6
1994	1,031,668	139,473	7.4
1995	1,324,202	227,529	5.8
1996	1,549,876	305,348	5.1
1997	1,412,953	272,397	5.2
1998	1,555,776	387,406	4.0
1999	1,579,010	470,449	3.4
2000	1,676,438	616,346	2.7
2001	1,266,214	449,675	2.8
2002	955,310	333,648	2.9
2003	931,557	347,263	2.7
2004	1,160,395	491,771	2.4
2005	1,189,075	439,079	2.7
2006	1,089,092	392,074	2.8
2007	876,704	378,239	2.3
2008	723,825	317,696	2.3
2009	556,041	241,673	2.3
2010	463,382	212,202	2.2
2011	340,252	123,285	2.8
2012	364,768	120,000	3.0
2013	420,789	120,939	3.5
2014	486,651	87,915	5.5

SOURCE U.S. Customs and Border Protection 2015.

would have spent hours (not days) crossing, and would have paid his coyote less than $500 for his services. However, the increase in the number of migrant deaths in Southern Arizona is not simply a function of an increase in migration in the area but rather the result of a higher probability of death as migrants are forced to walk for longer periods of time in order to avoid apprehension. One of the fundamental reasons that the prevention-through-deterrence strategy was adopted was that the Border Patrol anticipated that undocumented migration flows would be "forced over more hostile terrain, less suited for crossing and more suited for enforcement."[29] Ultimately, U.S. immigration officials understood that this preemptive military-style approach to immigration enforcement would result in the deaths of thousands of people, yet not only was this strategy adopted, it was also boasted about as a success early on. Thus, the increase in migrant deaths in Southern Arizona was a foreseeable and preventable consequence of enforcement efforts of the 1990s.[30]

DESCRIPTIVE STATISTICS AND ANALYSIS OF UBC DEATHS IN SOUTHERN ARIZONA

Data used in this study were collected from medical investigator reports conducted by officials at the Pima County Office of the Medical Examiner (PCOME) of UBCs who perished in Southern Arizona during a migration attempt. PCOME conducts medical investigations of unattended deaths in Pima County, and in some cases, adjacent counties. This includes the deaths of UBCs who die during the migration process. PCOME records are perhaps the best source of systematically collected data on UBC deaths in Southern Arizona, as it is estimated that this office conducts nearly 95 percent of all medical investigations of known migrant deaths that occur on the U.S. side of the Arizona-Sonora border.[31]

PCOME has experienced an exponential increase in the number of UBC deaths it has investigated since the mid-1990s. For example, between fiscal year 1990 and fiscal year 1999, PCOME was tasked with investigating the deaths of 120 UBCs. This number increased more than tenfold over the next decade to 1,537. More recently, between fiscal year 2010 and fiscal year 2014, PCOME investigated a total of 876 UBC deaths. In all, the agency investigated the deaths of 2,533 UBCs between fiscal year 1990 and fiscal year 2014. The drastic increase in the number of reported UBC deaths in Southern Arizona has been

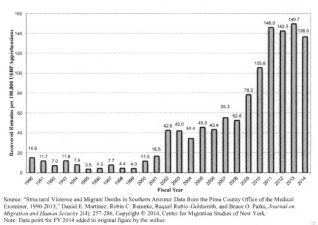

Source: "Structural Violence and Migrant Deaths in Southern Arizona: Data from the Pima County Office of the Medical Examiner, 1990-2013," Daniel E. Martinez, Robin C. Reineke, Raquel Rubio-Goldsmith, and Bruce O. Parks, *Journal on Migration and Human Security* 2(4): 257-286, Copyright © 2014, Center for Migration Studies of New York.
Note: Data point for FY 2014 added to original figure by the author.

FIGURE 6.2. Approximate death rate in the Tucson Sector using Pima County
Office of the Medical Examiner deaths coded as undocumented
border crossers, fiscal year 1990–2014 (*N* = 2,533)

directly linked to heightened border-enforcement efforts along the U.S.-Mexico border beginning in the mid-1990s.[32]

One could argue that the increase in the number of migrant deaths in Southern Arizona is simply a result of increased undocumented migration through the Southern Arizona. That is, more people are dying in the Southern Arizona because there are more people crossing through the area. One way to address this concern is to examine migrant death rates in the Tucson Sector, which encompasses a major portion of Southern Arizona, rather than a simple count of migrant deaths. Migrant death rates for the Tucson Sector can be estimated by using Border Patrol apprehension statistics as a proxy for undocumented migration though the area. While apprehension statistics may be problematic in that they do not account for recidivism, they are the best available data approximating undocumented migratory flows along the entire border. Figure 6.2 illustrates the change in the approximated migrant death rate in the Tucson Sector between fiscal year 1990 and fiscal year 2014.

Figure 6.2 suggests that before fiscal year 2002, the UBC death rate in the Tucson Sector was well below seventeen deaths per one hundred thousand apprehensions. However, between fiscal years 2002 and 2009, the death rate per year ranged between a low of thirty-four deaths per one hundred thousand apprehensions in 2004 and a high of seventy-eight deaths per one hundred thousand apprehensions in 2009. More recently, the UBC death rate in the Tucson Sector has consistently exceeded one hundred per one hundred thousand apprehensions since fiscal year 2010. Therefore, even after taking apprehension statistics into consideration (as a proxy for migratory flow), one can see that the rise in UBC deaths in Southern Arizona is not simply due to more unauthorized migrants crossing through the Tucson Sector. Rather, this pronounced change is a result of unauthorized migrants having to cross through more desolate areas for longer periods of time in order to avoid detection because of increased border-enforcement efforts. Similar patterns have been previously reported in other areas along the border, such as the eastern portion of the El Centro Sector.[33]

Table 6.3 provides descriptive statistics for biological sex, age, region of origin, and cause of death of the individuals whose remains have been recovered in a major portion of Southern Arizona between fiscal year 1990 and fiscal year 2013. Estimates for these factors were not available for fiscal year 2014 at the publication of this chapter. Sample sizes vary because some information about the deceased is much more easily attained than other characteristics. For example, the biological sex of an individual and the cause of death can, in most cases, be determined by a forensic anthropological exam. However, information such as a person's exact age or where they are from require that the individual be identified and that contact with their next of kin or other personal contacts be established. As one can see from table 6.3, 34 percent of undocumented migrants whose remains were recovered in the area are unidentified. In these cases, it is nearly impossible to know where the individual was from and their exact age.

The typical UBC investigated by PCOME can be described as a male (80 percent) around the age of thirty-one from Mexico (69 percent) who died of exposure (e.g., hyperthermia, hypothermia, dehydration, etc.) sometime within the past decade. Among UBCs who were positively identified, 13 percent were from the Northern region of Mexico, 15 percent were from the Traditional region, 22 percent were from the Central region, 19 percent were from the South/Southeastern region, and 14 percent were non-Mexican. Region of origin was unknown in 16 percent of cases among positively identified UBCs. As Martínez and colleagues (2014) note, there have been important changes in UBCs' region of origin across time that have coincided with major structural and political

TABLE 6.3. Specific causes of death and demographic characteristics of Pima County Office of the Medical Examiner deaths coded as undocumented border crossers, fiscal year 1990–2013

CAUSE/CHARACTERISTIC	PERCENT/MEAN	N
Causes of death		
Exposure	45	2,413
Undetermined	38	2,413
Motor vehicle accident	8	2,413
Other miscellaneous causes[a]	5	2,413
Homicide	4	2,413
Demographic characteristics		
Identified	66	2,413
Unidentified	34	2,413
Male	80	2,413
Female	17	2,413
Unknown biological sex	3	2,413
Age[b]	31 years	1,499
Region of origin among identified decedents		
North	13	1,583
Traditional (West-Central)	15	1,583
Central	22	1,583
South/Southeast	19	1,583
Non-Mexican	14	1,583
Unknown region	16	1,583

NOTE Percentages may not sum to 100 because of rounding.
SOURCE Martínez et al. 2014.
[a]"Other" causes of death include drowning, suicide, natural causes, cases pending investigation, electrocution, envenomation, overdose, and other miscellaneous causes.
[b]Among identified decedents.

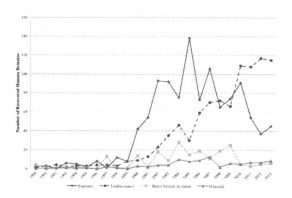

FIGURE 6.3. Leading causes of migrant deaths in Southern Arizona using Pima County Office of the Medical Examiner deaths coded as undocumented border crossers, fiscal year 1990–2013 (*N* = 2,290)

transformations in Mexico and Central America. For example, migrants from the South/Southeastern region only accounted for 9 percent of identified UBC deaths investigated by PCOME between fiscal years 1990 and 1999. However, this share increased to 23 percent in the 2000–2005 time period.[34] This increase coincided with higher levels of out-migration of Mexican campesinos who were systematically displaced by the long-term economic consequences of NAFTA. In a similar vein, non-Mexicans made up just 9 percent of UBC deaths investigated by PCOME between fiscal years 2000 and 2005. By the 2006–2012 time period, this share increased to 18 percent.[35] This increase in non-Mexican UBC deaths in Southern Arizona is likely a function of high levels of out-migration from Honduras, Guatemala, and El Salvador as people began to flee the region because of political instability and high levels of gang violence.

There have also been important changes in the leading causes of UBC death in Southern Arizona across time. As previously noted, increased border-enforcement efforts in the mid-1990s effectively funneled would-be migrants into remote and dangerous areas in Southern Arizona in an attempt to avoid apprehension by U.S. authorities. As illustrated in figure 6.3, the changes in the leading type of death across time speak directly to the effect that border-enforcement efforts have had on the increased lethality of attempting an unauthorized border crossing in Southern Arizona.

The rise in cases of death due to exposure began to increase around the same time that the migrant death rate in the Tucson Sector began to tick upward.

This suggests that migrants were being forced to cross through more desolate areas for longer periods of time in order to avoid detection. For instance, there was a pronounced increase in UBC deaths due to exposure after fiscal year 1999. This coincided with the increased border enforcements in the region. UBC deaths due to exposure, for the most part, continued to increase until fiscal year 2005, when they began to decrease, albeit not to the same pre-2000 levels.

Interestingly, the number of cases in which the specific cause of death was undetermined began to increase around the same time that the number of confirmed cases of death due to exposure began to decrease in the late 2000s and early 2010s. A definitive cause of death is often unable to be determined when the body is reduced to skeletal remains or is far too decomposed to yield a definitive cause of death. However, the remote locations where remains are recovered in these types of cases can offer some insight regarding the likely cause of death. In these cases it is very probable that the cause of death was indeed related to environmental exposure. Nevertheless, this cannot definitively be concluded from medico-legal standpoint, and such cases must be categorized as an undetermined cause of death. However, when one considers the increase in confirmed cases of exposure with the increase in cases in which cause of death was undetermined over the past fifteen years, it is hard to deny that the lethality of the unauthorized crossing experience increased as migrants began to be funneled into desert areas of Southern Arizona.[36]

DISCUSSION

Throughout this chapter I have attempted to illustrate how the border militarization efforts of the 1990s, in combination with the continued economic and social need to migrate, have resulted in horrible consequences: thousands of foreseeable and preventable deaths of undocumented migrants. Southern Arizona, in particular, has experienced a drastic increase in the number of migrant deaths and migrant death rate over the past fifteen years as a direct result of border-enforcement efforts forcing migrants to cross through dangerous desert areas.

Although unauthorized migration from Mexico has stalled in recent years, the United States and Mexico share a deep-rooted history of migration and have unique economic and social relationships that will continue to contribute to unauthorized migration from south of the U.S.-Mexico border. Furthermore, the agricultural displacement of campesinos as a direct consequence of NAFTA gave many people no choice but to seek alternative means economically to support themselves and their families. The reality is that people have migrated across the U.S.-Mexico border for generations and will continue to do so despite increased border militarization. The U.S. government's prevention-through-deterrence approach to immigration control has largely failed to deter people from crossing without documents and has resulted in the loss of countless human lives.

The increase in the migrant death rate is merely one of many consequences resulting from the border militarization efforts beginning in the 1990s. Some of these consequences directly relate to migrant deaths, while other consequences affect the lives of migrants while in transit. Consequences relating directly to the deaths of migrants include issues surrounding the handling of migrant remains once they are located and the financial costs incurred with this process as well as the challenges of attempting to identify and reunite the remains of migrants with their loved ones. This challenging process can take a financial and emotional toll on communities along the U.S.-Mexico border and throughout Mexico and Central America. Another consequence of heightened border enforcement that is often overlooked is the increased number of missing-person reports that have been filed over the past decade with Mexican and Central American consulates, medical examiner's offices across border, and nongovernmental organizations such as the Colibrí Center for Human Rights and the Coalición de Derechos Humanos (Coalition for Human Rights), both of which are located in Tucson. Every year, numerous people go missing and are never heard from again after attempting to cross the border without proper documentation. We must be aware of the social and psychological implications these events have on the family members, friends, and communities of undocumented migrants and even the effects they have on nearby border communities where people are disappearing or perishing.

In addition to the increase in the number of people who die or go missing while crossing and the complexities associated with these situations, border militarization also has other unintended social consequences along the U.S.-Mexico border specifically relating to the facilitation of undocumented migration. The funneling of migrant flows into less enforced areas along the border has made the undocumented crossing experience much more dangerous and has increased the vulnerability of an already extremely marginalized group. Elevated border enforcement has made undocumented migration a lucrative business venture for human smugglers and organized crime networks, as the demand for the facilitation of an undocumented crossing has risen substantially. This has led to the further commodification of undocumented migrants, resulting in increased crossing fees,[37] extortion, and kidnapping.[38] For example, the fees associated with undocumented crossing have risen because of the increased border-enforcement militarization efforts of the 1990s and 2000s.[39] One study, drawing on data gathered through the Mexican Migration Project, found that coyote prices had tripled from $400 in 1986 to nearly $1,200 in 2003.[40] A more recent study notes that undocumented Mexican migrants who used the services of a coyote reported paying, on average, $2,500 in smuggling fees during their most recent crossing attempt.[41] And such fees tend to be much higher for Central American migrants.[42]

Heightened border and immigration enforcement has also led to an increase in the number of undocumented migrants being held against their will in drop houses operated by human and drug smugglers in cities near the border. By 2009 media outlets began to describe Phoenix, Arizona, as the kidnapping capital of the United States for precisely this reason.[43] In most cases migrants are held against their will until their family members, friends, or prospective employers can pay all or part of the smuggling fee. In other cases, the family members, friends, and employers of undocumented migrants are extorted or deceived into wiring money to smugglers who claim to be holding someone when in fact they may have just briefly met the individual while they were preparing to cross the border in towns such as Altar or Sonora and managed to secure personal information from the potential migrant. Death, kidnapping, and extortion are not the only dangers people face during the migration process in the current era of increased border enforcement. Heightened border enforcement has also forced migrants into crossing corridors frequented by drug smugglers and *bajadores* (bandits), placing them at risk of being caught in the wake of drug-smuggling violence.

The issue of undocumented migration is not an easy one to address. All too often, discussions surrounding undocumented migration are politically charged and tend to focus on idealized visions of the ways things ought to be rather than on reality. While there is no easy solution to the issue of undocumented immigration, one thing is certain: the current prevention-through-deterrence strategy has not effectively addressed the issue and has resulted in numerous negative consequences. Not only are people continuing to migrate in large numbers without documents, but the number of migrant deaths and missing persons along the border has remained high and migrants' risk of experiencing drug-smuggling violence, extortion, or kidnapping has increased over the past two decades. Rather than attempting to control undocumented immigration through an ineffective and dangerous approach such as the prevention-through-deterrence strategy, perhaps efforts may prove to be more successful if greater attention were paid to issues of structural inequality that force undocumented migration in the first place.

NOTES

1. Eschbach et al. 1999; Cornelius 2001; Rubio-Goldsmith et al. 2006; Martínez et al. 2014.
2. De Genova 2002.
3. Massey et al. 1993, 2005; Massey, Durand, and Malone 2002.
4. Massey et al. 1993; Espenshade 1995.
5. Massey et al. 1993; de los Angeles Crummett 1993; Espenshade 1995.
6. Cornelius 1998; Massey, Durand, and Malone 2002.
7. Cornelius 1989; de los Angeles Crummett 1993; Hondagneu-Sotelo 1994; Donato and Patterson 2004.
8. Interviewed by the author, April 22, 2009.
9. Massey 1987; Massey and García España 1987; Massey and Espinosa 1997; Singer and Massey 1998; Aguilera and Massey 2003; Gathmann 2008.
10. *Visa Bulletin for August 2015*, vol. 9, no. 83 (Washington, DC: U.S. Department of State, 2015), http://travel.state.gov/content/visas/english/law-and-policy/bulletin/2015/visa-bulletin-for-august-2015.html.
11. Ibid.
12. Ibid.
13. Massey, Durand, and Malone 2002.
14. Passel, Cohn, and Gonzalez-Barrera 2013.
15. Anzaldo and Prado 2005.
16. Alanís-Enciso 1999.
17. Massey, Durand, and Malone 2002.
18. Ibid.
19. Massey and Espinosa 1997; Singer and Massey 1998; Aguilera and Massey 2003.
20. Alanís-Enciso 1999.
21. Marcelli and Cornelius 2001.
22. Massey, Durand, and Malone 2002.

23. Ibid.

24. Cornelius 2001.

25. Andreas 1998.

26. Ibid.

27. Andreas 1998; Eschbach et al. 1999; Cornelius 2001; Dávila, Pagán, and Soydemir 2002; Rubio-Goldsmith et al. 2006.

28. "Stats and Summaries," U.S. Customs and Border Protection, http://www.cbp.gov/newsroom/media-resources/stats?title=&page=1.

29. U.S. Border Patrol 1994, 7.

30. Rubio-Goldsmith et al. 2006.

31. Martínez et al. 2014.

32. Rubio-Goldsmith et al. 2006.

33. Cornelius 2001, 2005.

34. Martínez et al. 2014.

35. Ibid.

36. Rubio-Goldsmith et al. 2006.

37. Massey, Durand, and Malone 2002; Cornelius and Lewis 2007; Gathmann 2008.

38. Gonzales 2003; Felbab-Brown 2009; Quinones 2009.

39. Massey, Durand, and Malone 2002; Cornelius and Lewis 2007; Gathmann 2008.

40. Gathmann 2008.

41. Slack et al. 2013.

42. Durand and Aysa-Lastra 2015.

43. Quinones 2009.

BORDER MIGRANT DEATHS AND THE PIMA COUNTY MEDICAL EXAMINER'S OFFICE

BRUCE O. PARKS, ERIC D. PETERS,
CYNTHIA PORTERFIELD, DAVID WINSTON,
AND BRUCE E. ANDERSON

INTRODUCTION

LARGE NUMBERS OF UNDOCUMENTED IMMIGRANTS cross into the United States each year from Mexico. The most active area for this migration in the last decade has been the Arizona-Mexico border, perhaps the result of now unfavorable migration routes in safer, populated areas because of greater border enforcement by the U.S. government in these regions. Hundreds of thousands of border crossers are apprehended annually within the United States Border Patrol (USBP)–designated Tucson Sector (the middle and eastern divisions of Arizona), which may be the best available indicator of the magnitude of traffic. USBP apprehension data has been used previously as a sample estimate of the actual border-crosser volume because measuring the true population is impossible.[1]

The trek through Southern Arizona can be very dangerous, especially during the heat of the summer and late spring. Daytime high temperatures are often over one hundred degrees Fahrenheit. Water is scarce, and the terrain is rugged. If migrants are transported by vehicle, there are increased risks of crashes with overcrowded vehicles traveling at unsafe speeds. The Pima County Forensic Science Center (Office of the Medical Examiner), located in Tucson, Arizona, receives the majority of undocumented border-crosser deaths occurring in Southern Arizona. In this study, we will provide information about these individuals to give a better understanding of the scope of this issue, including changes in the Pima County Medical Examiner's Office as a result of such casualties.

METHODS

The majority of deaths investigated by the Forensic Science Center (FSC) occurred in Pima County, where Tucson is the county seat. Other deaths took place in the Southern Arizona counties of Santa Cruz, Pinal, and Yuma. Data from the FSC database and case files were evaluated. Historical information was based on our experience and FSC office records. Individuals were designated as a UBC (undocumented border crosser) if identified as non-U.S. citizens through the collaboration with a foreign consulate or family. If identity was unknown, and personal effects suggested foreign citizenship, a UBC designation was made. This was also the case when an anthropologic examination revealed an admixed Native American/Caucasoid heritage common to many within the Latin American population. The discovery of a body in the desert where corridors of illegal immigration were known to exist provided further support for the classification. Finally, a UBC designation was only applied to those who appeared to have died in transit and not to foreign nationals who had already established some form of residency. While it is assumed that the great majority were crossing in to the U.S., in some cases migrants may have been traveling back to Mexico. No distinction was made between migrants and smugglers.

Deaths of UBCs occurring during 2002 and 2003 were evaluated more extensively, including complete autopsies on the great majority of cases. If hospitalizations occurred and a diagnosis was established, then no autopsy was considered necessary. In the case of heat-related deaths, staff pathologists were asked to look specifically for previously reported findings. These findings included cutaneous petechiae (pinpoint hemorrhages), pulmonary edema, cerebral edema, pleural and pericardial petechiae, myocardial necrosis, centrilobular necrosis of the liver, disseminated intravascular coagulation (DIC), and acute tubular necrosis (ATN). Fluids, if available, were tested for drugs of abuse and alcohol. Glucose, electrolytes, vitreous urea nitrogen (VUN), and creatinine were quantitated if vitreous was available when a heat-related death was suspected. An anthropologic examination was performed in many cases, usually to assist with identification. Typical determinations included age, race, sex, stature, and sometimes separation of commingled remains (mixed remains of more than one individual).

The cause of death determination was based on the postmortem examination, the scene investigation, and historical information. A diagnosis of heat-related death or hyperthermia (considered synonymous) was made in each case when environmental heat exposure was most compelling because of the absence of other potentially fatal conditions coupled with the estimated time of death occurring during the hotter part of the year. An undetermined cause of death was typically applied when the extent of decomposition and historical information precluded accurate time of death estimates and/or when it was difficult to choose among one of several possible causes.

RESULTS

Since the year 2000, the number of recovered UBC bodies and skeletal remains has increased each year with the exception of a drop in the total for 2006. The following year, 2007, yielded the highest numbers of recovered UBCs, with a total of 218 (fig. 7.1). For the two-year period of 2002 and 2003, 304 four individuals were designated UBCs (147 and 157, respectively). Of those identified, ages ranged from seven to sixty (excluding one stillbirth), with a mean age of approximately thirty years. There were 232 males and 72 females. The great majority of UBCs were Mexican citizens, with others originating from Central and South America (table 7.1).

The most common cause of death of this group was heat related, certified as heat stroke or hyperthermia (fig. 7.2). The peak months of heat-related death, when time of death appeared to be within a few days of recovery, were June, July, and August (fig. 7.3). The second leading category is undetermined cause of death, followed by motor vehicle injuries, gunshot wounds, and natural conditions. The most common cause of death of UBCs for all years examined continues to be heat related (fig. 7.4). There were few potential exposure-related pathologic findings at autopsy in the heat-related group (see table 7.2). Linear abrasions of primarily the extremities were common, while blisters on the soles of the feet were observed less frequently (fig. 7.5). In ten cases individuals

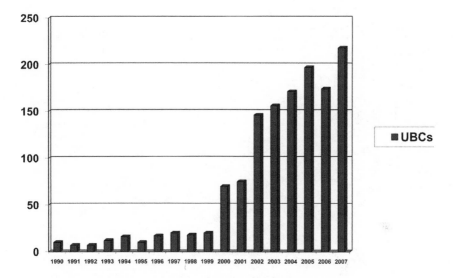

FIGURE 7.1. Annual number of undocumented border-crosser recoveries, Pima County Forensic Science Center

TABLE 7.1. Characteristics of undocumented border-crosser fatalities in Pima County, Arizona, 2002–2003

FINDING	%(N)
Male (N = 304)	76 (232)
Mean age (N = 233)	30
Mexican nationality (N = 230)	91 (209)
Heat stroke (N = 304)	62 (187)
Undetermined cause (N = 304)	22 (67)
Motor vehicle crash injuries (N = 304)	9 (26)
Homicidal injuries (N = 304)	4 (12)
Natural (N = 304)	3 (8)
Other (N =304)	2 (5)

NOTE N = number of cases for which data were available.

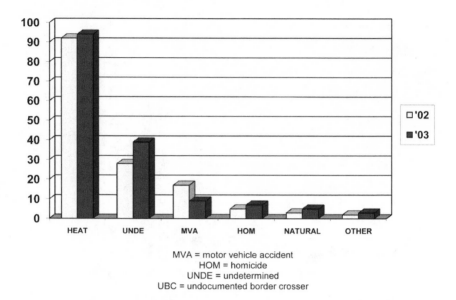

MVA = motor vehicle accident
HOM = homicide
UNDE = undetermined
UBC = undocumented border crosser

FIGURE 7.2. Undocumented border crosser cause of death, 2002–2003

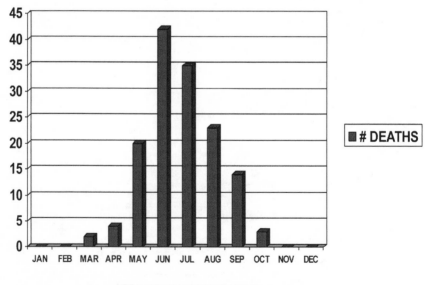

UBC = undocumented border crosser

FIGURE 7.3. Undocumented border crossers dying by month with short
postmortem interval recovered by month, 2002–2003

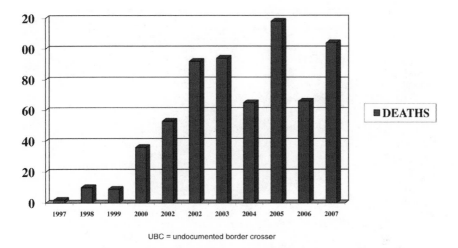

UBC = undocumented border crosser

FIGURE 7.4. Undocumented border crosser heat-related deaths, Pima County Forensic Science Center

TABLE 7.2. Characteristics of pathological morphology in 187 heat deaths

FINDING	% (*N*)
Abrasions	28 (52)
Foot blisters	4 (7)
Contusions	3 (5)
Cutaneous petechiae	2 (3)
Pulmonary edema	6 (11)
Cerebral edema	3 (5)
Pleural or pericardial petechiae	10 (19)
Other organ hemorrhage	3 (6)
Acute tubular necrosis	2 (3)
Myocardial necrosis	1 (1)
Hepatic centrilobular necrosis	0 (0)

NOTE *N* = number of cases for which data were available.

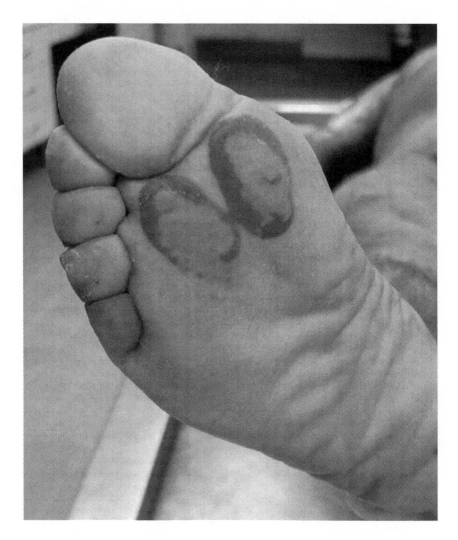

FIGURE 7.5. BLISTER ON SOLE OF FOOT

were found in distress, and medical care was provided. Their body temperatures before death ranged from 97.5 to 108 degrees Fahrenheit, with an average of 105 degrees Fahrenheit. The great majority of found remains exhibited at least some evidence of decomposition. Decomposition in many cases leads to mummification (fig. 7.6) and skeletonization. For those individuals recovered soon after death, the internal examination revealed few consistent findings, which include occasional petechiae of thoracic organs. Vitreous fluid was analyzed in seventy-four heat-related cases. Twenty-one revealed a dehydration pattern (elevated sodium, chloride, VUN), and all but eight of the remaining individuals showed elevations of one or more of the analytes. Finally, thirty-eight individuals showed an elevated VUN (table 7.3) without elevations of both sodium and chloride. The blood or cavity fluid of eighty-five cases was analyzed for ethanol, showing a result of forty-three positive, with a range of 0.01 to 0.110 g/dl. In two blood positive cases, another fluid was available for analysis, with vitreous negative in one and urine negative in the other. One hundred twenty eight individuals were tested for drugs, and most bodies underwent a drug-of-abuse screen. Fourteen were positive, and the most commonly detected drug was acetaminophen. Another five individuals were positive for controlled or illegal drugs.

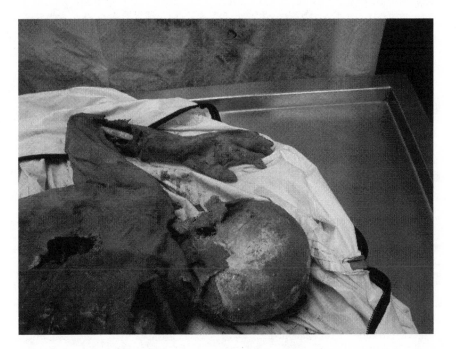

FIGURE 7.6. Partially skeletonized mummified body

TABLE 7.3. Characteristics of vitreous electrolytes in seventy-four heat deaths

ELECTROLYTE	% (N)
Elevated Sodium, Chloride, and VUN	28 (21)
Elevated VUN and creatinine	41 (30)
Elevated creatinine	53 (39)
Elevated VUN	51 (38)
Low or normal sodium, Chloride, VUN, and Creatinine	11 (8)

NOTE N = number of cases for which data were available. VUN = vitreous urea nitrogen.

DISCUSSION

The Pima County FSC was established in 1989. The office is involved with medical examiner death investigations in accordance with Arizona State Revised Statute 11-591. Currently this office performs work for not only Pima County but also Pinal, Santa Cruz, and seven other counties around the state. Included among categories of death under the medical examiners jurisdiction are unnatural deaths, deaths where no attending physician is available to sign the death certificate, and deaths due to violence. The medical examiner performs such duties as examinations, evidence collection, cause and manner of death determinations, documentation of injuries and disease, and body identification.

Before 2000, the FSC handled on average fourteen UBCs per year dating back to 1990.[2] A dramatic increase in the number of recovered bodies occurred beginning in 2000, and the numbers have generally increased steadily since, with an annual average over 150 from 2000 to 2007. This increase has led to both staffing and infrastructure deficiencies. A full-time forensic anthropologist was required because of identification issues, and the hiring of an additional pathologist was necessitated at least in part because of the greater workload.

In July 2005, Southern Arizona suffered one of the hottest months on record. The bodies of sixty-nine migrants were recovered and brought to FSC during this month, and the cold storage capacity of the office was exceeded. Migrants must often remain at the facility for an extended period of time since the identification process requires a careful examination of the body and belongings coupled with lengthy investigations made in cooperation with foreign consulates.

A refrigerated truck was leased at over $900/week to add additional temporary storage space. Months later, the office was able to purchase a refrigerated truck for $65,000 using federal Homeland Security funds. Within the next year, Pima County constructed a permanent auxiliary refrigeration building on the premises of the FSC for approximately $350,000. Between 2000 and 2006, Pima County estimated the unreimbursed additional UBC-related operating cost for the FSC to be approximately $140,000 annually.[3] This does not include infrastructure improvements.

The most common cause of death of UBCs examined at the Pima County FSC is heat related. In the United States, multiple fatalities from heat exposure are usually discussed in terms of heat waves affecting urban areas.[4] Criteria have been established for the diagnosis of heat-related illness, but they restrict hyperthermia and heat stroke to those instances in the living where an elevated body temperature exists. If after exposure to heat the person cools down before a temperature is taken and at the hospital elevated liver and muscle enzymes are discovered in addition to altered thought processes, a heat-related diagnosis may also be appropriate. Finally, if a person is thought to have died during a heat wave, then the death should be considered heat related either as the main cause of death or as a contributing cause depending on any preexisting conditions.[5] These criteria are better suited to the elderly living without air conditioning in cities with moderate climates and occasional heat waves but not for otherwise healthy, young, would-be migrants traveling through remote areas in an often perpetually hot desert. In this study, if the death was thought to be heat related, the pathologist used the terms *hyperthermia* or *heat stroke* for the cause of death. The term *heat related* was considered but was not used after discussions with the local Vital Registration department, who indicated the term would not be acceptable for their coding purposes. The fact that a high temperature was discovered for a few individuals found alive supports the hyperthermia/heat-stroke diagnosis as the primary cause of death.

Dehydration must also be considered as a contributing factor or cause of death. Twenty-one of seventy-four individuals tested showed a dehydration pattern as defined by Coe,[6] while only eight individuals had low or normal levels of sodium, chloride, and VUN. Because sodium and chloride levels decline over the postmortem interval, the dehydration pattern percentage is undoubtedly greater. Perhaps a better indicator of dehydration is an elevated, more stable VUN, which occurred in thirty-eight cases. However, relying only on VUN may exclude dehydration that has not progressed to renal failure.

The cause of death was classified as undetermined in sixty-seven deaths (22 percent) for UBCs during 2002–2003. Most of the time, this applied to skeletal remains found in the desert when the time of death could not be estimated with enough accuracy to correlate with the travel during a hotter time of year. Based on the fact that the vast majority of better-preserved crossers found in the desert die from heat exposure, it may be expected that most of the undetermined deaths are heat related as well.

GLOSSARY

ABRASION—A scrape, usually on the skin.

ANALYTE—A substance, usually a chemical, that is being measured.

ATN (ACUTE TUBULAR NECROSIS)—Death of cells making up part of the kidney.

CAVITY—A compartment in the body such as the chest cavity or abdominal cavity; with decomposition, fluids can leak from organs and accumulate in a cavity, especially the chest.

CREATININE—A protein in the body which in higher concentration indicates kidney problems.

DIC (DISSEMINATED INTRAVASCULAR COAGULATION)—A condition where clotting factors in the blood are depleted and bleeding into organs and other tissues occurs.

EDEMA—Leaking of watery fluid out of blood vessels causing swelling of an organ or tissue.

EXTREMITIES—The arms and/or legs.

HEPATIC—Pertaining to the liver.

HYPERTHERMIA—An elevated temperature that may cause death.

MUMMIFICATION—A form of decomposition where skin is dried and leatherlike.

MYOCARDIAL—Referring to muscle of the heart.

NECROSIS—Death of cells to include an organ or portion of an organ.

PATHOLOGIC—Abnormal, often referring to a biologic condition.

PERICARDIAL—Referring to the thin outer layer of the heart.

PETECHIAE—Small dot-like areas of bleeding in the skin and other organs.

PLEURA—The thin outer layer of the lung and the thin inner layer of the chest cavity.

RENAL—Pertaining to the kidney.

VITREOUS—A fluid within the back part of the eye.

VUN (VITREOUS UREA NITROGEN) — A measure of nitrogen in the form of urea, a product of protein breakdown that is eliminated from the body.

NOTES

1. Egan 2004; Hadden 2003; Hendricks 2004; U.S. Citizenship and Immigration Services 2003; Mrela and Humble 2004; Sapkota et al. 2006.
2. Rubio-Goldsmith et al. 2006.
3. Huckelberry 2005.
4. Basu and Samet 2005; Bernard and McGeehin 2004; Bouchama and Knochel 2002.
5. Donoghue 1997.
6. Coe 1993.

LOS DESAPARECIDOS DE LA FRONTERA (THE DISAPPEARED ON THE BORDER)

ROBIN REINEKE

---

cuando empezaron a desaparecer
como el oasis en los espejismos
a desaparecer sin últimas palabras
tenían en sus manos los trocitos
de cosas que querían
(when they began to disappear
like the oasis in a mirage
to disappear without any last words
in their hands they held the small pieces
of the things for which they longed)

—MARIO BENEDETTI, *DESAPARECIDOS*

THOSE WHO HAVE DISAPPEARED somewhere in the desert borderlands have left craters in the hearts of their families, abysses that threaten to swallow up nearby souls. The silence of the missing themselves is mimicked by the silence on the topic of disappearances of migrants on the U.S. side of the border with Mexico. If one seldom hears about the deaths on the border, one never hears about the missing. In this chapter, I will discuss the causes for this silence, the estimated number of missing migrants, and the effects these disappearances have on families. I argue that those crossing the border are already missing "persons" in a biopolitical system that appropriates migrants from the south as exploitable bodies for labor. The physical disappearance of migrants is a continuation of the violence they experience as being "the nobodies" of modernity.[1] Further, I argue that the deaths and disappearances on the border are indicative of the construction of the desert borderlands as a space of terror that creates an intimidated workforce in the interior of the United States.

The ethnographic work that informs this chapter comes out of ongoing dissertation research conducted from 2006 through the present. While fulfilling the requirements for a master's degree, and now for a PhD in the School of Anthropology at the University of Arizona, I also worked at the Pima County Office of the Medical Examiner (PCOME) on various projects focused on supporting efforts to identify the remains of migrants who died during their attempt to cross the U.S.-Mexico border into Arizona. In 2013, I cofounded with William Masson the Colibrí Center for Human Rights, a family advocacy organization that supports families in their search for information about missing loved ones last seen crossing the border. Colibrí collects missing-person reports from families, information that is then compared with records produced from examination of the unidentified dead. For my master's and dissertation research, I contacted relatives of the missing who had filed missing-person reports at PCOME and interviewed them off-site. The interviews were semistructured and almost always involved the collection of antemortem data that could aid in decedent identification in addition to information relevant to ethnographic study.

My dual role as ethnographer and applied practitioner is complex but not without antecedents in anthropological practice. My role can be most productively compared to that of medical anthropologists who work in a clinical setting but are neither doctors nor patients. In addition to the training I have received in ethnographic field methods, I have also been trained in the techniques of human identification within forensic anthropology. In what I think of as an ethnography of a body count, my participant observation has been physically located at the medical examiner's office but also in the community with families of the dead and disappeared. My stance between the relatives of the missing and forensic scientists has given me insight into the complexities, ambiguities, and inconsistencies in the "work" each side does to do the same thing—return the missing. My focus here will be on the work of the relatives.

I use the term *los desaparecidos*, or "the disappeared," to describe the missing. I do this because it is the term family members use when speaking of their missing loved ones and because the term draws historical links between Latinos missing on the border and those who were forcibly disappeared in Latin America throughout the latter half of the twentieth century. These links are important because *los desaparecidos de la frontera* are structurally the same people who were disappeared in Guatemala and El Salvador by military regimes backed by the United States government. Many migrants now crossing the border themselves survived repressive violence in their home countries during this era and into the present. Additionally, the deaths and disappearances on the border are structured, not random. Although there is an important distinction between the forced disappearance that occurred in Argentina in the 1970s, and the disappearances occurring along the border due to extreme vulnerability, the latter are congruent with the former in that they are preventable, predictable, and violent.

I will now turn to the numbers. Nancy Scheper-Hughes, who worked with displaced and extremely marginalized people in northeast Brazil, described how she, "the most interpretive and qualitative of ethnographers," became "an obsessive counter, a folk demographer . . . the village clerk, the keeper of the records recording and numbering the anonymous dead and disappeared."[2] Anthropologists are often interested in documenting the very same lives that the state and dominant sectors of society perceive as the most disposable. As of this writing, the Colibrí Center for Human Rights' database contains records for 2,035 missing migrants last seen crossing into Arizona. Over the past decade, Arizona has become the most heavily traversed point of entry for unauthorized immigrants. This was not always the case. The Tucson Sector of the U.S. Border Patrol, which includes about two-thirds of Arizona's border, accounted for less than 20 percent of all apprehensions in the mid-1990s.[3] Today, the Tucson Sector accounts for over 45 percent of all apprehensions.

This shift is a result of Clinton-era border-enforcement policy changes that effectively pushed unauthorized immigrants into the most remote areas of the international boundary. The Arizona desert became the most heavily crossed section of the border as well as the deadliest. The correlation between the border-security buildup and increased migrant fatalities has been demonstrated extensively.[4] Every time, calls to "secure the border" have resulted in more militarization, and subsequently, more death.[5] Closing the border to workers while opening the border to consumers and transnational markets is inherently violent.[6]

In order to understand how this violence is socially experienced, I will now turn to the story of one family missing someone last known to be crossing the border into Arizona. Through this case study, I will discuss themes apparent in many interviews and observations I have done for my ethnographic research. All names and identifiable places have been changed to protect confidentiality.

WHAT HAPPENED

During the fall semester of her sophomore year, in the middle of midterms, Adriana got an e-mail from her mother, Mayra, saying that she would be leaving Peru to make the journey to the United States to be with her. Mayra had been struggling ever since her business closed several months earlier. The nightclub she had owned for years was among a city strip of bars and restaurants that were simultaneously shut down because of, they were told, a lack of proper permits. In fact, a developer had purchased the land, and small businesses were being cleared to make way for a hotel. Most of what she had saved over the past eleven years was in that club. She lost everything. Desperate and depressed, she wanted to be with her two daughters and husband in New York. Adriana did not think that her mother was serious until she started getting e-mails from Ecuador, then Costa Rica, and then El Salvador. In a matter of weeks, her mother was calling from Sonora, Mexico, saying that she would be crossing into the United States the next day. Mayra told her husband that she would call when she got to Phoenix. The call never came.

Mayra is part of a small percentage of South Americans represented among the missing and dead and among migrants to the United States in general. There is very little known about the experiences of South Americans as they migrate through Central America and Mexico. I chose Mayra's story because what her family has experienced is very typical of families I have interviewed, and it was well articulated by Adriana in English.

The information about what happened came slowly, and many questions remained. After several weeks had passed with no word, Adriana and her father were able to find the family with whom Mayra had stayed in Sonora before she crossed the border. The family ran a hostel or shelter of sorts that housed migrants on their way to the United States. They had connected Mayra with the coyote (human smuggler) who led her across the border with a group. The coyote agreed to speak with Adriana and her father only after they paid a fee of $500. After speaking with the coyote and three other migrants who were in the group with Mayra, Adriana and her father were able to piece together an unsatisfying "story" of what happened—it did not make sense and had no clear ending.

Apparently the group crossed the physical boundary on foot and was then picked up in the desert on the U.S. side by an associate of the coyote in a van. As they drove north on Interstate 19, a Border Patrol vehicle appeared in the rearview mirror. Then, near Sahuarita, Arizona, only about a half hour's drive from Tucson, the vehicle began to have mechanical problems. The driver eventually stopped, and everyone who could ran. To get away from the interstate, they had to climb over two fences, one small, and one large. The fellow migrants who spoke to Adriana and her father said that Mayra had made it over the smaller fence but not the big one. She was left behind between the two fences. "And from there," Adriana explains, "she was just missing."

When interviewing family members, I often ask a question along the lines of "how did you find out that she is missing?" Despite its awkwardness, I ask this because many families received a call from someone in the group saying that the person was left behind. Others never heard from anyone. The awkwardness of this question, though, relates to the inadequacy of both the English and Spanish language and narrative structure to capture the ambiguity of the experience of "having a missing person." How can you have something that is missing? Relatives are enduring something terrible, but describing their condition is also challenging. They are not "bereaved," they are not "mourning," and they are not "grieving," as each of these implies a confirmed loss. They are survivors not of something but of the *absence* of something. Relatives of the missing remain in limbo, their status mimicking that of the missing person. The only cure for their condition is seeing the person in flesh or in bone. The search for this cure becomes all-consuming.

THE SEARCH

Adriana and her sister moved from Peru to New York in 2004 to join their father, who had been living and working in the area since 1998. All three of them are permanent residents and were working so that Mayra could join them. The economic situation was not good in either country. While Mayra fought to keep the nightclub and then lost everything when it was closed, Adriana's father struggled to make ends meet selling handicrafts at fairs in New York City. Adriana and her sister were enrolled in middle school immediately upon arrival in the city. Adriana excelled. After only three months in middle school, she began high school. "Even though it wasn't the best high school," Adriana said, "we decided, we're going to make the best out of this." By her sophomore year, she was in honors classes. She went on to study mathematics at a prestigious university, where she continued to thrive—getting straight As, participating in clubs, and garnering the support of faculty.

When her mother went missing, all of this changed. Adriana could not focus. Her grades fell. She dropped out of her clubs. She fought back tears during exams. After her finals that semester, Adriana and her father traveled to Arizona to search the area where Mayra went missing and to interview people who had traveled with her. They met with immigration, with the Mexican consulate, the Peruvian consulate, and several immigrant rights groups in Tucson. They traveled to Mexico and spoke with the family at the hostel where Mayra had stayed before she crossed. They met with the Instituto Nacional de Migracion (National Migration Institute) and filed a report. They posted fliers around Altar, Sonora, and Tucson, Arizona. They went to the spot where Mayra and the group got in the van and to the spot where everyone fled and she was left behind.

Families who are in search of a missing migrant face an incredibly decentralized setting for reporting. In the United States, missing-person cases are typically managed by the police jurisdiction where the person was last seen alive. In the border context, this process is no longer viable for a number of reasons, the first and most important of which is the fact that the families of missing migrants are highly vulnerable. Whether undocumented immigrants living in the United States or Oaxaqueños living in the *altiplano*, the families of missing migrants come from communities that are structurally vulnerable.[7] Contacting law enforcement can be a risky endeavor, one that could result in further family separation and trauma. In addition, many families say that police agencies turn them away when they attempt to report a missing loved one lost crossing the border. This was the case for Adriana, who said that the police told her to report to Border Patrol. Border Patrol does not have an institutional protocol for managing missing-person cases, and to date, there are no cases managed by Border Patrol in the National Missing and Unidentified Persons System (NamUs). Because the standard mechanism for reporting a missing person is out of reach for the families of missing migrants, they contact various other agencies, many of which were not designed to manage missing-person cases. Examples include foreign consulates, medical examiners, newspapers, immigrant rights organizations, or private investigators. Because Mayra is Peruvian, Adriana and her father reported her missing to the Peruvian consulate. Because she traveled through Mexico using a false Mexican ID, they reported to the Mexican consulate. In the United States, they reported to Immigration and Customs

Enforcement (ICE) as well as to Tucson-based immigrant rights organizations Coalición de Derechos Humanos and No More Deaths. These various agencies, whether governmental, private, or voluntary, do not have consistent systems for sharing information among themselves, and more importantly, for sharing information with those agencies that have accurate and detailed data about unidentified remains. The Colibrí Center for Human Rights was established to address this problem.

The information gathered about unidentified remains by medical examiners and coroners is also very decentralized. Although a national system was recently developed to prevent such occurrences, it is possible that a family could report a missing person to a coroner in one county only to have the remains be discovered in another. In many cases, there is still no consistent way for these records to be shared. In 2009, the National Institute of Justice launched the National Missing and Unidentified Persons System (NamUs), which is an online relational database designed to match missing-person records with records for unidentified decedents found throughout the country. Although NamUs represents an enormous step forward in the challenge of resolving the thousands of missing and unidentified cases in the country, there are limitations, especially when it comes to missing and unidentified migrants. The ability of NamUs to significantly aid in the identification of migrants will be severely limited until administrators relax the criteria for allowing missing-person cases to be entered into the system. NamUs follows the criteria of similar programs such as the National Crime Information Center, which requires missing-person cases to be overseen by law enforcement. This means that the only families NamUs will be capable of directly assisting are those that reported to law enforcement, something most families of missing migrants are unable or unwilling to do.

As Adriana and her father went about visiting and contacting various agencies in their search, they found kindness, indifference, and cruelty. At the first immigration and customs office they visited in Tucson, they had to wait for hours in a busy waiting room before meeting with anyone. Adriana's father wept, panicked for news. When they finally met with an agent, he refused to give them any information, saying that it was confidential "law enforcement-only information." The second immigration office was a little better, but not by much. An agent went through records for migrants deported the same day Mayra was left behind, looking for her name. He made sure to warn them, "If I find her, I'm going to deport her." Adriana and her father felt that their case was of little concern. Adriana explained, "You know, we're talking about a life-threatening thing. You know, and, it's someone's life out there, and they really didn't care. And we even said, like, we have papers, I mean, come on, we have the right to know."

The Peruvian consulate was similarly dismissive, focusing on Mayra's legal transgressions rather than her status as a missing and endangered person. After explaining that Mayra had used a fake Mexican ID card, the person at the Peruvian consulate scolded Adriana and told her that Mayra would get two years in jail for identification theft. Their own consulate refused to contact immigration, hospitals, jails, or other consulates. In turn, these other agencies would not give Adriana and her father information because they did not have the type of clearance the consulate would have had. Although Mayra went missing in Pima County, Arizona, none of the governmental agencies Adriana and her father contacted forwarded the report to the PCOME, where unidentified remains for the area are examined. It was thanks to Coalición de Derechos Humanos (Coalition for Human Rights), an immigrant rights group in Tucson, that Mayra's missing-person report made it to the medical examiner's office.

It was Kat Rodríguez, then director of Derechos Humanos, who took a full report and helped Adriana and her father find someone to stay with while they were in Tucson. Although Adriana and her father had saved for two months in order to afford the trip, their money was running out fast on hotels, food, and gas. A lawyer from No More Deaths, Margo Cowan, volunteered to host Adriana and her father in her home. During their stay, Margo drove them to Sahuarita, to the place where Mayra disappeared.

Adriana could not figure out how her mother could have gotten lost in the area. It is not particularly remote. When they were visiting, they saw farms, people out riding horses, traffic, mailboxes. "It would be really hard for someone to get lost there," Adriana said. Also, Border Patrol was right behind them. "She was stuck between two fences, they should have caught her," she said, "plus, there were helicopters, I mean, come on, they should have caught her."

When I ask relatives what they think happened in the desert, they often list a long and varied list of possibilities, each seemingly *the* one while they are talking about it. For Adriana, she believed that her mother was caught by Border Patrol and has yet to be released. She also worried that Mayra was kidnapped and was being held against her will. Her worst fear was that her mother was suffering. "What if she is being tortured right now?" Adriana also believed that Mayra never even crossed the border. She cannot reconcile this with the testimonies of those who crossed with Mayra, but, as she said, "I just don't know what to believe anymore." When I interviewed her, Adriana was a junior in college. She told me that she planned to save up money with her father so she could take a year off before graduation to search for her mother in northern Mexico.

Family members of the missing and dead, many of whom have crossed the border themselves, often speak of the desert borderlands as a strange space where it seems anything can happen. They describe it as *muy feo* (very ugly/awful) or *extraño* (strange), and the circumstances of the death or disappearance as suspicious, creepy, or mysterious. Although most of the confirmed deaths are due to environmental exposure (hyper- or hypothermia), relatives often do not believe this determination and are convinced that their loved one was murdered. Rumors circulate, and fears are intensified.

Anthropologists who have studied state terror have characterized spaces under regimes of terror as unpredictable, out of control, and dominated by a sense of uncertainty or unknowability. Following Scarry,[8] Begoña Aretxaga describes how terror operated during the Franco regime in Spain through a "fantasy space within which state violence operates that gives it a surreal, uncanny, and chilling feeling, a power to 'unmake worlds' as it 'unmakes' bodies."[9] Nancy Scheper-Hughes described her field site in northeastern Brazil as a "ruthless, unstable, amoral place . . . a place where almost anything can happen."[10] Michael Taussig argues that "cultures of terror are based on and nourished by silence and myth in which the fanatical stress on the mysterious side of the mysterious flourishes by means of rumor and fantasy woven in a dense web of magical realism."[11]

Anthropological studies of state terror have tended to focus on direct, somatic violence, where state or parastate forces act on the state's power to kill. Less attended to are settings where violence is manifested in the state's realization of the power to *let die*. Despite increasing emphasis on structural violence within anthropology,[12] there is very little scholarship that systematically focuses on the experience of structural violence among survivors of those who have died, been maimed, or disappeared as a result. Originally conceptualized by Johan Galtung,[13] theories of structural violence have been drawn on extensively to theorize the modern U.S.-Mexico border. Notably, Joseph Nevins has argued that the deaths on the border are "destined to happen as a result of structures and actions of violence not seen as such."[14] But structural violence is also present when whole sectors of a population are denied access to food, water, or medicine. Structural violence is present in the lives of migrants before they leave their homes, during their travels north, at the border, and beyond.

In short, structural violence is in effect whenever there is structured inequality. While this is certainly the case at the U.S.-Mexico border, as has been well elucidated, the violent mechanisms at the border reach well beyond those created by structural violence.

By this I am not referring to direct violence or trying to put various acts of violence on a continuum. Without question there is horrific direct violence along the border in the form of Border Patrol abuses, drug-cartel disputes, kidnapping, rape, and torture. However, viewing violence through typologies does not provide a lens strong enough to comprehend the creation and maintenance of a space where all forms of violence flourish. What has been constructed at the border is a space of terror that would-be migrants must pass through in a grotesque rite of passage. This space of terror is not limited to the U.S. side of the line but exists on the Mexican side as well. The discovery of the mutilated corpses of seventy-two Central American migrants in Tamaulipas in 2010 is one example of the horrors migrants face as they approach the international boundary. Although historically the frontier has been viewed as "lying at the margins of state power,"[15] the "frontier" today has more state presence in the form of Border Patrol, the National Guard, and federal police than any other region in the country. Aretxaga's question with regard to the Spanish Civil War is useful here: "How was one to regard this state that appeared at once in control and out of control?"[16]

The 1994 Border Patrol Strategic Plan, which laid out the enforcement strategy the agency would follow during the next decade, reveals this contradiction. While stating that the border would "be brought under control,"[17] effectively "restoring our Nation's confidence in the integrity of the border," the report also states that "violence will increase as effects of strategy are felt." This demonstrates that the simultaneous appearance of control and the fostering of lawlessness is strategic. State terror has been defined as "the use or threat of violence by the state or its agents or supporters, particularly against civilian individuals and populations, as a means of political intimidation and control (i.e., a means of repression)."[18] The nurturing of violence in the space of the borderlands can only be seen as state terror. It has been sustained by a public consensus that those crossing the border are not only noncitizens but are enemy combatants. The success of hundreds of thousands of migrants each year is further evidence that the "restoration" of the "nation's confidence in the integrity of the border" is a performance of intimidation and control. For the migrants themselves, the very real terror experienced at the border is maintained once they arrive at their destination through threats of deportation and other forms of violence, which may result in further family separation and the possibility that the desert gauntlet might have to be experienced again.

As families like Adriana's undertake the search for a missing loved one alone, the particular unknowability and terror of the desert borderlands becomes their day-to-day reality. They encounter the indifference of state actors who are either no longer bound to maintain the act of caring or who, despite their personal feelings, do not have the authorization to help. Adriana's experience with both ICE and the Peruvian consulate are indicative of a punitive state consumed with maintaining the construction of illegal bodies, which necessitates an erasure of the person.[19]

The search can also expose the family to further violence and abuse. Adriana's family experienced extortion and exploitation during their search for Mayra. Calls started coming to Adriana's father's cell phone shortly after Mayra went missing. The callers claimed to have Mayra and said they could only allow her to speak on the phone after they received money. One caller told Adriana that they would not free her mother from captivity until they were wired US$4,000. And a "lawyer" Adriana's father was paying to search for Mayra claimed to have found her in jail but demanded he be paid US$10,000 for her to be released. Although they did not pay this amount and severed the relationship with that particular lawyer, Adriana told me that most of her father's earnings go toward paying detectives and lawyers to search for Mayra. Adriana's family, unlike many families interviewed for this research, have documents demonstrating their legal right to be in the United States. For undocumented immigrants, the risks of exploitation and abuse are even higher.

THE EFFECTS

When this happened to our family, all our dreams just crushed. Just crushed. Everything stopped, especially me. You know, like, I used to do everything that my mother used to tell me. You know, get a good career, study, you know, she used to give me so many advices, and now, like, what am I doing this for? It really affected us a lot. I think when this happened, we stopped living in general. I feel like we have no other life than to find her. That's our only goal.

The effects of disappearances on families like Adriana's are devastating. Psychologist Pauline Boss has characterized what relatives of missing persons experience as "ambiguous loss."[20] Boss, who developed the concept while working with families of missing pilots from the American war in Vietnam, describes the experience as one where missing loved ones are "perceived by family members as *physically absent* but psychologically present, because it's unclear whether they are dead or alive."[21] She argues that ambiguous loss is similar to post-traumatic stress disorder in that it results from psychologically traumatic events that are outside the realm of usual human experience, "but with ambiguous loss, the trauma (the ambiguity) continues to exist in the present. It is not *post* anything."[22]

Anthropologists have traditionally placed the missing into the category of "the unquiet dead."[23] This category usually refers to those who died culturally stigmatized deaths, or "bad deaths." For example, in most Western cultures, those who died by suicide or as children or from violence can be considered the unquiet dead. They are liminal—they have not been successfully emplaced in the society of the dead but exist somewhere between the living and the dead. As such, they are threatening. Special care must be taken, usually in the form of regular rituals or special burials, so that these dangerous dead do not harm the living.[24]

For the relatives of the missing, however, the missing are not dead. There are no socially agreed on rituals to protect and heal families of the missing. With no body, anything could have happened to the person, and death is just one option among many. Rita Arditti, an Argentinian human rights activist, quoted a local Argentinian mental health expert describing how difficult it is to resign oneself to the fact that a missing person is dead:

> To presume the death of people you have not seen dead, without knowing the conditions of their death, implies that one has to kill them oneself. I believe that this is one of the subtler and complex mechanisms of torture for the relatives and for all the members of the community. . . . To accept their deaths, we have to kill them ourselves.[25]

For these reasons, the category of the missing should remain distinct from that of the dead. Like the unquiet dead, the phantom of the missing person threatens the well-being of the living, but unlike even the unquiet dead, there are no clear socially agreed on courses of action. The unquiet dead may be appeased through special postmortem rituals, burial practices, and spirit tending.[26] The materiality of the dead body, regardless of how mutilated, allows mourners of the unquiet dead a social legitimacy that the families of the missing do not have.[27]

In addition to providing emplacement for the dead and solace for mourners, funerals and collective burial rites are occasions where socially agreed on narratives of "what happened" are established.[28]

For relatives of missing migrants, often each family member has a different list of possible explanations to account for the person's absence. Some explanations may leave certain family members more or less culpable. Those I interviewed for this research describe intense family conflict after the disappearance of a loved one. In most cases, this has led to further family fracturing through divorce or estrangement. Adriana told me that she can no longer speak to her family in Peru.

> I remember before, I used to be really close to my cousins and grandparents, but not anymore, because as soon as I talk to them, they say, "have you heard anything about your mother?" You know, just the fact that they ask once is already affecting you. Even though they don't blame me, you already feel guilty. It's like, because she disappeared here, it's your fault. I just stopped talking to them.

Family members who live in other countries often feel powerless and do not know where to direct their anxiety other than onto those relatives living in the United States, who are perceived to have more recourse. Family members already in the states often help relatives who are planning to migrate by recommending the same coyote, helping to pay for the trip, or promising lodging once they arrive. In many cases, a close friend or family member was actually traveling with the person at the time of disappearance and was forced to leave them behind in the desert or risk dying or disappearing themselves. These people are often blamed and ostracized by other members of the family. Some family members are emotionally unable to engage in the search, which also causes resentment and mistrust.

The missing seem to consume the lifeblood of their families. Regardless of disagreements, family members find it difficult to be together. Individually, they are distracted, unable to find pleasure in their daily lives. They are haunted by the possibility that their loved one could be suffering while they are enjoying life. It is difficult to eat, difficult to sleep. Relatives have often described dreams to me where the missing person is begging for food or water, literally pleading with the living to be nourished. One woman missing her sister told me, "The only time I feel alive is when I'm looking for her." Adriana's friends had to talk her out of committing suicide the year after her mother disappeared.

In the 1970s, the Argentine military dictatorship used forced disappearance as a way of disciplining those who opposed state policies.[29] Antonius Robben describes how "the disappearances absorbed the political consciousness of the relatives into a desperate search."[30] He demonstrates how this was a precise strategy of state control. Military officers admitted to him that forced disappearance was opted for by the military over public execution because it was thought that it would debilitate the opposition. Most families of *desaparecidos* (disappeared) feared that any political action would endanger the missing person, who might still be alive in the hands of security forces. As Marcel Suarez-Orozco put it, the "sacred currency" of silence "became part of the madness as if it intervened in the causality of events."[31] State terror such as what occurred in Argentina during the "dirty war" was not aimed solely, or even mostly, at victims and their families, but at society at large. Regimes built on terror count on the fear and submission of those who perceive themselves as not so different from the dead and disappeared.[32] The "culture of terror," Michael Taussig argues, comes about through "the need to control massive populations through the cultural elaboration of fear."[33]

In a two-hour interview, Adriana repeated variations on the following sentence four times: "You know, it doesn't really matter what happened, if she got deported, or caught for selling drugs, or how much we have to pay . . . anything as long as we know that she is okay." When it came to confronting the state security apparatus that was ultimately responsible for Mayra's disappearance, Adriana was prepared to accept the criminalization of her mother and the physical act of forced removal from the country as long as she could know her whereabouts. Her anger at the system that disappeared her mother was sublimated by her fear and desperation.

The silence on the issue of deaths and disappearances at the border is part of a broader regime of terror experienced by immigrants in the United States. Their utility as an exploitable workforce without rights is dependent on fear.[34] The experience of terror is by no means limited to the desert borderlands, but it is punctuated in that geography, where disciplined, noncitizen subjects are created. Paul Sant-Cassia argues that for the modern nation-state, "borders are first and foremost symbolic boundaries, whose transgression is signaled by the production of dead bodies . . . and their post-mortem treatment."[35] The performance of sovereignty at the border teaches citizens and noncitizens alike what the nation is and who its members are and are not. According to Foucault, such a performance is a demonstration of biopower, or the right of the sovereign to "take life or let live."[36] Mmembe shows how through terror, the sovereign "marks" those who are citizens who "error" versus those who are disposable, who commit "crimes."[37]

Migrants crossing the border are allowed to enter the sovereign space of the United States, but they are also allowed to die trying, marking them as disposable. In the politics of "protection," performed at the border, they are not those who are protected.[38] In their home countries and within the United States, those sectors of the population that migrate are often reduced to "bare life" as their status as persons is reduced to that of exploitable bodies in the global economy.[39] Linda Green sees them as "the nobodies" of neoliberalism.[40] They could be seen, following Judith Butler, as "ungrievable lives" that "cannot be apprehended as injured or lost if they are not first apprehended as living."[41] De Genova, following Coutin,[42] conceives of "the social space of illegality" as "an erasure of legal personhood—a space of forced invisibility, exclusion, subjugation, and repression."[43]

In this context, even the act of reporting a person missing becomes an act of resistance. Jenny Edkins argues that in searching for a missing person, loved ones are demanding that a particular, irreplaceable person is returned and thereby are inherently challenging the dominant political-economic structure that is based on "*a politics that misses the person*, a politics of the *what*, not the *who*."[44] Such actions by family members "demand for a place for the person-as-such in politics."[45] In some ways, the missing are the inverse of bare life—they are pure personhood. There is no body, no bones, only memories and traces left behind. This status has given political voice to relatives of missing persons in other contexts, such as in Argentina among the Madres de Plaza de Mayo (Mothers of the Mayo Plaza), who transformed their anger and grief for the loss of their *desaparecidos* (disappeared) into one of the most powerful contestations of the state's actions during the dirty war. The permanent ambiguity of the disappeared created a space that could not be controlled by state narratives.[46]

Many families use the Spanish word *denunciar* (denounce) when referring to the act of reporting a person missing. The meaning, similar to the English word "denounce," is to "publicly declare to be wrong or evil."[47] Families calling the medical examiner's office often do literally denounce the disappearance as they are describing the physical characteristics of the missing person. "She was a good person; she didn't do anything wrong. She was just trying to help her family" is a sentiment expressed by many callers. "Esta situación es muy fea. Tan negra para nosotros y muy injusta" (This situation, it is very ugly. So dark for us and very unjust), remarked the sister of a missing man.

In Mexico and in several Central American countries, political activism among families of the disappeared is not limited to the denouncing of missing-person reports. In El Salvador, the Comité de Familiares de Migrantes Fallecidos y Desaparecidos de El Salvador (Committee of Relatives of Dead and Missing Migrants of El Salvador), "recognizing that we had a shared pain from the disappearance and death of our relatives, but also sharing the indifference of the government authorities," organized to protest the disappearances, demand that the missing be returned, and work to create a database of deceased migrants. The Foro Nacional para las Migraciones en Honduras (National Forum for Migration in Honduras) is an organization devoted to political action on behalf of migrant human rights. Part of the work that they do relates to searching for and decrying the absence of *migrantes desaparecidos* (disappeared migrants). Both groups organize and participate in caravans to Mexico, where they demand respect for the human rights of migrants. This type of political action will likely appear in the United States, especially as the children of the disappeared realize their rights as citizens.

CONCLUSION

The deaths and disappearances along the border are part of a strategy of state control within the United States. The construction of the borderlands as a space of terror is useful for the neoliberal state, which relies on the simultaneous unregulated flow of capital and the repression of laborers.[48] Disappearances have been at the core of many regimes of terror, where they were used to silence and intimidate the opposition. In the border context, the physical disappearance of migrants as they attempt to travel through the desert borderlands is a continuation of the disappearance of personhood effectuated by the current international neoliberal market, which exploits workers as "bare life."

For those in search of missing loved ones, the ambiguity and unknowable nature of the desert borderlands enters the space of the family, and whole families "go missing" themselves. As individual relatives imagine what their missing loved one might be enduring while they live a "normal life," they experience the suffering themselves—living the torture they fear their loved one might be experiencing. The desert borderlands has become a space of terror where some of the most blatant abuses of human rights are not only occurring but are occurring visibly. These abuses are accepted and even condoned by the public, because those suffering have been successfully characterized as "illegals" rather than human beings.

Although fear still silences the families in the United States, in other settings where there have been a high number of disappearances, it was only a matter of time until families took political action. As the children of the disappeared grow up, many of them citizens or taking part in movements such as Undocumented and Unafraid, we can expect to hear more about *los desaparecidos de la frontera* (the disappeared from the border).

NOTES

1. Green 2011.
2. Scheper-Hughes 1993, 216.
3. U.S. Department of Homeland Security 2009.
4. Eschbach et al. 2001; Cornelius 2001, 2005; Rubio-Goldsmith et al. 2006.
5. Dunn 1995.
6. Nagengast 2002.
7. Quesada, Hart, and Bourgois 2011.
8. Scarry 1985.
9. Aretxaga 1999, 46.
10. Scheper-Hughes 2004, 175.
11. Taussig 2004, 40.
12. Farmer 1997, 2004, 2005; Quesada, Hart, and Bourgois 2011; Green 2011.
13. Galtung 1969.
14. Nevins 2005, 17.
15. Alonso 1995.
16. Aretxaga 1999, 47.
17. U.S. Border Patrol 1994, 1, 2, 4.
18. Sluka 1999, 2.
19. De Genova 2002.
20. Boss 1999.
21. Ibid., 8.
22. Ibid., 24.
23. Hertz 1960.
24. Parsons 1939; Goody 1962; van der Geest 2004.

25. Angel Galli, quoted in Arditti 1999, 15.
26. Covarrubias 1947; Topley 1955; Endres 2008; Langford 2009.
27. Boss 1999; Suarez-Orozco 2004.
28. Cole 2004.
29. Arditti 1999; Robben 1999; Suarez-Orozco 2004.
30. Robben 1999, 96.
31. Suarez-Orozco 2004, 384.
32. Green 1999; Warren 1999; Pettigrew 1999; Scheper-Hughes 2004.
33. Taussig 2004, 40.
34. Nagengast 2002; De Genova 2002; Green 2011.
35. Cassia 2007, 16.
36. Foucault 1990, 136.
37. Mbembe 2003, 19.
38. Magaña 2008.
39. Agamben 1998.
40. Green 2011.
41. Butler 2009, 1.
42. Coutin 2000.
43. De Genova 2002, 427.
44. Edkins 2011, 9, emphasis in original.
45. Ibid., 12.
46. Arditti 1999; Robben 1999; Edkins 2011.
47. *New Oxford American Dictionary*, 3rd ed. s.v. "denounce."
48. Harvey 2007.

STATION 4

METAPHORS

We light this candle so that all our migrant sisters and brothers
who have died in the desert may not be forgotten.

A THEOLOGY OF THE DESERT

ALEX NAVA

LTHOUGH I WAS BORN AND RAISED in the desert regions of the U.S. Southwest, specifically in Tucson, Arizona, it was not until I lived elsewhere, especially in Chicago and Seattle for several years, that I began to notice the desert with new, more alert and fresh eyes. I left Arizona to study religion at the University of Chicago and was immediately cognizant of the distinctiveness of my new surroundings. If it is the unique and incomparable saguaro cacti that command one's attention in the deserts of Arizona, in Chicago it is the buildings and skyscrapers downtown and the skyline along the lake that evoke a feeling of awe. If the immensity of Lake Michigan reminds Chicagoans of their belonging and dependence on nature, the vastness of the desert terrain does the same for Arizonans. As I look back at my time in Chicago, I am convinced that besides preparing me for a life of study and teaching, the contrast of this great urban city with my desert experience in Arizona led me to reassess the desert and U.S.-Mexico border regions of my upbringing. Perhaps, in addition to the substance of my theological learning, the distance from the Southwest gave me the perspective that I needed to understand and interpret the desert and border regions in a new light.

After graduation and a couple of years in Seattle, I returned to Tucson to teach at the University of Arizona. A passage from T. S. Eliot's *Four Quartets* kept returning to my mind: "We shall not cease from exploration and the end of all our exploring will be to arrive where we started and know that place for the first time."[1]

Everything was indeed new to me. The distinct, fragrant scent of the summer rains falling on the parched desert ground was more poignant than ever. Ah, the wonderful smell of wet creosote bushes. The beauty and rarity of some of the cacti here—the saguaros, the organ pipe, the ocotillo—greeted me as if I were an explorer first entering this territory, a Cabeza de Vaca or Fr. Eusebio Kino. Indeed, I could see how surprising and unexpected some of this terrain might appear to someone who associates the idea of "desert" with Sahara-like desolation. The Southern Arizona desert is amazingly verdant and mountainous. Here the deserts are pregnant with life, home to a great diversity of animal and bird species. If some of the ancient Egyptian monks described the desert as a wasteland, they also saw in it the seeds of a potential paradise, a "desert blooming with the flowers of Christ."[2] This vision of a desert in full bloom is easily understood by anyone who has visited the Sonoran Desert regions of the U.S.-Mexico borderlands.

But there was something else happening in the desert that interrupted my contemplation of its surprising beauty: a growing number of migrant deaths. In the summer months the reports of women and men, children and infants dying in the desert is as endless and unforgiving as the heat of the sun. Almost inexplicably, every summer for the past several years seems to register a new record of deaths in the borderlands.

In my work with a couple of human rights groups, particularly Humane Borders and Borderlinks, I have come face to face with many immigrants beginning or in the midst of their journey to the north. Over 1,000 immigrants per day pass the doorstep of the small town of El Sasabe, Sonora, Mexico, with dreams that the ancient Israelites must have shared in their exodus from a land devoid of milk and honey. The first time I encountered a group of these pilgrims, besides being struck by the number of women and children, I could not help but recognize myself in their sunburned faces, as every American with an immigrant past might understand. If the Statue of Liberty was the welcoming symbol of past generations of European immigrants, the desert of our southern border is now the symbol of new generations of the tired and poor, of the huddled masses.

However, it is easy for many Americans to repress memories of their immigrant past. Perhaps such memories conjure feelings of insecurity and anxiety that prove too frightening to summon again. Or perhaps we fear that the recognition of our past as strangers might shatter our confident and self-assured, at times arrogant, identity as "Americans." Regardless, one thing seems quite clear:

most of us North Americans have a profoundly short-term memory. Forgetfulness is our common malady. We need to be reminded, as the ancient Israelites were reminded, that we, too, were once strangers in the land (Deut. 10:19).

While these reflections are motivated by the contemporary events along the border regions of the United States and Mexico, I would also like to consider in what follows some of the historical references to the desert in the Christian tradition as well as in the work of some modern poets before returning to the realities of death occurring in these regions today.

THEOLOGY OF THE DESERT

It is not surprising that the geography of the desert occupies a central place in the biblical imagination. The context of the Bible is, indeed, the stark, arid, desolate deserts of the ancient Near East. And it is in this difficult milieu that the ancient Jews interpreted and experienced the Divine, as have the Muslims. To any careful reader, it is clear that the desert landscape influences and informs the way in which God is represented and symbolized in biblical times. It left its mark on the theological language and beliefs of the ancient Jews, Muslims, and Christians. Indeed, one might see the desert as a major character in the biblical texts, beginning with the narrative of Exodus. In Exodus, this character is frightening and untrustworthy. The desert is synonymous with exile and often wears the mask of death. "Was it for want of graves that you brought us out of the land of Egypt. . . . Why did you bring us out of Egypt, to kill us and our children and livestock with thirst?" (Exod. 17:3). The faith in the "promised land'" that Moses sought to instill in the Israelites proved to be precarious and fragile when tested in the unforgiving and death-dealing environment of the desert. Even Moses's faith wavers: "Why have you treated your servant so badly? . . . Where am I to get meat to give to all these people? For they come weeping to me and say, 'Give us meat to eat.' . . . If this is the way you are going to treat me, put me to death at once" (Num. 11:10–15). And as we know, Moses dies in the desert. He never made it to the "promised land." Dr. Martin Luther King Jr. also invokes this narrative, fully aware that he, too, may share the fate of Moses: "I may not get to the promised land with you."

Anyone with experience in hot and arid desert regions will be able to understand the challenging and terrifying countenance of the desert. Inhospitable to human survival, impersonal and unrelenting to human needs and desires, the desert is a location where body and soul are easily wounded beyond recovery. Nothing seems to be in moderation here: the sun is fierce and excessive, deaf to the pleas of pilgrims seeking the refuge of shade. Any traveler to these regions will understand why clouds thus signal the presence of God to the wandering Jews in biblical times. Clouds not only hide the face of God (and hence are metaphors of Divine incomprehensibility) but they also hide the severe face of the sun, providing an exiled people with respite from its damaging power. And clouds, of course, indicate rain. In the Sonoran Desert, however, even the summer monsoon rains come with excess, announcing themselves with violent thunder, piercing lightning, and the suddenness of a flash flood, striking and pounding the earth with a violent force. Even the rains do not know gentleness. The desert terrain itself is immoderate, a parable of immensity, as vast as the sky. Surely to a migrant on foot, the terrain seems endless, a kind of cruel, banal infinitude.

In his study of the symbols of the desert in biblical and Christian thought, George Williams identifies at least four themes in the interpretation of desert: (1) the desert is a wasteland awaiting the blossoming of paradise; (2) the desert is a place of testing and punishment; (3) the desert is the location of God's nuptial union with Israel or the human soul; and (4) the desert is a place of refuge or contemplation.[3] Finally, as Bernard McGinn has explained with regard to the mystical traditions, the desert can become a symbol of the incomprehensible and inexpressible God (the God beyond God).[4] In this case, God's nature adopts desertlike characteristics. God is the "Divine Desert."

The Egyptian monks were among the first in the Christian tradition to take to the desert to encounter God (the Jewish community known as the Essenes had already done so at the beginning of the Common Era). Many of the above themes associated with the desert motivate and define their spiritual quests. For one, their journeys to the desert were interpreted as a step in their detachment from the attractions and distractions of the "world." By withdrawing to the desert, these ascetics would empty and void themselves of the comforts and pleasures of civilization. They welcomed the emptiness of the desert, an abyss or void, as a partner in their search for a naked, unearthly wisdom. Away from the noise of city life, they might hear God in the silence of the desert wind as Elijah once did. For these hermits, the model of the spiritual life was the nakedness and stillness of the desert. And they sought to cultivate this desert life within the depths of their own souls. Although there are no studies of the spiritual experiences of migrants crossing the desert through Arizona, it is difficult to believe that these immigrants experience the desert in the same way as the hermits did.

In the Middle Ages, Christian monks would appeal to desert metaphors for similar purposes, to advocate a turning away from the emptiness of the world and to sing of the benefits of solitude. In interpreting the desert as an inner condition of the spirit, many medieval monks dreamed of nuptial union with God in the inner recesses of the human heart, not literally in the geography of the desert. The Cistercian monk Isaac of Stella invokes the prophet Hosea in speaking of the followers of Christ in the desert: "They seek the desert and the secret places where they can be open to God . . . where he himself will answer and speak to their heart, as the prophet says: 'I will lead you into solitude and there I will speak to your heart.'"[5]

In spite of the belief among many Eastern and Western monks that God may be encountered in the simplicity and emptiness of the desert, however, very few of them actually referred to God as desert. Bernard McGinn insists that none of the early monks used desert language to describe the nature of God. It was left to medieval Christian thinkers to create "desert" language about God. Why was this theological language so slow in coming? Is it because the desert was a dwelling place of demons, not God? Was the emptiness and void of the ancient Near Eastern desert too life threatening to ascribe to God? For those monks with long-suffering experiences of the desert, like the migrants crossing the Arizona desert, was this region too hostile, too fierce to associate with the merciful God of scripture? And finally, why does this reluctance give way to a daring willingness to use desert language to describe God among some medievals?

In the West, it was Pseudo-Dionysius who first connected the Exodus story with the theory of Divine incomprehensibility. With Dionysius, reference to the desert suggested the unfathomable and vast nature of God, a nature that no intellect could plumb or exhaust. In this manner, a disciple of Dionysius, John the Scot Eriugena, expounds on the transcendent nature of God: "A more profound interpretation understands it as the desert of the Divine nature, an inexpressible height removed from all things. It is 'deserted' by every creature, because it surpasses all intellect, although it does not 'desert' any intellect."[6] This emphasis on the inaccessibility of the Divine nature to human conception would find a more elaborate and sustained formulation among various German theologians. It was in the verdant forests of Germany, ironically, that desert language of the Divine became more pervasive.

The work of the German beguine mystic, Mechtild of Magdeberg, is a step in this direction. She provides a prescription for dwelling in the desert and for speaking of the Divine.

> You shall love nothingness,
> You shall flee existence,
> You shall stand alone,
> And you shall go to no-one. . . .
> You shall drink the water of suffering
> And light the fire of love with the wood of virtue,
> Then you will live in the true desert.[7]

Besides recalling the ascetical traditions of desert language, this remarkable passage indicates a connection between the desert of the inner soul and the Divine Nothingness of the Godhead. In a manner reminiscent of Dionysius or Eriugena, Mechtild names the Divine as a reality beyond being, as a nothingness or emptiness that exceeds the realm of human knowledge and existence. God is no-thing. We see this position even more clearly with Meister Eckhart.

Eckhart explicitly and consistently uses the desert as a symbol of God. In one of his sermons, he discusses the nature of a noble or just person in this way:

> Who then is nobler than he who on one side is born of the highest and the best among created things, and on the other side from the inmost ground of the divine nature and its desert? "I" says the Lord through the prophet Hosea, "will lead the noble soul out into the desert, and there I will speak to her heart," one with One, one from One, one in One, one everlastingly. Amen.[8]

In this passage, Eckhart implies a union of indistinction in which the soul merges into God, or more precisely, into the unnameable desert of God, the God beyond our conception God. In this empty place of Divine oneness, where all human conceptions are empty, the soul is united with the "solitary wilderness" of the Divine: "God's ground and the soul's ground are one ground."[9]

Another German text called the "Granum sinapis" is similar in its theology. One passage describes the journey of the intellect first in climbing a mountain and then in fleeing to the desert.

> The mountain of this point, Ascend without activity, O intellect!
> The road leads you into a marvelous desert, So broad, so wide,

It stretches out immeasurably. The desert has neither time nor place,
Its mode of being is unique. . . . It is here, it is there, It is far, it is near,
It is deep, it is high, It exists in such a way that it is neither this nor that.[10]

The vastness of the desert terrain is an icon of the grandeur and inexhaustible nature of God. Other mystics—and surely many ancient peoples—chose the symbol of the ocean to make this point. The immeasurable depths and darkness of the abyss of the sea was a parable of the unfathomable abyss of the Divine. And the ocean symbol would have a further benefit: the analogy of a river flowing into the sea would resonate strongly with those mystics seeking union with the Divine Beloved. So, why is it that Eckhart and other German theologians turned to desert language in their God-talk?

As we have seen, part of the answer is the influence of Dionysius among many German intellectuals in the Middle Ages. Perhaps, however, as McGinn states, this is also explained by the fact that there are more forest deserts in Germany than anywhere else in Europe. Or perhaps the immensity of the desert sky and the brilliance of the sun proved alluring to these forest dwellers, to a people eager for the feeling of sunlight bathing one's body. Regardless what the exact answer is, it is questionable whether or not these theologians understood the life-threatening and hostile effects of desert terrain. Perhaps this is why the early desert-dwelling hermits, including the Egyptians, were unwilling to ascribe desert language to God. Even if they believed, vis-à-vis scripture, that the soul's betrothal to God occurs in the simplicity of the desert, they were too well schooled in the dangers and suffering of desert living to see the desert as a parable of Divine nature. The desert is indifferent, merciless, devoid of forgiveness, a place of demonic dominion, a place of death. If the desert is Divine, then it is a god too ambiguous and uncaring to be revered. A desert god shows signs of cruelty. This kind of god is all too close to the gods of tragedy, to the protests of Shakespeare, for instance: "As flies to wanton boys, are we to the gods, they kill us for their sport."[11] Perhaps this is what the biblical figure Job most feared, that his God is not a friend at all, but an enemy. As Job's life is undone by the experiences of physical and spiritual affliction, he files a lawsuit against the Almighty. Is the Almighty responsible for, or at least indifferent to, the suffering of his people? Does the Divine, after all, contrary to Eriugena's claim above, desert His people in the scorching heat of the desert?

Such daring questions naturally arise when one tries to make sense of the deaths occurring in the desert regions of our borders today. I, for one, cannot help but share the reluctance of early Christian theologians to name God as desert. In light of the harsh and meaningless deaths of immigrants in the desert regions of the border today, I find myself uneasy with a devotion to the "Divine Desert."

DEATH IN THE DESERT

If some mystics saw in the emptiness and nothingness of the desert a symbol of Divine emptiness, they also believed that the latter was a greater reality than anything humans could imagine or experience. Simone Weil put it this way: "Contact with human creatures is given to us through a sense of presence. Contact with God is given to us through the sense of absence. Compared with this absence, presence becomes more absent than absence."[12] In confronting the absence of God and the emptiness of much of our ideas and beliefs about God, Weil believed that we might clear space for the entrance of the true God. After voiding our lives of false attachments and comforting illusions and in entering a desert experience of vacancy and desolation, we will hear God speak to us "heart to heart." As Weil also knew, however, the experiences of the void or emptiness in history and society are real, destructive threats to the human body and spirit. The human spirit is not invulnerable to the blows of fate and the weight of suffering. Our modern age seems to sense more acutely the abyss of suffering or the threat of meaninglessness. In our time, a time out of joint, the threat of emptiness seems to fill the air that many great modern intellectuals breathe. Modern expressions of nothingness or emptiness, then, are far removed from the reverential postures of the classic Christian mystics, or of classical Buddhism, for that matter. Our age appears to be far more troubled. Robert Frost's poem "Desert Places" represents this modern experience of the desert of life:

> They cannot scare me with their empty spaces,
> Between stars, where no human race is.
> I have it with me, so much closer to home
> To scare myself with my own desert places.[13]

This experience of the terrifying countenance of emptiness is already signaled in early modern times by the figure Blaise Pascal, who cried out in terror, "The eternal silence of these infinite spaces fills me with dread."[14] Modern science, witnesses Pascal, emptied the universe of God. For many in modern times, then, the desert becomes a symbol of absence and loss, a representation of the death of God. Needless to say, this brand of emptiness is far removed from the meaningful descriptions of emptiness in Christian mysticism or in Buddhism (*sunyata*).

When Pablo Neruda wrote of the desert terrain of the mining regions of northern Chile, for instance, he recalled a traditional biblical setting, the desert as prophetic space, but now with characteristics of this modern age. Neruda speaks as a prophet of the old and new, of ancient and modern times. While Neruda's poetry evokes feelings of modern, existential anxieties ("I've come once again to lonely bedrooms, to have a cold lunch in restaurants, and once again I throw my pants and shirts on the floor, there are no hangers in my room, or pictures of anyone on the walls"[15]), he also summons language that echoes biblical precedents, as in his passionate words of the desert-dwelling people of northern Chile.

> I delivered myself up to the deserts and the man of the slag, came out of his hole,
> his mute harshness, and I knew the sorrows of my lost people ...
> And then I went through streets and told everything I saw, I showed
> the hands that touched the lumps full of pain, the lodgings of forsaken poverty,
> the miserable bread and the loneliness of the forgotten moon. And elbow to
> elbow with my barefoot brother, I tried to change the kingdom of dirty coins.[16]

If the desert prophets of Israel—Amos or Isaiah, Micah or Jeremiah—lived today, one could imagine such powerful words coming from their lips.

In addition to this poignant reading of the desert as a location of suffering and injustice, desert language in Neruda evokes the experience of exile. "I am a wandering son of that which I love," Neruda writes. "I am a wanderer, I live the anguish of being far from the prisoner and the flower."[17] Even before his exile from Chile, Neruda's works resound with a sense of alienation. He speaks to us from the perspective of a stranger and alien of this earth. As the title of one of his great works suggest, *Residence of Earth*, Neruda wrote a poetry of temporary residents, of pilgrims in exile. And his words reflect this tragic sensibility. His poems are filled with plaintive and black tones. Neruda's poetry is an elegy dedicated to all who feel the desolation of desert space and time, perhaps what many of the migrants crossing the desert through Arizona feel.

In *Canto General*, Neruda's desert language, however, describes the particular anguish of the downtrodden and destitute. In a poem titled "El desierto" ("The

Desert"), Neruda describes the nakedness of the terrain and the struggle for life in such landscapes: "The sun breaks its glass in the empty space, and the earth agonizes with a dry and drowning noise of crying salt." In this place "without plants, without claws, without dung, the land revealed to me its naked dimension."[18] This nakedness, this vulnerability is shared by Neruda the exiled poet and by all refugees and wandering peoples.

As the ancient Israelites knew firsthand, survival in such stark terrain is a battle. In awaiting God, man fights with death in the desert, and for many migrants in Arizona, the desert wins. The great Spanish poet, García Lorca—who describes Spanish culture as death obsessed—pictures death lurking in the empty desert, in this case in a vast dune:

> Atop that vast dune
> —most ancient light—
> I find myself lost
> with no sky, no road.
> The North near to death
> had switched off its stars.
> The skies were shipwrecked,
> slowly rising and falling.[19]

Here the traveler is lost in the immense dune, oppressed by the darkness of the sky, drowned in the vast sea of arid, scorched terrain. The North is no longer the beacon of freedom. Death has extinguished the light.

In another Lorca poem, Death interrupts the journey of an Andalusian on the way to Córdoba.

> Córdoba.
> Distant and lonely.
> Over the plain, through the wind,
> black pony, red moon.
> Death keeps a watch on me
> from Córdoba's towers.
> Oh, such a long way to go!
> And, oh, my spirited pony!
> Ah, but death awaits me

Before I ever reach Córdoba.

Córdoba.

Distant and lonely.[20]

GOD AND DEATH IN THE DESERT

If some Christian mystics interpreted the desert as a location of a possible Divine encounter or even as a parable of the incomprehensibility of the Divine nature, others, including the ancient Israelites, read more ominous and dark signs in the symbol of desert. The desert to these latter figures is a sinister realm where hunger and thirst, unforgiving heat and vast stretches of land become the occasion for death's visitation. In our own times, for too many immigrants from the south, the journey to the North is a battle with these demons. The North is distant and lonely, forever absent, forever unattainable. If it is not the heat and thirst, the cause of countless deaths is the sheer vastness of the desert and the number of miles they travel. Exhaustion comes quickly in this terrain, and dizziness and confusion often accompany the physical experience of the heat and insatiable thirst. In this condition, it is easy to lose one's way in the labyrinth of the desert. Lorca's description of being lost, of locating neither road nor sky, is a precise expression of many immigrant's experiences. The light summoning them to the "promised land" of the North has been extinguished, and the sky, dark and undecipherable, hides the way. These desert pilgrims are shipwrecked by the immensity and abyss of the desert landscape. It is not difficult to imagine them repeating the mournful and protesting words of the Israelites, "Was it for want of graves in Egypt that you brought us into the desert to die?" (Exod. 14:11). Our immigrants might echo, "Was it for want of graves in Mexico and Central America that you brought is to Sonoran Desert to die?"

I opened these reflections by speaking of the surprising beauty of the Sonoran Desert in Southern Arizona and northern Mexico. If there is a good amount of rain in the winter months, this terrain blooms with an intensity of color and scent and shape. Wildflowers are resurrected during the spring in locations that seem inhospitable to plant life. In staring at this sight, so unexpected, so holy, I recall what the Egyptian monks describe as a "desert blooming with the flowers of Christ." Perhaps for similar reasons, the Tohono O'odham people (the "Desert Dwellers") consider much of this land sacred (especially the mountain of Baboquivari, where the god I'itoi dwells in a cave). It is not an exaggeration to see in this terrain the aesthetical attractiveness of a garden.

I wonder, then, how to make sense of the garden-like beauty in light of the suffering and deaths of hundreds of immigrants. If the ecology of the Sonoran Desert cannot exactly be described as a wasteland, does not the reality of death witnessed by this terrain justify such a title nevertheless? Perhaps it is a wasteland, simply for the spent lives exhausted here if not for geography and flora. Or are there the seeds of a garden experience even here in the midst of death and suffering?

Perhaps what I am asking is the same question posed by many of us: how does one reconcile the stunning, even at times, ecstatic experiences of the beauty of nature with the horror of human history, with the experiences of exile and poverty, violence and war? Surely, Dante, another great poet of the desert, explored this terrain.[21] In *Inferno*, the pilgrim is lost in the *gran deserto* (great desert) until Virgil appears and guides him to the Garden of Eden. As many critics have suggested, the metaphor of desert in Dante represents the desert of Exodus and the experience of exile in Dante's own life and in human history. At the same time, Dante alludes to the hope (a hope sustained by the possibility of beauty and love) that a garden will reveal itself in the midst of the desolation and suffering of history. Recall that in *Paradiso*, the third part of the *Divine Comedy*, it is Dante's beloved Beatrice who takes over as the pilgrim's guide. It is now love that allures the pilgrim and that impels his will and causes his wings to sprout. It is Dante's experience of love that makes possible the ascent into paradise where he will be astounded and silenced by a vision of God (symbolized by the rose).

It is not surprising that images of a garden appear in much poetry of the desert, including the Bible. In the ancient Near East, a garden would have been a place of salvation in the context of the threatening desert. In the Song of Songs, for instance, the delights and intensity of love, the rapture of beauty, the sensual joy of both nature and the human body are celebrated in the context of a garden. This garden appears to be a refuge from the trials of history, a Garden of Eden in the context of exile on earth.

Perhaps in these contexts, the garden is nothing else but a symbol of hope. As I look across the expanse of the Sonoran Desert—its garden-like terrain and awesome immensity—I am filled with ambivalence. I witness beauty everywhere and yet also hear the laments of immigrants burnt by the sun. It is a tragic beauty that I recognize, a beauty that attests to the contradictory and ambiguous face of the human experience. This ambiguity is felt not only in the experiences of beauty and exile, nature and history, love and suffering, but also dwells with the experience of the Holy itself, as Rudolph Otto once suggested. For Otto, the Holy is a *mysterium tremendum et fascinans*.[22] This power and mystery is felt as an awesome, even terrifying mystery on the one hand and as an attractive, beautiful, trustworthy mystery on the other.

As holy space, the desert wears these different masks, not unlike the ancient god Janus, a god of doorways, thresholds, and borders. He stands on the border and looks north and at the same time south. He stands nowhere, in between two different positions and places, in liminal territory. Janus is a contradictory figure, situated in a location of contradiction. It seems to me that exiles and immigrants—if not us all—wear the masks of Janus, looking toward different cultural and religious horizons with lives marked by contradiction, paradox, and ambiguity. If this is true of the human condition itself, perhaps exiles and migrants understand these facts better than anyone else.

The tragedy of our contemporary border situation, however, remains the fact that the ambiguous and liminal space of the border has now become a gravesite for numerous pilgrims. While some North Americans blame the immigrants themselves for their own deaths (viewing their deaths as a kind of punishment for the sin of illegal trespassing), others see in these deaths a loud cry for a change in border policy. For this to happen, we need the prophetic voices of justice in biblical texts, in the poetry of a Neruda, Lorca, or Dante joined with the deep spirituality of the mystical traditions, traditions that are reflected in images of the Virgen de Guadalupe, for example, that many migrants carry though the Arizona desert. In following the paths of these great prophets, we might be led to the mysterious regions of the human soul, crossing and transgressing the limiting borders that confine and prevent our spirits from exploring new terrain and from discovering new possibilities that would allow us to grow as individuals and as a human community. In following the trails of the border crossers of history, past and present, we might be led to discover the faces of strangers within our very selves and thus to respond to the other with justice and compassion. Perhaps only when this happens will we be able to announce, with T. S. Eliot, that "fire and the rose are one."[23] Only then will the roses of the garden bloom in the scorched fire zone of the desert, and we might begin to find credible the hope of biblical texts and mystics that we will be united with God in an ecstatic and consuming love.

NOTES

1. Eliot 1943.
2. McGinn 1994.
3. McGinn 1994, 156–57. See Williams 1962, 18.
4. McGinn 1981.
5. McGinn 1994, 165.
6. Ibid., 162.
7. Ibid., 166.
8. Eckhart 1981, 247.
9. Ibid, 192.
10. McGinn 1994, 171.
11. Shakespeare (1606) 1993, *King Lear*, act 4, scene 1, line 173.
12. See Weil 1956, 239–40.
13. Frost 1936.
14. See Pascal 1995, 102.
15. See Neruda 1982, 92.
16. Ibid., 203.
17. Ibid., 193.
18. Ibid., 195–96.
19. See García Lorca 1994, 121.
20. Ibid., 143.
21. See Mazzota 1979.
22. See Otto 1950.
23. Eliot 1943.

METAPHORICAL IMAGERY IN NEWS REPORTING ON MIGRANT DEATHS

JANE ZAVISCA

N THE MID-1990S the U.S. government introduced Operation Gatekeeper to increase Border Patrol enforcement near cities such as San Diego and El Paso. Since then increasing numbers of migrants have been crossing through and dying in remote desert regions. As a result the leading cause of migrant deaths shifted from traffic accidents to weather exposure.[1] Local news media in border regions have heavily covered these deaths, from "just-the-facts" stories that frame migrant deaths as routine weather or traffic incidents to investigative reporting that explores the political and economic forces leading to death on the U.S-Mexico border.

News media influence how audiences think about issues by characterizing their *ontology*; that is, the nature of the problem at hand, as well as their potential causes and solutions. This chapter examines how journalists account for migrant deaths by analyzing metaphorical representations of death in two local newspapers, the *Arizona Daily Star* and the *San Diego Union-Tribune*, from 1999 to 2008. In choosing metaphors, journalists and their sources do more than make their writing more colorful and readable. Metaphorical reasoning is a fundamental cognitive process that helps people make sense of complex topics by comparing them to more familiar ideas.

Sociological research on media framing of social problems typically uses the method of content analysis to "code" or classify articles for the varieties of ontological, diagnostic, and prognostic claims that journalists make.[2] Such studies typically do not specify how the researcher identified frames beyond intuitively assessing an article's content in the course of reading it. Linguistic anthropologists and cognitive psychologists have identified and developed methods for analyzing specific linguistic devices, such as metaphors, that communicate meaning. Metaphors help people make sense of the world by mapping concepts from a familiar *source domain* onto a less familiar *target domain*. In a study of reporting on immigration in the *Los Angeles Times*, Otto Santa Ana found the dominant class of metaphors equates *immigrants* (target domain) to *animals* (source domain). Such metaphors are racist, he argues, because they deny migrants' humanity. There need not be any racist intent on the part of the journalist. Because metaphors are a cognitive shortcut, they subconsciously transfer ontological assumptions from the source domain to the target domain. Applying the imagery of animals, who rank lower than humans in Western culture, to immigrants implies that immigrants are less than human.[3]

This study analyzes metaphors that are applied to the topic of migrant deaths. The target domains of interest include death, the cause of death, and the person who dies. Whereas Santa Ana focuses on the ontological implications of metaphors, I am also interested in causal reasoning, in particular how metaphors *naturalize* versus *socialize* the causes of death. Border deaths are simultaneously natural and social events. The proximate cause of death in most cases is exposure of the body to heat or cold. The migrant's decision to enter the desert is causally before such exposure. Social factors drive people to risk death in the desert: poverty pushes them to enter the United States in search of jobs, while enforcement policies inhibit safe passage across the border. I therefore expect metaphors applied to migrant deaths to cluster into natural versus social source domains.

DATA AND METHODS

Reporting on border deaths was analyzed for Tucson's *Arizona Daily Star* and the *San Diego Union-Tribune* for the period from 1999 to 2008. Both newspapers serve regions close to the U.S.-Mexico border that have been the site of many border deaths, and both report frequently on immigration. The *San Diego Union-Tribune* is more conservative in editorial slant than the *Arizona Daily Star*. Articles were identified via full-text searches of databases indexing the two sources. Each article located by the search was checked for content, and only those discussing death or risk of death were selected.[4]

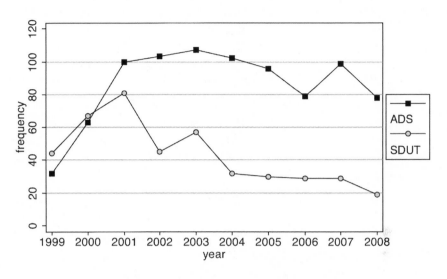

FIGURE 10.1. Articles discussing migrant deaths

Trends in coverage roughly track trends in incidence of death. Operation Gate-keeper increased enforcement around San Diego and other urban areas, causing migrant crossings to shift to the Arizona desert. The number of border-crossing deaths occurring in the Border Patrol's Tucson Sector spiked after 1998. Mean-while, deaths in the San Diego Sector, which peaked around 1990, steadily declined until 2000, after which rates stabilized at a relatively low level.[5] Reporting on migrant deaths in Tucson's *Arizona Daily Star* increased dramatically from 1999 to 2001 and remained high, whereas reporting in the *San Diego Union-Tribune* decreased after 2001 following the shift of deaths out of the region (see fig. 10.1).

Out of the 1,311 articles identified, 399 were selected for analysis of meta-phors. Twenty articles were randomly sampled for each year from each publica-tion (with the exception of 2008 for the *San Diego Union-Tribune*, with only nineteen total). The sample was balanced across years and sources to facilitate comparison. All sampled articles were coded for metaphors related to border deaths.[6] Only segments of text that discuss death or the risk of death were coded. I extracted *tokens*; that is, discrete segments of text employing metaphori-cal reasoning, along with surrounding text that clarifies the speaker and context. All tokens were coded for the following information: the source domain, the target domain, the voice (i.e., who is speaking—journalist, Border Patrol, gov-ernment official, activist, or migrant), and claims about the cause of death, if any.

Only metaphors that occurred at least twenty times (or on average in at least 5 percent of the sample) are discussed in this chapter. I also only discuss causes of death that are referenced in at least 5 percent of tokens for at least one category of metaphor. The following causes were analyzed and are defined below.

- *Economy*: Includes push factors of poverty in migrants' home countries and pull factors of available jobs and demand for low-wage migrant labor in the United States
- *Policy*: Refers to the legal framework for means of entry and associated enforcement efforts
- *Smugglers*: Guides who place migrants in harm's way, including deaths at the hands of robbers and rival smugglers
- *Migrant*: Deaths attributed to migrants' decisions to enter the United States illegally
- *Weather*: Exposure to the elements, such as heat, cold, and fire
- *Not otherwise specified*: Deaths described but not explained

These causes are listed in order from what I call "distal" to "proximate" causes. Most deaths are proximately caused by weather-related phenomena. Exposure to the weather can only happen after a migrant decides to enter the United States, and usually finding a guide, commonly referred to as a "smuggler," to lead the way. The path of entry is influenced by enforcement policies. Finally, economic push and pull factors stimulate migration despite the challenges of enforcement, finding a way in, and the risk of exposure that migrants face. As shorthand, I will refer to discourses on proximate causes as "naturalizing" and to distal causes as "socializing." Reporting on proximate causes naturalizes death because it does not suggest that anything can or should be done at a social or policy level to prevent them. In naturalizing discourses, prevention efforts happen at the point of exposure, in the form of humanitarian assistance from Border Patrol agents or Samaritans in the desert. Distal causes, by contrast, suggest collective, social solutions.[7]

CATEGORIES OF METAPHORS ON BORDER DEATHS

How common is metaphorical imagery in general in reporting on death? As figure 10.2 shows, about 60 percent of articles in the years 1999–2006 contained a relevant metaphor. Metaphorical language declined sharply to only about

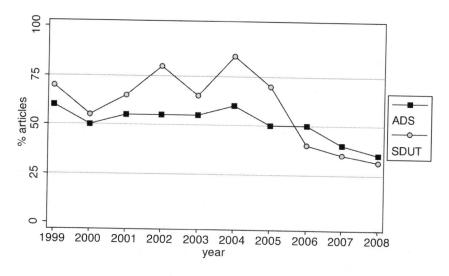

FIGURE 10.2. Articles using metaphors about death

35 percent of articles in 2007 and 2008. This is due to an increase in "just-the-facts" reporting in 2007 and 2008. These brief reports of discoveries of bodies, which provide little context or explanation, rarely use metaphors (30 percent vs. 68 percent in other types of articles). This trend may have been caused by declining interest in immigration during the 2007–2008 presidential election season, when news coverage was dominated by domestic economics and foreign policy.

Table 10.1 summarizes all categories of metaphor that occurred at least twenty times in reporting on border deaths. The first column tallies the occurrence of tokens, that is, discrete segments of text employing metaphors. The second column gives the number of articles having at least one occurrence of a particular type of metaphor (some articles have more than one instance of the same type). Economic metaphors on death as a cost, calculation, or gamble predominate, appearing in 36 percent of sampled articles. Metaphors characterizing death as the result of a violent place or policy also occur frequently, in 25 percent of articles. Dehumanizing metaphors, the focus of Santa Ana's work, appear in 21 percent of articles, constituting a significant but not predominant category. Humanizing metaphors that make migrant's personhood, or even sainthood, explicit are more rare (13 percent of articles) but provide an important counterpoint to dehumanizing metaphors equating migrants to animals, dangerous water, or cooked meat.

TABLE 10.1. Metaphors about migrant deaths

	N TOKENS	% ARTICLES
Economic metaphors	206	36
Death = cost/calculus	114	23
Death = gamble	94	19
Violent metaphors	141	25
Desert = vengeful	59	11
Border = war zone	44	10
Death = punishment	29	6
Policy = violent	23	5
Dehumanizing metaphors	104	21
Migrant = animal	71	15
Migrant = water	38	9
Migrant = cargo	20	5
Humanizing metaphors	71	13
Migrant = human being	55	11
Migrant = saint	22	5

NOTE Subcategories do not add up to category totals due to overlapping metaphors within tokens and articles.

Other than the overall quantitative decline in use of metaphors depicted in figure 10.2, there was little variation in the relative prevalence of the various types of metaphors across sources or over time. The consistency of metaphor types across news sources and over time is consistent with Santa Ana's finding that animal and water metaphors were equally prevalent regardless of the political slant or policy context of articles in his sample. The remainder of this chapter ignores source and year to focus on the more interesting variation in implicit causal claims across types of metaphors. Table 10.2 summarizes the findings quantitatively, showing, for each type of metaphor, the percentage of tokens that suggest a particular type of cause of death.

TABLE 10.2. Causal claims associated with types of metaphors about death

CAUSE OF DEATH (ROW %)

	ECONOMY	POLICY	SMUGGLER	MIGRANT	WEATHER	NOT SPECIFIED
Economic metaphors						
Death = cost/calculus	12	29	13	4	32	11
Death = gamble	33	30	17	40	14	3
Violent metaphors						
Desert = vengeful	6	32	5	3	61	0
Border = war zone	11	57	11	9	14	11
Death = punishment	14	32	7	24	45	0
Policy = violent	8	92	4	0	0	0
Dehumanizing metaphors						
Migrant = animal	11	20	52	4	15	1
Migrant = water	11	56	10	8	15	8
Migrant = cargo	0	0	80	5	5	15
Humanizing metaphors						
Migrant = human being	15	36	13	4	13	27
Migrant = saint	0	35	0	0	24	41

NOTE Row totals can exceed 100 because some metaphors imply multiple causes of death.

ECONOMIC METAPHORS

Economic metaphors are extremely common in discourse on death. Talk of death as a price to pay or as the result of a cost-benefit analysis predominates, appearing in 23 percent of articles, and is associated with a variety of implicit causes, both distal and proximate. Gambling metaphors suggest that migrants actively take a chance, and migrants are held partially culpable for their own deaths in 40 percent of instances of such metaphors.

DEATH AS A COST

Migrant deaths are often characterized as a price, cost, or toll. Metaphors related to price suggest a transaction, specifying both the agents that are paying and those that are collecting. Most obviously, migrants are the ones who are "paying with their lives." About one-third of cost metaphors naturalize death by making the desert the agent extracting a "toll" from those who cross it. For example, an article describes humanitarian water stations in the desert as a "response to the soaring migrant death toll from last spring's unseasonably hot, dry weather." Cold weather can also be the culprit. One headline reads, "Migrant Death Toll Due to Cold Now at 10." Deaths from fires and traffic accidents are also commonly described as tolls, for example, "Border Fire Takes Toll on Illegal Crossers." These tolls are routine: "Wrecks and rollovers of overloaded vehicles driven by smugglers are nothing new in Southern Arizona," reports an article on an accident that killed nine people, but "none [of the previous incidents] took a toll like last Thursday's crash."[8]

Why must a price be paid beyond the desert's demands? Rarely, the migrant is the culprit for daring to cross the so-called devil's highway: "Historical accounts of El Camino del Diablo make you wonder why anyone would choose to visit this harsh and silent stretch of Arizona desert. . . . Many unsuspecting travelers, including today's illegal border crossers from Mexico, have *paid* for their ignorance with their lives." More often, in about one-third of cost metaphors, death is the price of harsh enforcement policies. For example, policy is to blame for the metaphorical cost to an injured baby as well as the financial cost of his medical care: "Little Santana, caught between the tectonic plates of immigration policy and the lure of jobs, *costs money*. No one will really *pay the costs* but him." An article on Operation Gatekeeper claims that: "Critics and supporters agree the strategy has stemmed the flow of illegal immigration through San Diego County's urban areas. But human rights groups say it has come with a *price*: In the past decade, more people have crossed through desert and mountain areas where extreme temperatures have contributed to the deaths of several thousand migrants along the entire U.S.-Mexico border."[9]

If death is a price paid by the migrants who lose their lives, their dead bodies are an expensive burden on government and taxpayers: "For the moment, with immigrants pushed from San Diego's streets into the mountains and deserts, the *cost* of our anarchic immigration policy is invisible. Out of sight, out of mind. One person to whom the *cost* is not invisible is Luis Herrara-Lasso, Mexico's fine consul general. One of the consulate's primary jobs has become, as Herrara-Lasso indicated, 'picking up corpses.'" Humanitarian assistance is sometimes justified as a cost-cutting measure. In the words of Pima County Supervisor Richard Elias, water stations in the desert are "a moral response that also *saves taxpayers money* in terms of picking up those bodies, doing those autopsies." Likewise, a representative of U.S. Immigration and Customs Enforcement defends the policy of repatriating migrants to Mexico as cost effective in the same breath as she describes life as priceless: "U.S. officials consider it money well spent because it keeps those who take the flights safe and, as Nantel says, there is *no cost on human life*. 'It *saves the taxpayers money* and addresses a very critical life-safety issue for individuals who are out in the desert in these very dangerous months,' Nantel said."[10]

DEATH AS A CALCULATION

Another genre of economic metaphor suggests that death results from a cost-benefit analysis, with measurable, calculable risks and consequences. Smugglers put migrants in harm's way because they are "bringing people across *at any cost*" and "*value profits* more than life." If migrants do not die of exposure or in traffic, they may be killed by market forces that generate crossfire between rival smuggling gangs: "Authorities blame the surge of violence on the *law of supply and demand*." Both enforcement agencies and activists describe migrants' decisions to cross and Border Patrol's attempts to stop them as a (mis)calculation of worth. A Mexican government official describes prevention efforts as follows: "We've been telling them that even though it's their dream to come across, *it's not worth* their lives."[11]

Migrant deaths are also a disputed measure of policy worth. An editorial urging sanctions against U.S. employers described illegal immigration as "*win-win* until summer comes, and border crossers start to die from heat stroke."

Employer sanctions are "*an investment*" that "will have been *worth it*" if it reduces the number of deaths. Likewise, in discussing repatriation flights, a Mexican official says, "You can't try to *save money* when it comes to saving lives. . . . One life is *worth it*." By contrast, a Border Patrol official rejects migrant deaths as a policy evaluation principle, maintaining that "the number of deaths is not the only *yardstick to measure successes* of the border initiative." He proposes crime rates as an alternative metric.[12]

DEATH AS A GAMBLE

A related type of economic metaphor frames border crossing as a game of chance and death as a risk of losing the game.[13] Migrants calculate the odds of survival, believe they will be lucky, and gamble with their lives. Gambling metaphors, in 40 percent of cases, suggest that migrants bear some responsibility for their own deaths. In this discourse, migrants either know or should know the odds of dying when they decide to cross. They weigh the risk of death against the potential payout of a job in the United States. They will take such chances "as long as their *odds appear favorable* and jobs await. Hundreds of illegal entrants still cross each day in the middle of the summer even though they know the scorching desert claims the lives of crossers nearly every day, perhaps because the 237 deaths reported by county medical examiners in 2007 pale in comparison to the hundreds of thousands that likely made it across."[14]

When they lose the bet, migrants are portrayed as both victims and perpetrators in an illicit game of chance:

> How long does it take for criminals to become victims? About as long as it takes for a little boy's heart to stop beating. . . . Hailing from Mexico and Central America, those who started the journey knew that the United States, the country they were desperate to enter, had laws on the books to keep them out. Giving into desperation would thus be costly and treacherous. And yet, confident that they had a job waiting for them up north, they did it anyway and *gambled with their lives*. Every year, hundreds of people learn the hard way that *you can't beat the house*.[15]

Policies that seek to inform people of the risks presume that if migrants had all the information, they would recalculate the odds and payouts and choose to stay home. Public service announcements on television, in churches, and along the border warn migrants, "Don't Expose Your Life to the Elements! It's *Not Worth the Risk!*" A psychologist at a shelter in Mexico for prospective migrants shows a photo of a rotting corpse and then asks the audience: "Do you think it's right to *risk your child's life*?" On the other hand, opponents of humanitarian efforts such as water stations and guide maps claim they will "create a false sense of security for Mexican migrants, encouraging more of them *to risk the treacherous treks* across deadly desert terrain."[16]

Journalists are largely skeptical of the effects of either humanitarian or enforcement efforts on migrants' decisions to cross. Smugglers work at cross-purposes, "conning" migrants by deceiving them about the risks. And even if migrants have all the information, they continue to take risks: "At well-worn border trails, signs graphically warn of snow, sun, canals and rattlesnakes. Surely, the word is getting out. Still, the migrants come, *gambling with their lives*." Some journalists attribute this risk-taking to self-deception, "because people want to believe they'll be the *lucky ones* who make the journey unscathed." More commonly, journalists point to the power of the "jobs magnet" in rational calculus of risk: "Those who know something of the dangers often forge ahead anyway, assuming that *the risk of death* is low and therefore an *acceptable tradeoff for the chance* of a brighter future in America." The ultimate culprit is demand for cheap labor: "Undocumented immigrants wouldn't be *risking their lives* to come here if the American landscape wasn't dotted with 'Cheap help wanted' signs."[17]

One-third of gambling metaphors attribute death to economic factors, a higher proportion than for any other type of metaphor. Many articles quote migrants who point to the push of necessity to explain why they chance death: "It's dangerous, but *we take the risk* because we have such needs"; "If I could [help my parents] in my land, I wouldn't be *risking my life* here with these men." Economic push and pull factors interact with enforcement policies to transform the border into a gambling arena where life is the ultimate stake. Economic incentives render enforcement efforts hopeless: "The deployment of more equipment and more officers into this sector will never dissuade illegal entrants who *willingly risk their lives* in search of better-paying jobs." In pointing to the failure of enforcement strategies to stop illegal entry, humanitarians have framed U.S. policy as the ultimate con, a "deadly, exorbitantly costly *shell game*."[18]

VIOLENCE METAPHORS

Metaphors drawn from the source domain of violence are the second-largest category identified in the sample. In this section, I divide these metaphors into two subcategories based on causal reasoning. Metaphors of vengeance, which depict the desert as angry and death as a punishment, naturalize death by blaming the weather. By contrast, metaphors that describe the border as a war zone blame enforcement strategies for migrant deaths.

DEATH AS VENGEANCE

Many metaphors describe the desert or the weather as angry, violent, and vengeful. Summer heat is brutal, oppressive, harsh, or smothering, while the desert is devilish, pitiless, remorseless, hostile, and unforgiving. A headline reads, "Risky Crossing: Another Summer of Brutal Heat Places Migrants at Risk." The desert determines migrants' fates in "a pitiless trek through southwestern Arizona desert that can deliver a man to steady work—or to a whimpering death." The Border Patrol favors such metaphors: "The Border Patrol said the area is one of the harshest deserts in the country." Some agents call it "The Devil's Path." Similarly, "An oppressive mid-summer heat wave in Arizona, during which several Phoenix residents also died, is cited [by the Border Patrol] as the principal cause for the rising death toll."[19]

Such metaphors, by ascribing emotions and intentions to natural phenomena, typically blame the desert itself for deaths without referencing political or economic factors such as enforcement policies or labor markets. Attributing murderous intent to the desert is especially evident in metaphors that portray the desert as "punishing" or "unforgiving." An editorial praising humanitarian volunteers claims, "There are people in need wandering and staggering in the *punishing* desert." Another editorial casts migrants as the desert's victims: "The desert *did not forgive* them their innocent ambitions, adding them instead to the growing number of illegal immigrants killed by the desert heat." The climate "imposes the death sentence" on hapless border crossers.[20]

Another variant of punishment metaphor suggests that the agent doing the punishing is policy or the law rather than the desert per se. In this discourse, death is an excessive punishment that does not fit the crime. An editorial states, "The U.S. has every right to control its border, of course, and the dead had broken our immigration laws. But this shouldn't be a *capital offense*." As Humane Borders founder Robin Hoover puts it, "It's a relatively minor offense to cross the border and be deported. You shouldn't have to pay the *death penalty* for it." Another activist suggests that this punishment is a deliberate strategy: "I'm outraged that there are people in Washington who think the way to control immigration is to give people a *death sentence* for coming into this country."[21]

DEATH AS WAR CASUALTY

A related class of metaphors also employs violence as the source domain but characterizes policy as a killer, the border as a war zone, and migrants as refugees and casualties of war. Immigration policy is "lethal" and a "killer" because it "forces" migrants to risk death in the desert. For example, an editorial in the *Arizona Daily Star* claims that "so far the federal government has shown no inclination to change *policies that kill* illegal entrants looking for work. Our immigration policies still plug the borders at San Diego and El Paso. This pushes the migrants into the Southern Arizona deserts."[22]

Journalists usually employ the voices of humanitarian activists when employing such metaphors (in two-thirds of cases in the sample). For example, "Human rights advocates have said the Border Patrol's strategy of *intentionally forcing* migrants into the outlying areas puts them at greater risk." Similarly, "Local ACLU spokesman Jordan Budd said civil and human rights groups will continue to put pressure on the U.S. government to scrap Operation Gatekeeper. 'The U.S. government will have to face international scrutiny if it chooses to press forward with its *lethal enforcement strategy*,' Budd said yesterday."[23]

Violent enforcement policies have transformed the border into a "war zone," and deaths evidence a border war: "It is the cumulative number of dead that demonstrates that we have a *war* on the border. An estimated 200 to 400 individuals per year—at least 3,000 people over the past decade—have died because they tried to find work or reunite with family members who had found jobs in the United States. Every additional *weapon* used for border control has added to this rising death toll." Tokens using war metaphors overwhelmingly blame enforcement policies for "militarizing" the border and causing deaths in an atmosphere of war. For example, Ray Borane, the mayor of Douglas, Arizona, said, "This is a *military* operation, and everything that's happening is as if they were fighting a *war*. . . . They're doing everything in a *war* against people who are looking for work and in the process causing tragedy and death, and one death is one too many."[24]

What role do migrants play in this metaphorical war? Migrants usually appear as innocent bystanders in a war not of their making. In this discourse, favored by humanitarian activists, a war zone was created by Operation Gatekeeper and then exacerbated by the "recasting of the border as a *battleground in the war on terror*." Migrants are thus akin to refugees: "Others talked about the *militarization* of the border since the Sept. 11, 2001 terrorist attacks—even though the overwhelming number of illegal immigrants entering from Mexico are looking for work. 'They're crossing not because they want to—they have to,' said Enrique Morones of Border Angels, which provides emergency relief to migrants in danger. 'They're hungry.'" If migrants are civilian casualties, then their deaths are, in the words of activist Isabel García, "a *crime against humanity* perpetrated by the government of the United States," which "turned the border into a '*militarized zone.*'"[25]

An alternative discourse describes migrants as an invading army. Frustrated residents of border towns are often quoted describing migrant traffic as an "invasion." In the discourse of immigrants as invaders, the warlike atmosphere and associated deaths are created not by enforcement but by lack of it: "The mass migration of illegal entrants is largely the result of federal policies that tacitly encourage *invasive* border crossings."[26]

These alternate interpretations of migrants' role in a "border war" have corollaries in the framing of pro- and anti-immigrant activists. The name of the group "Samaritans Patrol" suggests a police force that keeps the peace and assists the innocent. However, critics of such groups say they "provide aid and comfort to an *invasion* the U.S. government is unable or unwilling to stop." On the other hand, the names of groups such as "Minutemen" and "American Border Patrol" cast proenforcement activists as legitimate warriors: "With the *war on terror* an ongoing campaign, one would think the federal government would welcome major volunteer assistance in monitoring U.S. borders for illegal entries." Such assistance will also help to save migrants from themselves: "An added benefit to this presence would be the *deployment* of responsible, trained individuals who could aid would-be crossers who succumb to extreme heat and cold in these remote areas." Humanitarian activists by contrast frame the Minutemen as dangerous vigilantes: "With an alleged force of 800 volunteer *vigilantes*, the Minuteman Project could stir up more problems than rights of access. It could end up costing lives."[27]

DEHUMANIZING METAPHORS

The most significant categories of metaphor in media coverage of border deaths are related to cost and violence. However, the dehumanizing metaphors identified by Santa Ana are also present. Mirroring Santa Ana's findings, the most significant dehumanizing discourse equates migrants to animals, followed by secondary metaphors of migrants as water and cargo. The dehumanizing ontology of migrants as water is partially mitigated, however, by the implication that migration flows are responding to social forces. Water metaphors typically socialize rather than naturalize the cause of death.

MIGRANTS AS ANIMALS

Animal metaphors overwhelmingly frame migrants as hunted. They are "lured by an unending supply of jobs and the urge to flee dire economic prospects at home." Who is hunting the migrants? Most commonly, migrants are the "prey" of smugglers or bandits. In a common turn of phrase, smugglers "prey on human misery." The isolation of the desert makes migrants "easy prey for bandits and other criminals." The "prey" metaphor blames smugglers and criminals for migrants' deaths. This metaphor usually occurs in quotes from law enforcement officials or in editorializing on why smugglers should be charged with murder. For example, in covering the trial of the driver of a truck in which migrants suffocated, the journalist writes, "For preying on the weak and profiting from it, the guilty should be punished—severely."[28]

Activists against illegal immigration constitute a second set of hunters. Humanitarian groups often employ this metaphor to characterize activists on the other side of the immigration debate. A member of the Border Action Network said, "These groups have *hunted* Mexicans and other immigrants with dogs, guns and hi-tech surveillance equipment." One critic sarcastically wrote, "Hopefully the civilian border watchers will *hunt* the terrorists down with the ferocity they use to *capture* their gardeners and auto mechanics." Supporters of the "border watchers" reject this depiction (although news coverage of their objections repeats and thereby reinforces the metaphor). For example, congressman Tom Tancredo "took direct aim at President Bush's recent description of the [Minutemen] group as 'vigilantes.' Mexican president Vicente Fox, who was meeting with Bush at the time last week, used the term *cazamigrantes—immigrant hunters.*"[29]

Like smugglers and vigilantes, Border Patrol agents are also "hunters." They chase migrants in a "chaotic, often deadly *cat-and-mouse game.*" However, the preferred metaphor for Border Patrol agents is "trackers" rather than beasts of prey: "Early Sunday morning, an Ajo agent *tracking* a set of footprints belonging to what he believed was a group of illegal entrants discovered the body of another man in the same general area." The tracker metaphor reinforces the humanity of the Border Patrol while it dehumanizes migrants by portraying the Border Patrol as "saviors." One article describes rescue efforts as follows:

"they are Border Patrol *trackers* whose *humanity* leads them into this wilderness in vehicles or small planes. They are there to enforce immigration laws, but the *hunters* invariably become the *rescuers*."[30]

A related metaphor depicts enforcement agents as humane shepherds tending a flock: "At night, [Mexican Grupo Beta] agents won't enter the lawless desert because they have no way to stay safe since they stopped carrying guns three years ago and are not allowed to make arrests. 'That leaves no one to *tend* to the migrants out there,' Enriques said." A more sinister livestock metaphor depicts smugglers as "polleros," or chicken ranchers. "People they smuggle into the United States are called pollos, a reference to the barnyard treatment they receive at the hands of their herders."[31]

MIGRANTS AS WATER

According to Santa Ana, journalists depict immigrants as dangerous waters threatening the nation, with the nation in turn being a metaphorical home. Such metaphors also occur in discourses on death. The rise in the number of deaths is a "surge," and the bodies are part of a "flood" of migrants that overwhelm Border Patrol agents and medical examiners. Dr. Bruce Parks counts both (skeletal remains and smugglers) and any other death he can link to the *human flood washing* though his jurisdiction. Bodies that do not fit in the morgue and must be stored in a refrigerated trailer are an "overflow."[32]

The idea that migration is a flood is reinforced by the metaphor of enforcement as attempting to "seal" or "plug" the border. The "flow" of migrants increased in Arizona when urban areas were "sealed": "Our immigration policies still *plug* the borders at San Diego and El Paso. That pushes the migrants into the Southern Arizona deserts." "What is occurring on the border is the result of a border squeeze at California and in Texas that *squirts* illegal entrants directly into the desert lands of the Tucson sector." This redirection of flows is called "the funnel effect."[33]

Santa Ana argues that water metaphors, whether referring to flows or floods, are ontologically dehumanizing because immigrants appear as an undifferentiated mass. Causally, however, the "flow" metaphor is less dehumanizing than metaphors of immigrants as animals or cargo. As table 10.2 shows, about two-thirds of water metaphors point to the role of policy or economic forces in leading migrants to cross the border in hazardous places versus less than one-third of animal metaphors.

HUMANIZING METAPHORS

Activists who are sympathetic to migrants often point to migrants' humanity to justify humanitarian aid in the desert and to urge changes to enforcement policy. It may seem odd or even racist to classify descriptions of migrants as human beings as metaphors. Recall the definition of metaphor as the mapping of a target domain onto a source domain. Humanizing metaphors make explicit the ontological connection between migrants and human beings. The fact that advocates find it necessary to explicate this connection implies that migrant's humanity is not taken for granted and must be asserted with reference to an external source domain.

MIGRANTS AS HUMAN BEINGS

Some humanizing metaphors directly assert that migrants are human. "*These are human beings* that are being forced into this walk for survival," said a Samaritan who maintains desert water stations. A relative of a disappeared migrant stated, "We have to search. *She is a person*—not just any old thing." Likewise, activists believe that naming the dead humanizes them. "We don't want the dead to be an abstraction. They had a *name*. They had a *face* because they had a family that saw them leave with great expectations and never heard from them again."[34]

Another variant of humanizing metaphors asserts the value of human life. Border Patrol spokespersons favor this metaphor in drawing out the moral failings of smugglers. "This is an absolute atrocity regarding the ruthlessness and the callousness of the smugglers. Their lack of care for *human life* is evident in this situation." Proenforcement activists also assert this value, and their own humanity, in countering charges that they are racist hunters.

> He said he and his brother are determined to protect the ranch from trespassers, but that doesn't make them insensitive to the difficulties that migrants face. "*Human life is a pretty precious thing*," said Don Barnette. "*That woman was a human being* in trouble who had her child with her. . . . I'm no different than 95 percent of the rest of the people out here. If I see someone in trouble, I'll help them."[35]

Humanitarian activists, by contrast, question the humanity of proenforcement policy and activists. As an editorial in the *Arizona Daily Star* reads, "This is the death sentence Arizona's harsh climate imposes on dozens of border crossers each year. Incredibly, it is one that some Arizonans seem content to see visited upon their *fellow human beings*."

MIGRANTS AS SAINTS

Religious activists for humanitarian treatment of migrants go even further by elevating migrants to blessed and even godly figures. "Christ would be weeping over the *crucifixion* of people in the desert," says Pastor John Fife. Catholic bishops have urged "parishioners to see *Jesus Christ* in the faces of the men, women and children who continue to make grueling illegal border treks into the United States from Mexico." Participants in border demonstrations often carry crosses to represent the holiness and humanity of dead migrants.[36]

Migrants are also given religious stature by equating them with other biblical figures such as the people of Israel or the stranger assisted by the Samaritan. For example, "The [No More Deaths] camp is named for the Old Testament Ark of the Covenant, a wooden box that symbolized the presence of God traveling with the people of Israel as they wandered in the desert." "The group says it operates on a premise from the Torah: 'Know the heart of the stranger, for you too were strangers.'"[37]

Although Samaritans as represented in media occasionally refer to policy as "sinful," the majority of religious metaphors do not point to any particular cause of death or attribute death to the proximate cause of dehydration (see table 10.2). Equating migrants with Christ or God's people is humanizing, but these metaphors do not necessarily encourage the audience to consider the distal causes or broader policy solutions. The focus is on person-to-person acts that reinforce the godliness of the Samaritan as well as the migrant: "'If Jesus Christ were here, he'd be offering water and welcoming the stranger,' says Humane Borders director the Rev. Robin Hoover of Tucson's First Christian Church. 'Water in the desert means life.'" Hoover avoids taking a public stance on policy, a position he buttresses by invoking the metaphor of Jesus in the desert.[38]

CONCLUSION

Journalists employ a variety of metaphors in writing about border deaths. Some of these metaphors are familiar from Otto Santa Ana's work on dehumanizing metaphors of immigrants as animals or dangerous waters. This chapter identifies three additional classes of metaphor in writing about migrant deaths: death as a cost, death as violence or vengeance, and dead migrants as human beings.

These varieties of metaphors invoke different forms of causal reasoning in accounting for deaths, causes that are more or less naturalizing versus socializing. Economic metaphors typically point to social explanations for death: a "cost" of the push and pull of poverty abroad and jobs in the United States and/or the "price" of enforcement policies. However, gambling metaphors also implicate migrants as calculated risk takers who gamble with their lives. Violence metaphors are naturalizing when the perpetrator of violent acts is the hostile, harsh, cruel desert that punishes those who try to cross it. On the other hand, violence metaphors are socializing when the perpetrator is a policy that has transformed the border into a "war zone."

Dehumanizing metaphors of migrants as victims tend to point away from policy factors by placing the focus on the individuals at the scene of death: smugglers as "predators," Border Patrol as "trackers," and migrants as "prey" who are lured into the desert's trap. On the other hand, water metaphors point to the policies that determine migrant "flows." Finally, humanizing metaphors are often invoked by humanitarian activists who seek to change policy. Nevertheless, the religious variant on these metaphors, which casts both migrants and humanitarians as biblical figures, tends to concentrate on the physical phenomenon of dehydration in the desert rather than on the distal causes that led migrants into the desert in the first place.

This analysis of metaphors illustrates their rich and complex contributions to cognition. In choosing metaphors (often unconsciously), journalists and their sources do more than make their writing more lively and readable. They import ideas from source domains of economy, violence, and (in)humanity into the target domain of migrant deaths, thereby making implicit arguments about the nature and causes of death.

NOTES

1. U.S. Government Accountability Office 2006.
2. Benford and Snow 2000; Marx Ferree et al. 2002.
3. George Lakoff's theory of metaphors has been influential in scholarship on political discourse. For an accessible introduction to his ideas, see Lakoff 2002.

Otto Santa Ana applies Lakoff's theory to news reporting on immigration (Santa Ana 1999, 2002). See Santa Ana 2002, chap. 2, for a concise review of the literature on metaphor in cognitive linguistics; see Lakoff.

4. Articles less than one hundred words were excluded. Articles about the Elian Gonzales case were excluded as were articles about the arrest of No More Deaths volunteers that only discussed legal details of the cases and did not link to the broader issue of migrant deaths.

5. U.S. Government Accountability Office 2006.

6. Following Santa Ana (2002, 339), I exclude foundational metaphors and orientation metaphors that are ubiquitous and found in any target domain.

7. Attributions of cause do not inherently suggest a specific policy solution. I have set aside analysis of prognosticating discourses for future analysis.

8. Carol Ann Alaimo, "Humane Help for Migrants," *Arizona Daily Star*, September 27, 2000; "Migrant Death Toll Due to Cold Now at 10," *Arizona Daily Star*, April 8, 1999; Leslie Berestein, "Border Fire Takes Toll on Illegal Crossers," October 28, 2007; Brady McCombs and Brian J. Pederson, "9 Killed, 10 Hurt as Packed SUV Rolls on Rte. 79 South of Florence," *Arizona Daily Star*, August 8, 2008. Article citations are given in order of corresponding quotes appearing within footnoted paragraph, here and throughout.

9. Mitch Tobin, "'Devil's Highway' Has Long History of Deadliness," *Arizona Daily Star*, March 4, 2002; Ernesto Portillo Jr., "Immigration Issue Has a Face: He's 2, and He's Barely Conscious," *Arizona Daily Star*, December 22, 2000; Anna Cearley, "Pressures Continue on a Bolstered Border," *San Diego Union-Tribune*, July 11, 2004. Emphasis in quoted text here and in the remainder of the article has been added by the author to highlight metaphorical tokens.

10. James O. Goldsborough, "We Only Pretend to Block Immigration," *San Diego Union-Tribune*, May 17, 1999; Erica Meltzer, "Vote Set on County Aid for Desert Water Stations," *Arizona Daily Star*, October 7, 2008; Brady McCombs, "U.S. Is Out $51M for Flying 64,000 Illegals to Mexico," *Arizona Daily Star*, August 10, 2008.

11. Marisa Taylor, "Man Pleads Guilty in Immigrant Smuggling Crash Case," *San Diego Union-Tribune*, December 5, 2002; Joe Cantlupe, "Border Patrol Targets Arizona," *San Diego Union-Tribune*, March 17, 2004; Charlie LeDuff, "A New Crime: Kidnapping the Smuggled," *San Diego Union-Tribune*, November 11, 2003; Sandra Dibble, "It's a Wintry No-Man's Land," *San Diego Union-Tribune*, April 8, 1999.

12. "Patrolling the Border," *Arizona Daily Star*, March 17, 2004; Carla McClain, "154 Illegal Crossers Fly Back to Mexico," *Arizona Daily Star*, June 11, 2005; "Facing Reality," *Arizona Daily Star*, September 29, 2004.

13. I do not classify as gambling metaphors references to migrants as being "at risk" in the epidemiological sense.

14. Brady McCombs, "Zero Tolerance Working, Says Border Patrol," *Arizona Daily Star*, April 6, 2008.

15. Ruben Navarrette, "America's Broken Promise," *San Diego Union-Tribune*, May 21, 2003.

16. Anne Krueger, "A New Zone of Contention," *San Diego Union-Tribune*, August 17, 2004; Michael Marizco, "Illegal Migrants Warned of Dangers," *Arizona Daily Star*, August 16, 2005; Carol Ann Alaimo, "Humane Help for Migrants," *Arizona Daily Star*, September 27, 2000.

17. Peter Rowe, "In Desperation, Migrants Ignore Laws of Nature," *San Diego Union-Tribune*, April 8, 1999; Ignacio Ibarra and Chris Richards, "Destination USA: Thousands Flock to Sasabe," *Arizona Daily Star*, March 2, 2004; Tim Steller and Ignacio Ibarra, "Desert's Heat Deadly for 7 Migrants," *Arizona Daily Star*, June 9, 2002; "Framing the Debate: The Root Causes of Illegal Immigration Are . . . ," *San Diego Union-Tribune*, March 22, 2005.

18. Tim Steller, "Betrayal and Banditry: Danger Is Part of the High Cost of Illegal Entry," *Arizona Daily Star*, July 12, 1999; Ignacio Ibarra, "Heat Leaves No Place to Hide," *Arizona Daily Star*, July 12, 1999; Foster Klug, "14 Border Crossers Die in the Desert," *San Diego Union-Tribune*, June 11, 2002; "Bordering on Failures," *Arizona Daily Star*, July 16, 2000; Brady McCombs, "U.S. Is Out $51M for Flying 64,000 Illegals to Mexico," *Arizona Daily Star*, August 10, 2008.

19. Time Steller, "Risky Crossing: Another Summer of Brutal Heat Puts Migrants at Risk," *Arizona Daily Star*, May 20, 2002; Laura Brooks, "Photojournalist Lives Border-Crosser Life," *Arizona Daily Star*, July 18, 1999; Daniel J. Chacon and Gregory Alan Gross, "Migrant Toll Rises to 14 in Desert Tragedy," *San Diego Union-Tribune*, May 25, 2001; Leslie Berestein, "Record Number Have Died Trying to Cross Border," *San Diego Union-Tribune*, September 4, 2005.

20. Ernesto Portillo Jr., "Group Searches for Illegal Entrants to Aid," *Arizona Daily Star*, June 16, 2006; "Where Everything Is Wrong," *Arizona Daily Star*, June 11, 2000; "Water in the Desert," *Arizona Daily Star*, June 14, 2002.

21. Peter Rowe, "Dash for Border Should Not Be a Capital Offense," *San Diego Union-Tribune*, March 9, 2000; Carol Ann Alaimo, "Humane Help for Migrants," *Arizona Daily Star*, September 27, 2000; L. Anne Newell and Carol Ann Alaimo, "Desert Kills 12 Migrants," *Arizona Daily Star*, May 24, 2001.

22. "Sinful Border Policies," *Arizona Daily Star*, July 2, 2002.

23. Tim Steller, "Mexican Dies in Desert; It's 5th Death in 10 Days," *Arizona Daily Star*, June 26, 1999.

24. Fred Krissman, "Our Border War," *San Diego Union-Tribune*, June 27, 2003; Ignacio Ibarra, "Illegal-Immigrant Detentions Declining," *Arizona Daily Star*, August 6, 2001.

25. Michael Marizco, "More Border Aid," *Arizona Daily Star*, July 8, 2004; John Fanestil, "Expanding the Border Fence in the San Diego Sector," *San Diego Union-Tribune*, August 16, 2008; Jeff McDonald, "Death and 10 Years of Border Fence," *San Diego Union-Tribune*, October 3, 2004; Doug Kreutz, "Border Battler," *Arizona Daily Star*, February 29, 2004.

26. "A Persuasive Man," *Arizona Daily Star*, August 3, 1999; "Federal Funds Fall Short for Illegal Entrants' Care," *Arizona Daily Star*, May 12, 2005.

27. Ignacio Ibarra, "Providing Assistance Along the Border," *Arizona Daily Star*, March 2, 2005; Michael Waterman, "Put Minutemen to Work at Border," *San Diego Union-Tribune*, April 29, 2005; "Minutemen Vigilante Project Could Be a Disaster," *Arizona Daily Star*, March 31, 2005; Leslie Berestein, "Rugged Routes, Deadly Risks," *San Diego Union-Tribune*, September 29, 2004; Leslie Berestein, "Border Fire Takes Toll on Illegal Crossers," *San Diego Union-Tribune*, October 28, 2007; Ignacio Ibarra, "Chancy Crossings: Desperate Aliens Take More Risks," *Arizona Daily Star*, April 25, 1999; Ruben Navarrette, "America's Broken Promise," *San Diego Union-Tribune*, May 21, 2003; Serge Dedina, "Waiting for the Border Watchers," *San Diego Union-Tribune*, September 16, 2005.

28. Eunice Moscoso, "Citizens Group to Monitor Border with Aircraft Drones," *San Diego Union-Tribune*, August 24, 2003; Serge Dedina, "Waiting for the Border Watchers," *San Diego Union-Tribune*, September 16, 2005; Jerry Kammer, "Border Volunteers Descend on Tourist Town," *San Diego Union-Tribune*, April 2, 2005.

29. Marcus Stern and Brianna Sannella-Willis, "Deaths of 14 Immigrants Loom over Border Talks," *San Diego Union-Tribune*, June 6, 2001; Ignacio Ibarra, "Border Patrol Recovers 4 More Bodies in Desert," *Arizona Daily Star*, August 20, 2002; Ernesto Portillo, "Death in the Devil's Desert," *San Diego*

Union-Tribune, July 4, 1999. I do not include the terms *humane* or *humanitarian* when coding metaphors as "humanizing" in the next section. *Humane* refers to the humanity of the person providing assistance, not the one receiving assistance (who may be an animal, as in the Humane Society).

30. Michael Marizco, "Clinic Gets Ailing Migrants in Shape for Illegal Entry into United States," *Arizona Daily Star*, March 4, 2004; Charlie LeDuff, "A New Crime: Kidnapping the Smuggled," *San Diego Union-Tribune*, November 11, 2003. The most common animal metaphor for smugglers is *coyote*, accounting for one-third of all animal metaphors in the sample. This metaphor is less dehumanizing than other animal metaphors, however, as it is rarely used to depict migrants as hunted prey. Rather, *coyote* describes the smuggler's wiliness in evading enforcement and toughness in the desert environment.

31. Marcus Stern and Brianna Sannella-Willis, "Deaths of 14 Immigrants Loom over Border Talks," *San Diego Union-Tribune*, June 6, 2001; Stephanie Innes, "Scores of Unnamed Entrants Lie Here," *Arizona Daily Star*, September 22, 2006; Michael Marizco and Ignacio Ibarra, "$28 Million Fails to Slow Deaths," *Arizona Daily Star*, September 26, 2004; Lourdes Medrano, "Entrant Deaths Down," *Arizona Daily Star*, July 24, 2006.

32. "Sinful Border Policies," *Arizona Daily Star*, July 2, 2002; "Bordering on Failures," *Arizona Daily Star*, July 16, 2000; Brady McCombs, "'Funneling' Raises Entrant Toll in AZ," *Arizona Daily Star*, February 15, 2007.

33. Erica Meltzer, "Vote Set on County Aid for Desert Water Stations," *Arizona Daily Star*, October 7, 2008; Tim Steller, "Migrant Returned to Look for Missing Wife," *Arizona Daily Star*, July 28, 2001; Leonel Sánchez, "Group Casts Light on Lost Immigrants," *San Diego Union-Tribune*, July 3, 2000.

34. Ignacio Ibarra, "Vigilantes Help Save Migrant," *Arizona Daily Star*, May 19, 2001.

35. L. Anne Newell and Carol Ann Alaimo, "Desert Kills 12 Migrants," *Arizona Daily Star*, May 24, 2001; Stephanie Innes, "Bishops Plead for Border Crossers," *Arizona Daily Star*, April 24, 2004.

36. Stephanie Innes, "Group's Aim: 'Flood Desert' to Aid Migrants," *Arizona Daily Star*, July 21, 2005; Stephanie Innes, "Volunteers to Work with Border Patrol," *Arizona Daily Star*, May 20, 2006.

37. Carmen Duarte, "Samaritan Patrol Will Try to Save Entrants," *Arizona Daily Star*, July 1, 2002; Michael Marizco, "Praying for a Safe Journey: Before Setting Out, Crossers Seek Strength in Church," *Arizona Daily Star*, June 5, 2003.

38. Marizco, "Praying for a Safe Journey."

STATION 5

EXPRESSIONS FROM THE LIVING DEAD

Peace is flowing like a river,
Flowing out of you and me,
Flowing out into the desert,
Setting all the captives free.
Hope is flowing like a river . . .

ETHICAL AND BIOPOLITICAL DIMENSIONS OF MIGRANCY, LIFE, AND DEATH IN MEXICO'S SOUTHERN BORDER

JAVIER DURÁN

O N JANUARY 9, 2009, members of the state of Chiapas' Policía Estatal Preventiva (State Preventive Police) opened fire on a large truck carrying a group of twenty-six undocumented migrants near San Cristobal de Las Casas. Apparently the truck failed to stop when prompted to do so by the agents. As a result, three migrants were dead (Levis Clarisa Moina Cabrera and Norma Dután Parrapi, from Ecuador, and Kevin Pérez Carias, from Guatemala), and eight others were wounded and hospitalized.[1] The remaining migrants were sent to a migratory station for their eventual deportation. According to press dispatches, the three agents were reported to have been placed under arrest after the shooting. Although Mexico's Comision Nacional de los Derechos Humanos (CNDH; National Commission of Human Rights) opened an investigation,[2] the case was not taken to any judicial instance, and no record of further inquiry by the Mexican authorities can be found in the press. It is highly doubtful that the surviving migrants were going to be allowed to stay in Mexico to press charges against the policemen. It is also not clear how and when the bodies of the victims were sent to their countries of origin. All in all, it seems just like any other typical case of impunity concerning undocumented migrants on Mexican soil. The only difference from other such cases is that this one received press coverage mainly because of the location of the incident and the tragic result. Moreover, it was significant that the CNDH, by acting promptly in opening an investigation, helped in bringing attention to the incident. What I find interesting about this case is the high degree of press coverage of an aggression against a group of migrants by Mexican authorities. Furthermore, the case seems to suggest that the frequency of these types of episodes in which human rights are only a vague reference is escalating to the degree that jurisdictional lines dealing with immigration law enforcement continue to be blurred and even erased in Mexico's southern border area despite official rhetoric to the contrary.

As U.S.-inspired notions of territorial security and border reinforcement are transferred to Mexico's southern border, the levels of violence and the incremental rise in deaths seem to point to a direct correlation between these models and a continued disregard for human rights and for the value of life itself. Besides press coverage, there have been recent efforts to document this situation, mostly coming from human rights organizations allied with migrant shelters and with limited participation by some academics. These efforts have translated into a few recent cultural artifacts, both textual and visual, that attempt to expose and denounce these dynamics. The emergence of testimonial narratives as viable records of the migrant experience has become an important locus of enunciation for this subaltern experience. Inasmuch as testimonial narratives have a strong tradition in Latin American and in particular Central American cultural representations, contemporary migrant testimonies challenge, in my view, established notions of the genre by attempting to document not only the experience of "crossing" borders but also the ethical and biopolitical dimensions of violence in the migrant experience along with issues of gender and sexuality.

In this chapter, I want to undertake a critical reflection of the conference theme *No vale nada la vida, la vida no vale nada* (Life has no worth, life has no worth). I would like to notionally examine some ethical and biopolitical dimensions connected with migrancy, life, and death in Mexico's southern border. To this end, I first establish an engagement with some etho- and biopolitical notions. Here, I am interested in exploring the notion of "bare life," which comes to equate with that minimal condition of life, the minimum "value" of life ("el valor mínimo de la vida"). My argument is that in the etho-biopolitical dimensions of today's global immigration debate, in which the politics of fear play a major role, the migrant, as subject, adheres closely to this notion. Yet, there seems to be a parallel process under which the opposite effect appears to occur: that human trafficking and the economic value of migrant life have become more profitable. Second, I briefly revise current views and perceptions of Central American migration within the Mexican sociopolitical context using this etho-biopolitical lens. And finally, to illustrate how this plays out culturally, I briefly analyze how works such as the collective testimonial *La migra me hizo los mandados* (2002) by Alicia Alarcón and the documentary film *De nadie* (2005) by Tim Dirdamal, document and problematize the trials and tribulations of unauthorized migrants, stressing the place of Mexico as a living hell in the migratory hemispheric maps. Moreover, I want to underscore ways in which Mexico's anti-illegal immigration enforcement practices mirror and sometimes exceed those emanating from the United States.

In a recently published study titled *Targeting Immigrants: Government, Technology and Ethics*, Jonathan Inda proposes a theoretical revision of the various ways in which globalized governments/nation-states institute new tactics for the incorporation or disincorporation of citizenship. A binary opposition arises within this system in the form of a new citizenry that Inda designates "prudential" and "imprudent" citizenship. In terms of the latter, its racial makeup and unethical condition vis-à-vis an attitude of personal responsibility that is required in a "prudential" or mainstream system is quite evident. In this ethopolitical landscape, as Nikolas Rose would contend, those individuals incapable of integrating into a system that requires more and more financial and social self-responsibility in the face of real-life insecurities are excluded from such a system and many times end up being criminalized.[3] Discipline and punishment act, then, as society's filters to decant layers of "irresponsible" individuals. The system has changed to incorporate the new needs of a post–welfare state power. Population control has taken new forms beyond just surveillance on criminality. This political state of permanent exception is tightly linked to the ideology of governance and of security. As Slovenian thinker Slajov Zizek suggests, today's predominant mode of politics is the "post-political bio-politics": "post-political is a politics which focus on expert management and administration while 'bio-politics' designates the regulation of the security and welfare of human lives as its primary goal. . . . For this reason, bio-politics is ultimately a politics of fear, it focuses on defense from potential victimization or harassment."[4]

The relations between state of exception and biopolitics are also theorized by Italian philosopher Giorgio Agamben in his Homo Sacer series. For Agamben, the *homo sacer* is an individual who exists as an exile in the law. In this, there seems to be a paradox: it is only because of the law that society can recognize the individual as homo sacer, and so the law that mandates the exclusion is also what gives the individual an identity, albeit referential, but not necessarily agential. Agamben contends that life exists in two capacities. One is natural biological life (Greek *zoë*), and the other is political life (Greek *bios*). As "bare life," the homo sacer is submitted to the sovereign's state of exception, and, though biologically alive, she or he has no political significance.[5]

In this framework, human life is politicized the moment it occupies space; that is, when it is exposed to death. In the sovereign sphere it is permitted to kill without committing homicide and without celebrating a sacrifice, while sacred life is that which has been captured in this sphere of double exclusion and double capture (from the law and from religion). The sacred man (homo sacer) is a living dead. He or she constitutes the law through its externality as well as indicating its limits of operation. Sacred man is a pariah of society, which Agamben identifies with migrants held hostage in detention camps as well as the prisoners in Guantanamo Bay.[6] Thus, as Agamben argues, the so-called sacred and inalienable rights of "man" prove to be completely unprotected at the very moment it is no longer possible to characterize them as rights of the citizens of a state. This dialogues with Hannah Arendt's reasoning concerning the 1789 Declaration of the Rights of Man and of the Citizen, which tied human rights to civil rights (Arendt 1998). Arendt shows how although human rights were conceived as the ground for civil rights, the privation of those civil rights—for instance, in the case of stateless people, such as refugees (and some unauthorized migrants)—made them comparable to "savages," setting the stage for the extermination of many during the New Imperialism period. Arendt seems to suggest that respect of human rights depends on the guarantee of civil rights and not the other way around, as argued by the liberal natural rights philosophers. In this context, I suggest that Agamben's tripartite biopolitical proposal (bare life, political life, and the state of exception) collides with and problematizes the issue of the "value of migrant life" in Mexico's southern border.

It is not, then, an exaggeration to say that migrant's rights (political and human) are barely existent. On the other hand, the crude conditions of clandestine crossing through Mexico make bare life the norm. In this complex scenario, the border itself seems to fall under a continued state of exception whereby the suspension of rights and the increased role of state violence become the ruling guidelines. Migrancy then becomes a permanent status of exposure under which bare life and the state of exception exert their full force. Nonetheless, and perhaps as suggested by Jacques Rancière, the issue of humanitarian rights is also part of a process of dehumanization, exclusion, and violence exerted against "the other,'" where

Any kind of claim to rights or any struggle enacting rights is thus trapped from the very outset in the mere polarity of bare life and state of exception. That polarity appears as a sort of ontological destiny: each of us would be in the situation of the refugee in a camp. Any difference grows faint between democracy and totalitarianism and any political practice proves to be already ensnared in the biopolitical trap.[7]

With this argument, Rancière problematizes and challenges Arendt's assumption (that the Rights of Man are those of either the citizen who has rights or of those deprived of those rights) by submitting that "the Rights of Man are the rights of those who have not the rights that they have and have the rights that they have not."[8] This apparently confusing statement acquires meaning when, rather than being set in a binary opposition, it defines rights as an active part of political processes of subjectivization whereby

The Rights of Man are the rights of the demos, conceived as the generic name of the political subjects who enact—in specific scenes of dissensus—the paradoxical qualification of this supplement. This process disappears when you assign those rights to one and the same subject. There is no man of the Rights of Man, but there is no need for such a man. The strength of those rights lies in the back-and-forth movement between the first inscription of the right and the dissensual stage on which it is put to test. This is why the subjects of the Soviet constitution could make reference to the Rights of Man against the laws that denied their effectivity.[9]

In this scenario, it is thus possible that "even the clandestine immigrants in the zones of transit of our countries or the populations in the camps of refugees, can invoke them."[10] But what complicates the issue here is that in addition to a vicious cycle or impasse within the binary, there is indeed a process of depolitization that in fact disempowers the migrant subjects from exerting those rights through a process of consensus where the aim is to equalize the law with the natural life of society. To put it in other terms, *consensus* is the reduction of democracy to the way of life of a society, to its *ethos*—meaning by this word both the abode of a group and its lifestyle. Rancière elaborates in this long but essential quote:

As a consequence, the political space, which was shaped in the very gap between the abstract literalness of the rights and the polemic about their verification, turns out to diminish more and more every day. Ultimately, those rights appear actually empty. They seem to be of no use. And when they are of no use, you do the same as charitable persons do with their old clothes. You give them to the poor. Those rights that appear to be useless in their place are sent abroad, along with medicine and clothes, to people deprived of medicine, clothes, and rights. It is in this way, as the result of this process, that the Rights of Man become the rights of those who have no rights, the rights of bare human beings subjected to inhuman repression and inhuman conditions of existence. They become humanitarian rights, the rights of those who cannot enact them, the victims of the absolute denial of right. For all this, they are not void. Political names and political places never become merely void. The void is filled by somebody or something else. The Rights of Man do not become void by becoming the rights of those who cannot actualize them. If they are not truly "their" rights, they can become the rights of others.[11]

But do those rights really become the rights of those "others"? And if so, how, and who are those "others"?

As reported by the Mexican daily *La Jornada*, in April 2008 during a meeting with members of the Mexican Senate, United Nations Special Rapporteur for the Human Rights of Migrants Jorge Bustamante, a migration expert, publically accused the legislators of avoiding their responsibilities on this matter: "Desde hace 20 años están en deuda, no han modificado la Ley de Población, que considera criminales a quienes ingresan sin documentos al país" (You have been in debt during the past twenty years: you have not modified the General Population Law, which considers criminals those who come undocumented to the country). Bustamante's comments went further: "Lo que hacemos a los centroamericanos que ingresan al territorio nacional sin papeles tampoco nos coloca como un país ejemplar. Hay violaciones a sus derechos peores de las que padecen nuestros compatriotas en Estados Unidos" (What we do to the Central Americans that enter Mexican territory without papers does not place us as an exemplary nation either. There are violations to their rights much worse than those suffered by our countrymen in the United States). Perhaps Bustamante's comments refer to some of the 236,000 Central Americans deported from Mexico in 2005 out of an estimated 350,000 that entered through the southern border. Of the remaining total it is estimated that fifty-six thousand were deported by the Border Patrol, ten thousand stayed in Mexico, and forty thousand managed to cross into the United States.

Bustamante's comments are indeed an imperative reminder that the magnitude of the human crisis in Mexico's southern border is comparable or perhaps

even greater in magnitude than that of the northern region. Claudio Lomnitz has commented that death has become an important referent in Mexico's
northern border representations. The increased deaths of migrants along this
region have greatly contributed to this repositioning in the face of increased
deaths of migrants in the region.[12] Yet there is need to further research not only
the "idea" of death from a sociosymbolic and representational stand but also the
parameters of a large humanitarian crisis in the southern border where, I contend, "bare life" then comes to equate that minimal condition of life, the minimum "value" of life, *el valor mínimo de la vida*: the *zoë*, bare minimum zoological
condition of any human being. In the etho-biopolitical dimensions of today's
immigration debate, the migrant, and in particular women and children from
Mexico and Central America, are defined and treated according to this category. In addition, there is also an economic argument here. The minimum value
of life, the *zoë*, also has a sort of surplus value in economic terms. Paradoxically, the lives of migrants become economically viable to the degree that their
deportability and "illegality" are profitable, and their capacity to generate ransom funding exists.

In July 2008, Mexican president Felipe Calderón announced the decrimi-
nalization of undocumented migrants. With prison terms ranging from eighteen months to ten years, migrants found illegally in Mexico will have to pay a
series of fines depending on their situation.[13] In a press release, the Secretaría de
Gobernación (Mexico's secretary of the interior) specifically commented on how
these changes should benefit Central American migrants and their situation in
Mexico: "Nuestros hermanos centroamericanos, que diariamente ingresan a nuestro territorio con el fin de buscar mejores oportunidades de vida, no pueden ni
deben ser tratados como criminales"[14] (Our Central American brothers, who
daily enter our territory in order to seek better opportunities in life, cannot and
should not be treated as criminals). As stated by Nicholas De Genova (2002,
438) regarding Mexican immigration to the United States, "Deportability is de-
cisive in the legal production of Mexican/migrant 'illegality' and the militarized
policing of the U.S.-Mexico border, however, only insofar as some are deported
in order that most may ultimately remain (un-deported)—as workers, whose
particular migrant status has been rendered 'illegal.'" In the same fashion, Inda
(2005) proposes that deportability becomes a technology of anticitizenship that
the state uses as recourse in times of crisis.[15]

The case of Elvira Arellano is highly representative of this process. Arellano,
a Mexican citizen, became a symbolic figure for many undocumented migrants
in the United States. She was working illegally at Chicago O'Hare Airport

when she was arrested on a post-9/11 security sweep in 2002. In 2006, she evaded a deportation order and took refuge at the United Methodist Church of Adaberto on Division Street in Chicago, where she remained for twelve months. She was eventually deported to Mexico in 2007 after leaving Chicago to travel to Los Angeles. It is not my intention to discuss the Arellano case in full detail here, but I want to suggest that what deportability also provides, or rather undermines, is the possibility to establish a judicial case against the state, or what Jean Francois Lyotard has called the *differend*. In this sense, deportability, in particular abrupt and violent deportations, contributes to the increased production of differends among migrant subjects. Lyotard has explained the differend as a case of conflict between parties that cannot be equitably resolved for lack of a rule of judgement applicable to both. In the case of a differend, the parties cannot agree on a rule or criterion by which their dispute might be decided. A *differend* is opposed to litigation—a dispute that can be equitably resolved because the parties involved can agree on a rule of judgement.[16] From my perspective, abrupt deportations under which the migrants are unable to undergo a legal recourse to establish their status before the law are examples of *differends* and uphold a continued state of "illegality" for migrant subjects since due process and presumption of innocence are completely absent in this procedure. What the result of the Arellano case shows is that the legal apparatus is also determined to silence any challenges that these differends may bring. As soon as Elvira Arellano began to create discursive means to contest and defy the state in public, the state acted on her, removing her from the national territory. Arellano's removal also sanctions her behavior and agency by linking her "illegal" status to criminal activity, in this case, speaking in public about migrant rights.

If deportability plays a crucial role in the making of the migrant's surplus value, it is also profitable to keep the migrants as "illegal," or stateless. In this context, kidnapping and sequestering the migrants for profit has become another strategy used not only by human traffickers but also by Mexican authorities, as stated in a recent UN report given to the Mexican government:

Jorge Bustamante, Relator Especial de la ONU para los derechos humanos de los migrantes, entregó recientemente al gobierno de Felipe Calderón un informe exhaustivo y demoledor sobre la actuación de las fuerzas públicas en esta materia. Una de las conclusiones más inquietantes es que existe en nuestro país una especie de "red de extorsión" integrada por miembros del "Ejército, la Marina y la policía" que violan de forma sistemática los derechos básicos de "miles de migrantes" centroamericanos al año.[17] (Jorge Bustamante, UN Special Rapporteur for human rights of migrants, recently gave the government of Felipe Calderón a comprehensive and damning report on the performance of the law enforcement in this area. One of the most disturbing findings is that in our country a kind of "extortion racket" composed of members of the "army, navy, and police" systematically violate the basic rights of "thousands of migrants" from Central America yearly.)

In other words, migrants are not becoming "highly disposable," as the levels of reported violence may lead to believe, but in many cases they are not even being deported. On the contrary, by keeping them "subject to deportation" (sometimes barely alive) un-deported, but "illegal," and without legal recourse to invoke their rights, many migrants generate more profit depending on the value scale used by their traffickers. What really seems to dictate the migrants "surplus" value is indeed migrancy itself, their mobility; that is, the longer the migrants are able to travel along the migratory networks, the more opportunities will the traffickers have to exploit them. In some cases, the migrants face constant robberies and assaults by the authorities. In others, the bodies generate surplus value either as free/cheap labor or sexually exploitable bodies. Yet, in other situations, migrancy and illegal privation of freedom generate profit as the migrants are kidnapped for ransom several times during the journey through Mexico.

Perhaps, as Rancière suggests, the mere existence of the notion of humanitarian rights is also an element that compounds the problematic of migrancy:

If those who suffer inhuman repression are unable to enact the Human Rights that are their last recourse, then somebody else has to inherit their rights in order to enact them in their place. This is what is called the "right to humanitarian interference"—a right that some nations assume to the supposed benefit of victimized populations, and very often against the advice of the humanitarian organizations themselves. The "right to humanitarian interference" might be described as a sort of "return to sender": the disused rights that had been sent to the rightless are sent back to the senders. But this back and forth movement is not a null transaction. It gives a new use to the "disused" rights—a new use that achieves on the world stage what consensus achieves on national stages: the erasure of the boundary between law and fact, law and lawlessness. The human rights that are sent back are now the rights of the absolute victim. The absolute victim is the victim of an absolute evil. Therefore the rights that come back to the sender—who is now the avenger—are akin to a power of infinite justice against the Axis of Evil.[18]

In this convoluted state of affairs, it is possible to identify five main layers of obstacles and filtering that exist across the southern Mexican border and that have become tight elements in the devaluation of life and rights in the region, all of which are very well developed in the works selected in this essay: first, the recent overempowerment of the Mexican Migra as exemplified in the Instituto Nacional de Migracion (INM) Plan Frontera Sur; second, the constant abuses by regional military authorities and local law enforcement agencies; third, the excessive violence exerted with impunity by the Mara Salvatrucha and related gangs; fourth, the exploitation and quasi slavery of women migrants by abusive "coyote" networks; and fifth, the constant casualties produced accidentally and intentionally by the so-called killer trains. Furthermore, during a very recent fact-finding visit to Mexico last year, members of the National Alliance of Latin American and Caribbean Communities (NALACC) announced that according to written testimonies from several migrant shelters in Oaxaca, most of the abuses and rights violations against the migrants came from the police force (at all levels) as well as from the military and the gangs: "Se registran secuestros exprés, violaciones sexuales de mujeres, extorsiones y ataques con armas blancas y también de fuego, tanto de parte de los llamados *maras*, como de miembros del Ejército y de policías. Hay emigrantes que son asaltados y vejados hasta tres veces en un solo día" (There are express kidnappings, sexual assaults and rapes, extortions, knife and gun attacks from the so-called Maras and members of the military and the police. Some migrants are assaulted and attacked up to three times a day). Angela Zambrano, current president of NALACC, urged Mexican president Felipe Calderón to seriously consider undertaking immigration reform that can help end these abuses and at the same time solidify Mexico's ethical position when defending the rights and lives of unauthorized Mexicans in the United States.

RIGHTS AND LIVES

In the ethical and biopolitical dimension of migrancy and rights, Rancière's conclusion makes us reflect on the complex ways in which migrant life and human rights are subjected to systematic processes of depolitization.

Ethics is indeed on our agendas. Some people see it as a return to some founding spirit of the community, sustaining positive laws and political agency. I take a
fairly different view of this new reign of ethics. It means to me the erasure of all
legal distinctions and the closure of all political intervals of dissensus. Both are
erased in the infinite conflict of Good and Evil. The "ethical" trend is in fact the
"state of exception." But this state of exception is no completion of any essence of
the political, as it is in Agamben.

Instead it is the result of the erasure of the political in the couple of consen-
sual policy and humanitarian police. The theory of the state of exception, just as
the theory of the "rights of the other," turns this result into an anthropological or
ontological destiny.[19]

Migrant testimonies challenge established notions of the genre by confronting
the growing number of differends and attempting to document the etho- and
biopolitical dimensions of violence in the migrant experience and its links to
issues of gender violence. They also seem to defy traditional views of *testimonio*
(testaments).

In a recent work, *Can Literature Promote Justice? Trauma Narrative and Social
Action in Latin American Testimonio* (2006), Kimberly Nance revises the rhetor-
ical foundations of testimonial narratives. Following her analysis, it would be
difficult to locate migrant testimonies within "canonical" modes of this genre:
"*testimonio* will be defined as the body of works in which speaking subjects who
present themselves as somehow 'ordinary' represent a personal experience of
injustice, whether directly to the reader or through the offices of a collaborat-
ing writer, with the goal of inducing readers to participate in a project of social
justice."[20] Describing their repeated traumatic suffering during their journey and
denouncing the abuses and exploitation suffered at the hands of multiple participants in the human traffic chain are essential aspects of these narratives. However, promoting social change, inspiring reader participation in a particular cause,
and achieving social justice do not seem to be fundamental elements of migrant
testimonies. Perhaps migrant testimonies could be placed closer to a "Latin
American subset of trauma narrative with social intentions."[21] And yet, assessing the issue of social effect for these narratives seems rather problematic (and
could be the subject of another study). While it is not my intention to engage
in an deep discussion of testimonial narrative as a genre or narrative mode, I
would still like to concur with Nance when she states that "As a part of a social
project, *testimonio* (testaments) is not a matter of speaking of one's suffering for
therapeutic, archival, or judicial purposes, *but rather of speaking of one's suffering*

in such a way that readers will be induced to act against the injustice of it."[22] I also would like to suggest that works such as *La migra me hizo los mandados* (2002) by Alicia Alarcón and the documentary *De nadie* (2005) by Tim Dirdamal seem to adhere to the above prescription.

La migra me hizo los mandados, translated into English as *The Border Patrol Ate My Dust*, gathers twenty-nine short narratives or vignettes. There is no preface or introduction from the author or compiler of the collection. In fact, Alicia Alarcón's words are completely absent from the book. What the reader finds regarding the author is a sketchy description of how the stories in the volume were compiled. According to the back cover of the English edition,

> Radio personality Alicia Alarcón invited listeners who had migrated to the United States to call and share their stories. In these pages, Alarcón collects the footsteps of these travelers, through their flight and their falls. Their stories highlight the true American experience for immigrants from all over South and Central America who decide to leave their respective homelands.

The book describes in detail migrants' journeys from their homelands to the United States following what Nance would call a "epideictic form of *testimonio.*"[23] And yet it is important to return to the text itself to better grasp the implications of the project. As the back cover of the English edition reminds us,

> These intriguing but heartbreaking passages reveal young and old, men and women, who must overcome the impossible as they hope to find a better place than the one they've left behind. These difficult and gritty stories are the stories of the successful, the ones who make it across, past the natural and the bureaucratic obstacles along the border, only to scratch together lives on the other side.

Alarcón, the mediator, or *gestora*, as those who gather other people's testimonies are also called, comes from an immigrant background as well. Her biographical information in the back cover of the English edition states

> ALICIA ALARCÓN was born in Jocotepec, Jalisco, Mexico. Her parents moved their large family to Mexicali, on the border of the United States, to provide a better living for their children. She has been a journalist for La Opinión, Univisión, and CNN Radio in Los Angeles. She currently hosts a program on Radio Única 1580 AM in Los Angeles.

Considered a radio journalist, the website aliciaalarcon.com features an interview with Alejandra Bouza titled "La comunicadora de Los Angeles" (Los Angeles's communicator), which reveals more information about the genesis of the book.

> Fue precisamente, durante uno de sus programas de radio que la conductora se le ocurrió lanzar la invitación: "Platíquenme como llegaron al Norte, los que lo hicieron sin documentos."
>
> "La respuesta fue inimaginable. Me llegaron cientos de cartas con historias que reflejaban una experiencia que debía de ser documentada. De ahí surgió la idea de escribir el libro: *La migra me hizo los mandados*. Me tomó dos años terminar el libro que incluye 29 relatos de indocumentados de diferentes países de Latinoamerica."
>
> (It was precisely during one of her radio programs that she thought of inviting her audience: "Tell me how you arrived to the North [United States], those of you that did it without documents."
>
> "The response was unimaginable. I received hundreds of letters with stories that reflected an experience that should be documented. From there, the idea of writing a book emerged: *The Border Patrol Ate My Dust*. It took me two years to finish the book, which included twenty-nine stories of undocumented people from different Latin American countries.")

Compare the above paragraph with this one.

> Southern California radio personality Alicia Alarcon invited her immigrant listeners to call in and share their stories: The *Border Patrol Ate My Dust* (translated into English by Ethriam Cash Brammer de Gonzales) is her recorded collection of these stories of hardship and deprivation suffered by those who struggled to enter this country. Natural and man-made obstacles are recounted in recollections of making it across the border and making a new life in America.
> (backcover of the Spanish edition of *The Border Patrol Ate My Dust*)

While reading the above excerpts, it is clear that there seem to be some contradictions regarding the way in which Alarcón gathered the materials for the book. This in itself would constitute an interesting research topic about this work since it could perhaps guide the reader to better grasp the possible political and ideological spheres of the project. Did she receive phone calls or letters from her audience? If phone calls were received, who transcribed the contents from the audiotapes? If letters were received, did Alarcón correct their style and add features of her own to the stories? How many did she receive? How did she select the ones for publication? Despite the conflicting versions regarding the methodology for obtaining the testimonies from Alarcón's audience, the anonymous signing of each story, and the fact that we are only told the first name of the protagonist as well as the place of current residency in the United States, what interests me the most is the diverse representation in the stories themselves. Moreover, the vignettes grapple with the issue of the value of life in a broad spectrum of manifestations. Of the twenty-nine stories, twelve are authored by Latin American women, and seven are from Mexico. It is difficult to date the testimonies; some stories allude to particular time frames or make direct reference to historical events. Moreover, all or most of the stories suggest that the protagonists, by virtue of having made it across the U.S. border, had "triumphed" over the Border Patrol's efforts to stop them. What is interesting from the narratives are the ways in which Mexico becomes an absolute nightmare for the Latin American migrants, in particular those from Central America. The narratives seemed to foresee dynamics that today have become generalized for the migrant experience. Dated from the late 1970s, 1980s, and 1990s, these stories are no different from contemporary accounts of Central Americans crossing Mexico in 2009 mentioned at the beginning of this chapter. What is worrisome is not so much that violence and injustice permeate these crossings but the mechanisms and the increased number of actors involved in the process. If in the past, some coyotes and a few corrupted law enforcement officers were involved, now the actors are part of full networks with very violent and competitive agendas in a context where the distinction between authorities and criminals is constantly blurred. Moreover, there seems to be growing evidence that the human trafficking networks have close ties with drug traffickers, making the issue even more complex and dangerous for migrants.

EL VALOR RELATIVO DE LA VIDA (THE RELATIVE WORTH OF LIFE)

"A dónde vas que más valgas migrante" (migrant, where are you going that you'll be worth more), asks Carlos Monsivais in an article of recent publication.[24] The same question is posed by María's mother, a Mexican migrant who shares her testimony in one of the book's vignettes titled "Me vendió con el armenio" (He sold me to the Armenian), in *La migra me hizo los mandados*. In this account, María decides to leave her home somewhere in Mexico where she has endured abuse and violence during most of her life. Upon arrival in the United States, María is sold by her U.S. coyote to an Armenian, becoming practically a slave. Eventually she returns to Mexico, but realizing that there is no future for her there, she embarks again on a long journey to El Norte with her mother's words tagging along with her: "Pinchi huevona, a dónde vas que más valgas . . . cabrona te estoy hablando . . . pendeja no sirves para nada" (Damn jerk, where you going that you'll be worth more . . . bitch I'm talking . . . you're a worthless asshole). At the crucial time when she is about to be inspected by an immigration officer at a checkpoint, María gathers enough *valor* (courage) to affirm her citizenship:

> Cuando lo tuve frente a mi, había reunido el valor que no tuve antes. El valor que me hizo falta para reclamarle a mi madre por sus insultos, el valor de reprocharle a mi padre su abandono, el valor de desenmascarar a Mr. Mike (el coyote). Lo junté todo y lo usé para decirle, mirándolo a los ojos:—American Citizen. . . . Llegamos a Los Ángeles al amanecer.[25]
>
> (When I confronted him, I gathered the courage that I didn't have before. The courage that I needed to complain to my mother for her insults, the courage to blame my father for having abandoned us, the courage to unmask Mr. Mike (the smuggler). I gathered all this courage and used it to tell him, looking at him straight in the eye: American citizen. . . . We arrived to Los Angeles at dawn.

¿A DONDE VAS QUE MÁS VALGAS? (WHERE ARE YOU GOING TO BE WORTHIER?) ¿DÓNDE VALES MÁS? (WHERE ARE YOU WORTH MORE?) ¿VALE ALGO LA VIDA? (IS LIFE WORTH ANYTHING?) LA VIDA NO VALE NADA . . . (LIFE HAS NO WORTH . . .)

Following Nance (2006), testimonial narratives have undertaken many different media forms, from narrative texts to films, performances, and documentaries. In this multimodal approach, "Testimonio is not only a text. It is a project of social justice in which the text is an instrument. . . . Although the genre is frequently characterized as didactic, that description fails to recognize that the goal of testimonio (testament) is not only to educate readers about injustice, but to persuade those readers to act."[26] In Alarcón's case, she acknowledges that

> Estoy muy contenta con que haya salido el libro en inglés, así muchas personas de otras culturas van a conocer parte de nuestras historias. Yo espero que al leerlas sean más sensibles a los indocumentados.
>
> Alarcón finalizó la entrevista con una frase definitiva. "Para mi los indocumentados no se trata de un problema de legalidad, sino de moralidad. Y es inmoral el que se castigue a un hombre o a una mujer por querer trabajar y darle mejor sustento a sus familiares, sea donde sea."
>
> ("I am very happy that the book has been published in English; thus, many people from other cultures are going to know our stories. I hope that when they read them, they become more sensible to [the plea by] the undocumented.")
>
> Alarcón finished the interview with a resounding statement: "To me the [issue of the] undocumented is not a problem of legality but a moral problem. And it is immoral that punishment be infringed upon a man or a woman who wants to work to support her family, be it where it may be."[27]

It is obvious that for Alarcón, her collective testimonial is an ethical and textual appeal to the "problematic" of undocumented migration. Yet, the social and political implications of Alarcón's collection are not clearly articulated since she never explicitly comments on what the real intention of the work may be. That does not seem to be the case in the award-winning documentary *De nadie* (2005). In this eighty-minute movie, Mexican filmmaker Tim Dirdamal follows a number of Central American refugees in a southern Mexican refugee center, from where they hitch illegal rides on freight trains to the northern border. In addition to the Mexican immigration service and police, the migrants are threatened by the security service of the railroad companies, the criminal Mara Salvatrucha gang, and the train itself. That is, we become witnesses of how the five layers of obstacles mentioned previously operate in continued and exchangeable actions in the region. In the documentary, we see how sixteen-year-old José from Honduras lost an arm when he fell under a train and how young Adolfo witnessed the murder of his parents by La Mara. The film shows how protagonist María Ponce, whose house was destroyed in Hurricane Mitch, barely survived an encounter with the violent gang. Contorted with fear and worries, her face speaks volumes. Director Dirdamal visits María's relatives who stayed behind in a poverty-stricken Honduran town. The horror stories of refugees, filmed with a handheld camera, are alternated with interviews with employees of the railroad company, the immigration service, and a relief organization, and they are complemented by factual background information. The only hope along the way comes from a volunteer organization that hands out food to passing refugees near the railroad tracks as they board a train toward an uncertain future.

EL VALOR DE LA VIDA (THE VALUE OF LIFE): OR IS IT THE "BARE VALUE" OF LIFE?

While a close reading of *De nadie* could illuminate a number of different issues, I would like to suggest that the documentary is better viewed within a social justice project aligned with Nance's definition of testimonial narratives. As *De nadie*'s director Dirdamal responds when asked about the original idea of the film, "As I was working as a volunteer in an immigrant project, there was an urgent need to tell others about these terrible deaths and injustices, in an attempt for them to end" (IndieWIRE). The director also acknowledges the support of a religious organization that aids migrants: "A bishop that has an immigrant shelter wanted to make a video on Central American immigration. So what was supposed to be a video turned out to be this feature film with the help of the 7,000 dollars Raúl Vera, the bishop, gave me." Vera is listed in the credits as the executive producer of the film. Moreover, the shelter becomes the epicenter of its migrant protagonists and their experiences. This is the narrative space where Lyotard's differends are confronted and where Agamben's *zoë* and *bios* come together. It is also the place where those human rights are temporarily restored to the migrants and the site where these rights will be—as Rancière has suggested—handed down to other yet unknown migrants who will follow. The shelter not only provides room and board for the migrants but also the opportunity to enunciate their experiences as *De nadie*, of no one, *los nadie*, the nobodies, the disposed, or dispossessed, those who have nothing: "Los nadies: los hijos de nadie, los dueños de nada. Los nadies: los ningunos, los ninguneados, corriendo la liebre, muriendo la vida, jodidos, rejodidos. . . . Que no son aunque sean" (The nobodies: nobody's children, owners of nothing. The nobodies: none, the nobodies, running like rabbits, dying through life, screwed, doubly screwed. . . . That aren't even though they are). These are the words from Uruguayan poet Eduardo Galeano, which make the lyrics of the documentary's theme song composed by Alberto Ruibal. Those nobodies who "no figuran en la historia universal, sino en la crónica roja de la prensa local. Los nadies, que cuestan menos que la bala que los mata" (don't count in the universal history, but rather in the crime reports in the local press. The nobodies, who cost less than the bullet that kills them). And these are precisely those others that Rancière argues are the recipients of human rights and of the so-called humanitarian interventions under which they are policed and scrutinized so that their "rights" can be guaranteed in the name of order and security.

There is another dimension of "value" involved in this. Are we talking about *valor*/value in the courage sense: *valor, tener valor*, to be brave, in Spanish? As María says in *De nadie*, "No voy a tener valor para hablar con mis hijos, para decirles lo que me pasó . . . no tener valor" (I will not have the courage to talk to my children, to tell what happened to me . . . not having value). Does that translate into not being worth a thing or simply not having the courage to tell her family of the assault and rape at gunpoint she suffered at the hands of three members of the Mara Salvatrucha after jumping from the train in the jungles bordering Chiapas and Veracruz?

¿Sigue valiendo la vida después de eso? Is life worth living after that? But which life? Bare life, *zoë*? Or is it *bios*? If so, what, then, delineates the border between the biological and the ethical? What about the border between the ethical and the political? Where is the human being in all of this? Let us think and reflect on that.

NOTES

1. Henríquez 2009.
2. Ballinas 2009.
3. Inda 2006.
4. Zizek 2008, 34.
5. Agamben 1998.
6. Agamben 2005.
7. Rancière 2004, 301.
8. Ibid., 302.
9. Ibid.
10. Ibid.
11. Ibid.

12. Lomnitz 2005.

13. *La Jornada* 2008.

14. Ibid.

15. Inda 2006.

16. Lyotard 1988.

17. Tejeda 2008.

18. Rancière 2004, 308–9.

19. Ibid., 309.

20. Nance 2006, 7.

21. Ibid., 9.

22. Ibid., 19 (emphasis in the original).

23. Ibid., 23.

24. Monsivais 2007.

25. Alarcón 2002, 128.

26. Nance 2006, 9.

27. Interview posted at http://www.aliciaalarcon.com (accessed June 25, 2010; no longer posted).

SIN EL DERECHO DE VIVIR
(WITHOUT THE RIGHT TO LIVE)

Migration Songs, Corridos, *and Death*

CELESTINO FERNÁNDEZ AND JESSIE K. FINCH

MIGRATION SONGS

MIGRATION IS A UNIVERSAL HUMAN EXPERIENCE that has touched countless lives around the world. Throughout the history of humanity, people have moved from their place of origin for various reasons, including in search of adventure; as a result of natural disasters such as floods, earthquakes, or droughts; because of wars; or because of religious or political persecution, to name a few.[1] However, the overwhelming majority of people who migrate do so in search of work, looking for opportunities to improve the quality of life for themselves and their families, or simply as a means of survival because of low employment and harsh economic conditions in their place of origin.[2] Under stable conditions, with employment resulting in incomes on which people can sustain themselves and their families, most people would rather remain in their place of origin than to have to migrate, particularly to foreign counties and cultures with different customs, traditions, and languages.

Given the widespread and powerful emotional turmoil that is engendered by migration, like other deeply meaningful human experiences, this experience has been captured in many forms of cultural expression, including art, film, literature, and songs.[3] Specifically, various aspects and details of the migration experience have been captured in the songs of both sending and receiving countries, as illustrated by some of the examples presented below.

Although migration themes can be captured in any song genre, certain forms, such as ballads and traditional folk songs, lend themselves better than others to documenting both general migration themes and specific, true-life stories and events of a particular individual, family, or group. The list found in appendix A illustrates the broad range of genres (from folk and country to rock and rap), themes (employment, discrimination, deportation, etc.), and performers (Neil Diamond, Sting, Joan Baez, Bruce Springsteen, etc.) of migration songs found in the United States.

These songs capture many themes pertaining to the migration experience, and these themes are presented from various perspectives, including that of the immigrants, border officials, the general receiving community, concerned observers, and others. The verses below serve as examples of the variety of themes, perspectives, and artists found in migration songs in the Unites States. The first verse is from the song *Across the Wire* by Calexico, a group from Tucson, Arizona, and it captures the experience of thousands of undocumented immigrants as they make their way into the United States through the desert in Southern Arizona, but the description could easily apply to the experience encountered by immigrants in any rural crossing area along the 2,000-mile U.S.-Mexico border.

Crossing in rural areas spiked as a result of the U.S. Border Patrol initiative known as Operation Gatekeeper, an initiative that increased enforcement in urban areas and that channeled migrants into the deserts, canyons, and ravines.[4] These rural areas are much more difficult to traverse and thus are significantly more dangerous for crossing than crossing in urban areas. Consequently, the result has been a major increase in migrant deaths.

Alberto y Hermano on the coyote's trail
and dodging the shadows of the Border Patrol
out in the wastelands wandering for days
the future looks bleak with no sign of change.
"Across the Wire" (Calexico)

No more deaths, I'll keep them alive
the Minutemen hunt their hides
the desert heat burns their feet
and what they have won't help them eat.
"Traces of Identity" (Ted Riviera)

Across the border now but the little ones are tired
she knows they can't go down, they need the guide they hired
they've been out of water now for several hours or more
youngest child is been getting sick and their feet are full of soars
what she wouldn't sacrifice to have a life like yours or mine
though she's close to freedom she knows she's running out of time.
"Everyone" (Marny Kennedy)

The following four examples—"The Line" by Bruce Springsteen, "California Snow" by Dave Alvin, "Trailways Bus" by Paul Simon, and "Land of Plenty" by Kevin Pakulis—capture the migration experience from the perspective of the Border Patrol. Given the increased dangers of walking during daylight (e.g., greater chance of being spotted by enforcement agents or of dying from the elements such as heat exposure), migrants do most of their walking at night. The Border Patrol is aware of this and thus has increased its night-enforcement efforts, including patrolling, the use of stadium lighting, and of technology such as sensors and night-vision goggles. In fact, as a result of the increased funding received by the Border Patrol from Congress during the past decade, particularly since the acts of terrorism committed on September 11, 2001 (now popularly known as "9/11"), enforcement efforts have been greatly enhanced, and one can regularly see Border Patrol agents everywhere on the U.S. side of the U.S.-Mexico border, including in airports and bus stations and patrolling in their automobiles, ATVs, horses, helicopters, and light planes.

Drug runners, farmers with their families,
Young women with little children by their sides
Come night we'd wait out in the canyons
And try to keep 'em from crossin' the line.
"The Line" (Bruce Springsteen)

I catch the ones I'm able to
and watch the others slip away
I know some by their faces
and I even know some by name
I guess they think that we're all
movie stars and millionaires
I guess that they still believe

that dreams come true up here.
"California Snow" (Dave Alvin)

The border patrol outside of Tucson boarded the bus
Any aliens here? You better check with us
How 'bout you son?
You look like you got Spanish blood
Do you "habla ingles, Am I understood?"
"Trailways Bus" (Paul Simon)

Of course, there have been many periods in the history of the United States when immigrants, particularly from northern and western Europe, were openly recruited and highly welcome. With the exception of paupers and people with mental-health problems, the United States has welcomed and continues to welcome certain categories of immigrants depending on the nation's biases and needs.[5] Generally, professionals have always been welcomed, as have a certain number of unskilled works (particularly during boom economic periods), but people of color (other than slaves) have generally not been welcome (witness federal legislation such as the Chinese Exclusion Act, Gentleman's Agreement, etc.). The following three verses are from songs that document the welcoming experience.

Of all the mighty nations
in the East and in the West
oh, this glorious Yankee nation
is the greatest and the best
we have room for all creation
and our banner is unfurled
here's a general invitation
to the people of the world.
"Uncle Sam's Farm" (E. P. Christy and Jesse Hutchinson)

Lovely Lady Liberty
with her book of recipes
and the finest one she's got
is the great American melting pot
the great American melting pot
what good ingredients,

liberty and immigrants.
"The Great American Melting Pot" (Lynn Ahrens)

I'm an alien, I'm a legal alien
I'm an Englishman in New York
I'm an alien, I'm a legal alien
I'm an Englishman in New York.
"Englishman in New York" (Sting)

Often, however, immigrants who initially perceived the United States as the land of opportunity, where a hardworking individual can earn enough money to eventually rise into the middle class (the American dream), the land where "the streets are paved with gold," have had a rather sobering experience upon arrival as they have faced bigotry and discrimination simply because of the color of their skin or the language they speak; a land where they have been forced to live in poverty and work for unfair wages in demeaning and dangerous conditions. Such experiences have also been captured in songs, as the following three examples illustrate.

When you reach the broken promised land
and every dream slips through your hands
then you'll know that it's too late to change your mind
'cause you've paid the price to come so far
just to wind up where you are
and you're still just across the borderline.
"Across the Borderline" (Ry Cooder)

I started off to find the house, I got it mighty soon;
there I found the ould chap saited: he was reading the *Tribune*.
I tould him what I came for, whin he in a rage did fly:
No! says he, you are a Paddy, and no Irish need apply!
Thin I felt my dandher rising, and I'd like to black his eye—
To tell an Irish Gintleman: No Irish need apply!
"No Irish Need Apply" (John F. Poole)

He says . . .
these hands

have washed the clothes
these hands have served the food
heaven knows
and this neck has felt a mob's rope
and it's been behind barbed wire
these arms have built the
railroad track
this back has been for hire
and these hands have
fought injustice
and this soul has been on fire.
"Tired of Proving We Belong" (Chris Iijima)

Assimilation is a major component of the immigration experience, a theme explored in many immigration songs. Often, as has been the case in the United States throughout its history, the host community complains about the immigrants' lack of assimilation. Frequently, immigrants speak of the difficulties encountered in the process of taking on a new culture, such as learning a new language, and about the strange new customs and traditions that they are experiencing. In the end, however, most immigrants do assimilate, as the literature clearly documents and the following verse illustrates.[6]

They don't know the language
they don't know the law
but they vote in the country of the free
and the funny thing when we start to sing
My country Tis of Thee
none of us know the words
but the Argentine, the Portuguese, and the Greek.
"The Argentines, the Portuguese, and the Greeks" (P. D.)

A few migration songs have been composed from the perspective of the indigenous populations that were in the United States before the Europeans arrived. "Song of the Red Man" notes how the people ("red man") living in the Americas were happy and free before the arrival of the Europeans ("palefaces"), implying that such conditions changed as a result of outsiders coming in even if they were at first welcomed by the indigenous peoples.

When the palefaces came in their white-winged canoes
long ago, from the sun-rising sea
when they asked for a lodge, and we did not refuse
happy then was the red man, and free.
"Song of the Red Man" (Henry C. Wok)

As a human experience, migration can evoke the full range of feeling, pas-
sions, and emotions, from tragedy and deep sadness to humor and laughter,
among all of the protagonists. The following three songs illustrate both humor
and satire in the migration experience.

Would you ever go over to Czechoslovakia, marry me daughter for me
she's the finest girl in Prague, you'll ever see
her name is citizen Gertie, a communist is she
she wants to come to America, be a capitalist like me.
"Czechoslovakia" (Black 47)

If I could be a superhero
I'd be Immigration Dude
I'd send all the foreigners back to their homes
for eating up all of our food
and taking our welfare and best jobs to boot
like landscaping, dishwashing, picking our fruit
I'd pass a lot of laws to get rid of their food
'cause I'd be Immigration Dude.
"Superhero" (Stephen Lynch)

Border man can't let you through
what's a poor man gonna do
businessman got work for you
who's the criminal here?
"Who's the Criminal" (Ted Warmbrand)

We conclude this section with a quote from a song by Woody Guthrie,
"Deportee (Plane Wreck at Los Gatos)" (originally a poem; Martin Hoffman
later added music, and it became one of Guthrie's best-known compositions),
that deals with one of the main topics of this paper: death in migration songs.
"Deportee" was inspired by an airplane accident in Los Gatos Canyon (Fresno

County, California) on January 28, 1948, which resulted in the death of all aboard, including four American men (the crew and one guard) and twenty-eight Mexican migrant workers (twenty-seven men and one woman) who were being deported to Mexico. Guthrie was specifically struck by the fact that all newspaper (including the *New York Times*, January 29, 1948) and radio reporting mentioned only the individual names of the American victims, giving them personal, human identities, while the Mexicans were simply referred to as generic "deportees." Moreover, he was appalled by the racist treatment of the migrants, a condition that one could argue has remained relatively unchanged since then (as exemplified by SB 1070, passed by the Arizona Legislature and signed by the governor during the spring of 2010). The Mexicans were all buried in a mass grave in Fresno, California; only twelve were ever identified. With this song, Guthrie paid tribute to the migrants, even giving some of them symbolic names (Maria, Juan, Jesús, and Rosalita), as he speaks about the contribution Mexican migrants make to the United States working in agriculture and of the fact that Mexican immigrants have died everywhere (hills, deserts, valleys, plains) on American soil. This song is well known and has been covered by many artists, including Bob Dylan, Joan Baez, Judy Collins, Pete Seeger, Dolly Parton, the Kingston Trio, the Byrds, Arlo Guthrie (Woody's son), Emmylou Harris, Bruce Springsteen, Peter, Paul and Mary, and many others.

> We died in your hills, we died in your deserts,
> we died in your valleys and died on your plains.
> we died 'neath your trees and we died in your bushes,
> both sides of the river, we died just the same
>
> The sky plane caught fire over Los Gatos Canyon,
> a fireball of lightning, and shook all our hills,
> who are all these friends, all scattered like dry leaves?
> the radio says, "They are just deportees."
> "Deportee (Plane Wreck at Los Gatos)" (Woody Guthrie)

THE *CORRIDO*

The Mexican song genre that has best captured the migration experience in rich detail during the past one hundred years is known as the *corrido*. The *corrido* (a type of Mexican folk song or ballad) is an essential component of the

Mexican lyrical oral tradition that dates to the Conquest and whose popularity continues throughout Mexico and to wherever Mexicans have migrated and settled.[7]

Over time, many significant as well as day-to-day experiences of *el pueblo mexicano* (the common folk or working-class segment of the population) have been documented and preserved in *corridos*. Natural disasters (earthquakes), wars (Mexican Revolution, World War II, the Gulf War, etc.), the lives of folk heroes (Gregorio Cortez, Fernando Valenzuela), world-changing events (Sputnik, 9/11), assassinations (John F. Kennedy, Luis Donaldo Colosio), smuggling (drugs, narco-*corridos*), immigration (undocumented), towns and states (Mazatlan, Chihuahua), horse races (black, white, and bay horses), and miraculous occurrences (Padre Romo) are among the many diverse topics that have been documented and discussed in *corridos*.

Héctor Pérez Matínez provides the best summary of how subject matter and themes are selected for *corridos*:

> The corrido unfolds out of historical experience, imbedding itself in the oral tradition, from those episodes that popular spirit intuitively selects, if they represent, to a certain degree, what is characteristic of the times; better stated, that which could be taken as final expression of the essence and inner character of the period. Thus, everything that moves, disturbs, or affects the common spirit, everything that influences the lives of the masses; that which produces unforgettable commotion or excitement, becomes subject matter for the corrido.[8]

In some respects, the *corrido* may be compared to the editorial page of a newspaper; both begin with real or true events, document such events, provide analysis and perspective, and often offer an opinion.[9] *Corridos*, like editorials, are quite accurate in documenting the dates, locations, names, and other facts and details associated with actual issues and events.[10] Both the *corrido* and the editorial often express an opinion or relate a moral message about the story/issue. As Vicente Mendoza, the late Mexican musicologist and foremost expert on the *corrido*, noted, "The *corrido* is from beginning to end a description that comes to us from the lips of an eyewitness or an exceedingly knowledgeable informant."[11] Thus, *corridos* reveal how *el pueblo* (common people) perceives, interprets, explains, and understands its day-to-day experiences.

For many scholars the only folksong that qualifies as a true *corrido* is one with a particular structure: a verse form (such as octosyllabic lines arranged in

quatrains with a specific rhyming scheme) and such other features as an introduction, presentation of the story (with names, dates, locations, etc.), and a
farewell.[12] Although purists may insist on this narrow format, the average listener to *corridos* does not. For example, Dorothy Mull, while collecting songs
about drug trafficker Rafael Caro Quintero and former Mexico City Chief of
Police Arturo Durazo Moreno, found that her Mexican informants identified
as *corridos* songs not consistent with the form noted above.[13] Fernández and
Officer found that Mexican Americans in the United States also held a broader
definition of what constitutes a *corrido* than that denoted by the purists.[14] We
have chosen to apply the "popular" definition of *corrido* in all of our research,
including in the work presented in this chapter; in other words, if *el pueblo*
identify a song as a *corrido*, we treat it as such, regardless of its structure.

IMMIGRATION *CORRIDOS*

The migration experience is one that deeply touches the lives of participants,
their relatives and friends, and in some cases the entire communities (even
nations) from which they come and in which they settle.[15] Although the individuals who migrate may experience the process as a personal and emotional
experience, one may also view it as a cultural and sociological phenomenon
in that the migrants are linked to social networks,[16] often possess information
provided by others, and carry with them the hopes and good wishes of those
with whom they will share the benefits of their travels. Personal and collective
strategies, fears, and aspirations, along with both tragic and amusing incidents
of the migration experience, provide appealing subject matter for *corridistas* (com-
posers of *corridos*), many of whom have trod the migration trails themselves,
including the lead author of this paper.

Just as public interest in Mexican undocumented ("illegal") immigration has
soared in the United States during the past forty-five years and particularly in
recent years,[17] so, too, has this theme been a major focus of contemporary *corridistas*. Songs focusing on the various experiences associated with emigrating
to the United States have been heard regularly on Spanish-language radio stations in both Mexico and the United States since 1970, although there are many
immigration *corridos* that date to the early part of the twentieth century, such
as "El lavaplatos" (The dishwasher), which humorously relates the story of an
immigrant who came to the United States during the period of the Mexican

Revolution (1910–20) in hopes of becoming a movie star in Hollywood but who, because of the discrimination he encountered against Mexicans, was able only to find work in manual labor enterprises such as in the California agricultural fields and construction trades and as a dishwasher.

The list of immigration *corridos* is long (the lead author has a collection of about one hundred), and many popular performers have recorded them, including Vicente Fernández (Mexico's top *ranchera* [country] singer; he has been performing since the early 1960s and has recorded over fifty albums and made forty films), Los Tigres del Norte (the most popular Norteño band; this group had been performing since 1968 and has recorded over fifty albums and appeared in over fifteen films), and Joan Sebastian (a highly prolific composer who has been performing since 1968 and has recorded over forty albums and has appeared in soap operas and several films; he died July 13, 2015).

Corridos have captured almost every aspect of the immigration experience, including places of origin, the beginning of the trip and the pain and sorrow of having to leave family behind, the economic reasons for having to emigrate (e.g., lack of employment and low wages), the pull factors (e.g., employment and wages) that attract Mexican immigrants to the United States, the costs associated with crossing the border (such as having to pay a "coyote" or "pollero" [human smuggler]), dealing with the Border Patrol, being apprehended, working under unjust and unfair situations for American employers, and so forth.

Several immigration *corridos* have been composed and recorded about San Toribio Romo, now dubbed the "patron saint of undocumented immigrants" or "Santo Pollero/Santo Coyote" (the human smuggler saint). Since the late 1970s, although picking up greatly in the 1990s just about the time that Operation Gatekeeper began to force immigrants to cross the U.S.-Mexico border in the most inclement weather and inhospitable terrains, a number of undocumented immigrants (apparently the first one was from the lead author's home state of Michoacán) began reporting that whenever they found themselves in trouble in the process of crossing the border, a man dressed in black would suddenly appear and help them cross safely, giving them water, food, and money when they needed it as well as information on how to obtain jobs in the United States. Sometimes he came upon immigrants suffering from heat exhaustion or illnesses, and he healed them. The immigrants initially thought he was a real human being; not a guardian angel or priest.

Immigrants did not learn of this man's true identity until visiting his home town of Santa Ana, Jalisco (Mexico). There they learned that Fr. Toribio was born in Santa Ana in 1900 and was killed in Tequila, Jalisco, by soldiers in 1928 during the Cristero War (the Mexican government's persecution of Catholic clergy during the late 1920s and early 1930s). They learned that he had a reputation for serving the poor and that he was canonized by Pope John Paul II in 2000. Since the 1970s, Saint Toribio has become very well known and highly revered among immigrants. On the outskirts of Guadalajara, Jalisco (Mexico), on the freeway heading north to Nogales and Tijuana, at the last gas station as one heads out of the city, there is a statue of San Toribio covered with rosaries left behind by individuals heading "al Norte" (to the United States) and who prayed for his protection. The shrine in his hometown is visited by five thousand people every weekend who go there to thank him for helping them cross into the United States or by relatives of immigrants making their way north praying for safe crossings into the United States. Today, Saint Toribio Romo's image can be seen everywhere,[18] including on religious cards carried by immigrants, an item often found in the Arizona desert left behind by passing immigrants. Following are some of the lyrics from the *corrido* "Santo Toribio Romo"; they speak of the how Saint Toribio helps immigrants with various needs (food, water, money) as they make their way to and cross the border.

Por el río bravo su chate o el desierto traicionero
hay los salva del peligro ese santo misionero
cuentan que a veces les da agua, comida y dinero.

Ya son miles de ilegales que lo empiezan a adorar
le piden al Padre Romo que los ayude a cruzar
fronteras, ríos y desiertos para sus sueño alcanzar.

Como un ángel o un fantasma se aparece al ilegal
los cuida y hasta los cura pa' que puedan continuar
y luego desparece, señal que van a llegar.
"Santo Toribio Romo" (Los Originales de San Juan)

(Through the Rio Grande or the betraying desert
there this mysterious saint saves them from danger
they tell that sometimes he gives them water, food and money.

There are thousands of undocumented migrants who now pray to him
they ask Fr. Romo to help them cross
borders, rivers, and deserts in order to fulfill their dreams.

Like an angel or ghost he appears to the undocumented
he helps them and even heals them so they may continue
and then he disappears; a sure sign that they will make it.)

The list of *corridos* in appendix B is representative of the hundreds of immigration *corridos* that have been composed and performed. The titles give the reader a general sense of the many topics and issues these ballads cover.

DEATH IN MIGRATION CORRIDOS

In addition to our contributions, other scholars, such as Paul S. Taylor and Maria Herrera-Sobek, have also written about immigration *corridos*, but we are not aware of anyone who has written specifically of immigration *corridos* that focus on death.[19]

The present study is based on a subset of the lead author's collection of about one hundred songs dealing with immigration, including two of his original compositions. We have identified several that deal with migrant death and, thus, that give us a sense of how *corridistas* have treated this tragic event (see appendix C). The analysis is based on the methodological techniques of grounded theory.[20] Basically, we reviewed the lyrics several times, allowing major recurring themes to emerge phenomenologically from the data themselves. The three *corridos* presented below can be thought of as case studies and representative of those *corridos* that deal with death in the immigration experience.

Interestingly, when we were beginning to conduct the research for this chapter, in late 2008 and early 2009, the U.S. Border Patrol issued a five-*corrido* CD titled *Migra corridos* (*Migra*, short for immigration [officers], is the term used by Mexicans to refer to the Border Patrol). These *corridos* were intended to be played on Mexican radio stations (initially twenty-five communities in six states with the largest number of U.S.-bound émigrés, such as Michoacán, which is mentioned in three of the five *migra corridos*). The plan also called for releasing the *migra corridos* in a few Central American countries and to serve as a sort of public information announcement; that is, as a means to deter immigrants from crossing the U.S.-Mexico border. The CD was part of the Border Patrol's "No More Crosses on the Border" campaign (part of a larger effort known as the "Border Safety Initiative"), which purchased airtime on Mexican television and radio to provide cautionary information for those thinking about heading to the United States.

The jacket cover, all in Spanish, speaks about how "year after year, thousands of people die on the U.S.-Mexico border. . . . This album is a collection of *corridos* that supposedly tell the stories of some of these people." All five *migra corridos* end in death and basically convey one overriding message: if you attempt to cross the U.S.-Mexico border without proper documentation, you will die.

Although one can acknowledge that the use of the *corrido* to convey a message to the immigrant community demonstrated good instinct (given the popularity of *corridos* among the working class, the group that makes up the majority of Mexican undocumented immigrants), in reality it demonstrated rather poor judgment. It should be noted that instead of these *corridos* serving their intended purpose, the Border Patrol was heavily criticized for attempting to appropriate a popular Mexican art form for its use.[21] All media accounts that we were able to locate spoke negatively about this project. Perhaps what is most disturbing about the *migra corridos*, a point not captured by the media, is their lack of authenticity. *Corridos* are authentic, based in fact, stories of real people and events, which is one of the reasons they are popular with *el pueblo*. The stories related in the *migra corridos* are generic, albeit based on all-too-familiar stories, and although they may work at some level when the listener is unaware, they do not function as true *corridos* because they are fabrications that lack the specificity and authenticity of the stories of real human beings. The deception also is evident in the fact that although the U.S. Border Patrol funded this project through a contract with *Elevación*, a Washington, DC–based advertising firm, nowhere on the CD can one find the Border Patrol's imprint, recognizing and anticipating, perhaps, that disclosure would compromise any potential effectiveness of this *corrido* project. Finally, *el pueblo* does not want to be deceived nor does it want to hear government propaganda, of any sort or through any means, particularly not through one of its most traditional and cherished musical art form—the *corrido*.

The following *corrido*, "Vendiste los bueyes," dates from the 1940s and documents the story of a family from central Mexico that gets caught up in the immigration stream because of the family's poverty. The husband/father sells the family's means of livelihood, a pair of oxen with which they tilled the fields, to pay for the trip to the United States. The wife/mother is left behind to both take care of the children and to work the fields. As bad luck would have it, that year there is a severe drought, the corn does not grow, and there is nothing to live on, so the mother is forced to steal food to feed her hungry children. Her misery gets only worse when the Americans send a "bunch of money" and she learns that it is restitution for her husband's death. Apparently he had died while working in the United States. The lead author's father, who was recruited as a bracero in the 1940s, used to play this *corrido* while he was growing up. Although he did not die in the United States, he was working here when his own father, the lead author's grandfather, died in Mexico in 1952. Given the means of communication of the period (e.g., no telephones) and the fact that even today embalming is not practiced in rural Mexico, by the time the lead author's father learned of the death, his father had already been buried.

Mi negro del alma
te jüites pa' el norte
dejates la siembra
por una ilusión

Vendiste los bueye
para el pasaporte
maldita miseria
la de esta región

Con un burro Viejo
hicimos la branza
hicimos la escarda
con un azadón

Miramos al cielo
con una esperanza
las nubes se fueron
como maldición

Los niños lloraban
muriéndose de hambre
me fui pa' la tienda
y quise robar

Los güeros mandaron
la plata a montones
con unos papeles
que había que firmar

Mi prieto había muerto
el las condiciones
no quise la plata
y me puse a llorar

Mi prieto había muerto
el las condiciones
no quise la plata
y me puse a llorar

(The love of my soul
you left for the U.S.
you left the seeding
for a dream

You sold the oxen
to pay for the trip
damn the poverty
of this region

With an old donkey
we plowed the field
we sowed the seed
with a hoe

We looked to the sky
with much hope
but the clouds left
as if damned

The kids cried
dying of hunger
I went to the store
and wanted to steal

The Anglos sent
a bunch of money

with some papers
that needed to be signed

My loved one had died
while working
I didn't want the money
and began to cry

My loved one had died
while working
I didn't want the money
and began to cry)
"Vendiste los büeyes" (Fernando Ocampo)

The following *corrido*, "José Pérez León," tells the story of a young (nineteen years of age), working-class, recently married man who is on his way to the United States where his cousin had arranged a job (picking cotton) for him. Although José is quite sad on the trip because of having to leave his wife in Mexico, he, like so many Mexican immigrants during the past hundred years, is motivated by the desire to do well for himself and his family. When he arrives at the U.S.-Mexico border, he finds a smuggler who early the next day puts him and twenty-nine other undocumented immigrants into a sealed train box-car where, almost seven hours later, "one-by-one," including José, they die of asphyxiation because they cannot get the door open. To make matters even worse, the listener learns that José died without knowing that his wife back home was pregnant and, thus, that he was going to be a father but would never know it. The singer concludes by noting that José's death is only one of many such deaths of migrants who have died crossing the U.S.-Mexico border in search of a better life.

Él era un hombre de campo
oriundo de Nuevo León
tenía apenas 19 años
su nombre, José Pérez León

Tenía un primo lejano
que de mojado se fue
al poco tiempo le envía un telegrama

diciendo ven pronto Jose
pues un trabajo le había ya encontrado
piscando algodón como él

Y se fue, y se fue ahogando el llanto
en el adios con su mujer
y se fue sin saber que de ese viaje
ya jamás iba a volver
pobre José

Cuando llegó a la frontera
con Willy entrevisto
era el pollero más afamado
y astuto de la región
le dijo Pepe hoy estás de suerte
mañana te cruzo yo

La madrugada de un viernes
en una vieja estación
30 inocentes pagaban su cuota
entre ellos José Pérez León
y sin dudarlo a todos metieron
en el interior de un vagón

El tren cruzó al otro lado
casi siete horas después
fue cuando el aire empezó a terminar
y nada pudieron hacer
nadie escuchó aquellos gritos de auxilio
y la puerta no quiso ceder
uno por uno se fueron cayendo
y así falleció el buen José

Y se fue, se fue a cruzar el cielo
Con sus ansias de crecer
Se fue sin saber que ya su esposa
Un hijo suyo iba a tener
Pobre José

Aquí termina la historia
No queda más que contar
de otro paisano que arriesga la vida
que muere como ilegal
y aquel José que mil sueños tenía
y a casa jamás volverá

(He was a man from the country
coming from Nuevo León
he was barely 19 years old
his name, José Pérez León

He had a distant cousin
that went as a "wetback"
and shortly he sent him a telegram
saying come soon José
because he had found him a job
picking cotton like him

He went, he went drowning in tears
of the goodbye with his wife
he went without knowing that
he would never return from that trip
poor José

When he got to the border
he met with Willy
the best known [people] smuggler
and most astute of the region
he told him, "You are in luck
I'll take you across tomorrow"

Early on a Friday morning
at an old train depot
30 innocent people paid their fees
among them, José Pérez León
and without doubt they put them
inside a boxcar

The train crossed to the other side
almost seven hours later
when the air started to end
and they couldn't do anything
no one heard the cries for help
and the door would not give
one-by-one they started to fall
and that's how the good José died

He went, he went to cross the sky
with his desire to mature
he went without knowing his wife
was going to have his child
poor José

The story ends here
there is nothing more to tell
of another man who risks his life
and dies as an undocumented
and José with a thousand dreams
but who will never return home)
"José Pérez León" (Los Tigres del Norte)

The lead author composed the following *corrido* to warn migrants of the danger of crossing the U.S.-Mexico border through the desert, particularly during the time of year (May–September) when the temperature regularly reaches above one hundred degrees Fahrenheit during the day, even in the shade, and can remain quite warm throughout the night. The lyrics speak of both the natural danger posed by the heat as well as of the fact that some coyotes do not hesitate to take advantage of the migrants they are guiding; as long as the coyotes receive their cash payments, they do not care whether the migrants live or die en route. The *corrido* notes that each year hundreds of migrants of all categories (young/old, men/women, etc.) die of exposure to the elements, particularly from heat exhaustion and dehydration.

In the *corrido* tradition, when the story has included someone dying, the first line of the penultimate or last verse usually begins "Vuela, vuela palomita" (Fly, fly, little dove). Because so many immigrants have died (literally thousands[22]) during their trips across the desert since Operation Gatekeeper was launched by the U.S. Border Patrol in 1994, the I intentionally wrote two verses (the third verse from the end and the last verse) that begin with this familiar wording.

The *corrido* also comments on the fact that I am not against immigration per se nor am I interested in keeping undocumented immigrants from crossing the U.S.-Mexico border but, rather, that my goal is simply to keep migrants from dying.

This *corrido* has been disseminated widely throughout the U.S.-Mexico border region and has been played on several radio stations and at various events. Additionally, the *corrido* has been covered in numerous newspaper and other media (including electronic media) accounts in both Mexico and the United States and in both Spanish- and English-language publications, including, for example, the *Yuma Sun* ("Song Warns About the Risks Immigrants Face Crossing the Desert," May 11, 2010) and *Ariete Caborca* ("Corrido alerta a migrantes de altas temperaturas," May 13, 2010). It is also available on YouTube.

Así comienza el corrido
que aquí les voy a cantar
el desierto es peligroso
y a todos quiere matar

Se pone bravo el desierto
siempre que llega el calor
escuchen este corrido
que les dará el pormenor

No es fácil ser inmigrante
y cruzar como ilegal
los coyotes te maltratan
les da todos por igual

Ni de día ni de noche
hay clemencia en el desierto
de aquí pocos salen vivos
cada año fallecen cientos

El desierto y el calor
no es buena combinación

muchos encuentran la muerte
por la deshidratación

Esto ténganlo presente
no se les vaya olvidar
que por ganarse la vida,
muertos pueden terminar

La temperatura sube
y la probabilidad
de que mueran inmigrantes
sin saber su identidad

Niños, hombres y mujeres
en el desierto han quedado
sin auxilio de ninguno
muertos ya y abandonados

Queremos que el inmigrante
nos escuche y nos entienda
no queremos que no vengan
simplemente que no mueran

Nuestra meta es impeder
las muertes en el desierto
con el calor sube el riesgo
eso ténganlo por cierto

Si quieren sobrevivir
préstenme ya su atención
la mejor defensa siempre
es bajo la prevención

Vuela, vuela palomita
párate en aquel pitayo
no es lo mismo ir caminando
que montado en un caballo

Aquí termina el corrido
no se les vaya olvidar
protéjanse del calor
si el desierto hay que cruzar

Vuela, vuela palomita
vuela hasta aquellos gigantes
sigue rogándole a Dios
por todos los inmigrantes

(This is show the ballad begins
that I'm going to sing for you
the desert is very dangerous
and it wants to take everyone's life

The desert becomes dangerous
with the arrival of the heat
listen carefully to this ballad
it will provide all of the details

It's not easy being an immigant
and having to cross illegally
the coyotes will mistreat you
as they mistreat everyone

Not at night or during the day
is there any relief in the desert
few make it out alive
each year hundreds die

Desert and the heat
not a good combination
many encounter death
as a result of dehydration

Keep this foremost in your mind
and don't you forget it

in search of a better life
one can end up dead

As the temperature rises
so does the probability
that immigrants will die
without knowing their identity

Men, women and children
their remains are in the desert
without assistance whatsoever
dead and abandoned

We simply want immigrants
to listen to us and to understand
it's not that we don't want you here
we simply don't want you to die

Our goal is simply to prevent
more deaths in the desert
the risk increases with the heat
of that you can be certain

If you want to live
lend me your ears
as the best defense
is always prevention

Fly, fly, little dove
land atop that organ pipe (cactus)
it's not the same crossing on foot
as riding on a horse

The ballad ends here
but please don't forget
protect yourself from the heat
if you must cross the desert

Fly, fly, little dove
fly all the way to those tall trees
and continue praying to God
for all of the immigrants)
"Peligro en el Desierto" Celestino Fernández[23]

CLOSING COMMENTS

As we completed a draft of this chapter during June, July, and August 2009, the hottest and most dangerous months of the year in the Arizona desert, not a day passed that the local news media did not report that human remains were found in some isolated part of this desert. On Friday, July 31, 2009, for example, the Border Patrol was called by an immigrant who told them that he was "dehydrated and needed help, and had spotted another man in really bad shape. Agents went to the area and, after treating the caller with fluids, began backtracking the caller's footprints in an attempt to find the other man in distress. About a half-hour later, they found the man's body in the foothills."[24] On that same weekend, on Sunday, August 2, 2009, a sixteen-year-old youth found the Border Patrol about 4:00 pm and told agents "that his 64-year-old grandmother had been left behind. He said that he and his grandmother had been walking without food or water for three days."[25] By the time Border Patrol agents found his grandmother, "nearly two hours later," she and another woman had already died.

Since 1994, with the Border Patrol's launching of Operation Gatekeeper, which forced immigrants into harsh terrain and climates, deaths of migrants such as those reported in the preceding paragraph, regrettably, have become common daily occurrences in the Arizona desert. Such deaths have become so common that most people, with the exception of those few individuals involved in humanitarian groups such as No More Deaths, Coalición de Derechos Humanos (Human Rights Coalition), and Humane Borders, no one seems to notice them, to be offended by them, or to be moved to action by the deaths of so many innocent people.

Although since 1998 the U.S. Border Patrol has been operating a search and rescue unit (Border Patrol Search, Trauma, and Rescue [BORSTAR]), and undoubtedly this special unit has rescued many immigrants (and agents) in distress, the Border Patrol has not changed its policy of forcing immigrants into the most isolated areas, the harshest terrains, and most severe climates. Thus, the deaths continue pretty much unabated. Even when the Border Patrol does act, its actions are short of addressing the problem, as reported in a story in the local Tucson (Arizona) newspaper with the this headline, "Deadliest SW Border Stretch Is Getting 209 More Agents."[26]

> An additional 209 U.S. Border Patrol agents will be in Arizona starting today in an attempt to address border deaths in the Southwest border's deadliest stretch. The agency's "Operation Guardian" initiative kicks off after the two deadliest months for border deaths—June and July—have already passed. While the extra help is welcome, the initiative is too little, too late, said Robin Hoover, president of Humane Borders, which operates water stations in the desert. "They are responding kind of late in the game," Hoover said. "The numbers are higher, the rate is higher and the feds are just now responding to it. It looks to me like they don't monitor this situation closely."

In fact, thousands of agents have been added to the U.S.-Mexico border during the last decade with no significant decrease in the number of migrant deaths. As long as the economic disparities between Mexico and the United States continue to exist, Mexican immigrants will attempt to cross the border in search of employment regardless of the number of Border Patrol agents and/or barriers (such as the fences and electronic surveillance) found in the desert. Moreover, as long as the U.S. Border Patrol continues its policy of forcing undocumented immigrants into the harshest terrains and climates, the number of migrants dying in the Arizona border is unlikely to decrease. And *corridistas* will continue documenting the tragedies and bringing attention to this atrocious and appalling situation.

APPENDIX A: REPRESENTATIVE LIST OF MIGRATION SONGS

The following migration songs are listed in alphabetical order by song title followed by recording date or issue date when available and the name of the artist (followed in parentheses by the name of the composer, if different).

"Across the Borderline" (1981), Ry Cooder (Ry Cooder, John Hiatt, and James Dickson)

"Across the Wire" (2003), Calexico

"America" (1981), Neil Diamond

"The Argentines, the Portuguese, and the Greeks" (1928), the Duncan Sisters (P. D.)

"Ballad of the Tucson Two" (2005), Howe Gelb

"Born in East L.A." (1985), Cheech and Chong (Cheech Marin)

"California Snow" (1998), Dave Alvin (Dave Alvin and Tom Russell)

"Czechoslovakia" (1996), Black 47

"Dixieland" (1999), Steve Earle

"Elvira's Song," The Certones

"Englishman in New York" (1987), Sting (Gordon M. T. Sumner)

"Five Points" (1996), Black 47

"Give Me Your Tired, Your Poor" (1883; poem by Emma Lazarus engraved on the Statue of Liberty; set to music by Barbara Silberg)

"The Great American Melting Pot" (2007), Schoolhouse Rock (Lynn Ahrens)

"Icky Thump" (2007), the White Stripes (Jack White)

"Illegal Alien" (1983), Genesis (Phil Collins)

"The Immigrant" (1975), Neil Sedaka

"Immigrant Punk" (2005): Gogol Bordello

"The Immigrant Song" (1070), Led Zeppelin (Jimmy Page and Robert Plant)

"Immigration Blues" (recorded late 1920s), Duke Ellington and Kentucky Club Orchestra

"Immigration Man" (early 1979s), David Crosby and Graham Nash (Graham Nash)

"Kilkelly Ireland" (1860), Peter Jones (Peter and Steve Jones)

"The Line" (1995), Bruce Springsteen

"Little Ah Sid" P. D.

"Living in the Promiseland" (1998), Willie Nelson (David L. Jones)

"A Matter of Time" (2004), Los Lobos (David Hidalgo and Louie Perez)

"Mojado Power" (1980), Alfonso Arua (Guillermo de Anda)

"My Name Joe" (1992), David Massengill

"New Immigration Law" (1997), Cocoa Tea (Calvin Scott)

"No Irish Need Apply" (1863), recorded by Tony Pastor and several artists since (John F. Poole)

"The Perfect Nanny," Louis Prima and Gia Maione (a jazzed-up version of the original from the movie *Mary Poppins*, though there have been many versions

"Superhero" (2003), Stephen Lynch

"Teenage Immigrant Welfare Mothers on Drugs" (1996), Austin Lounge Lizards

"Thousands Are Sailing" (1988), the Pogues (Philip Chevron)

"Thousands Are Sailing to Amerikay," Dick Gaughan and Andy Irvine (P. D.)

"Tired of Proving We Belong" (1983), Chris Iijima

"Trailways Bus" (1997), Paul Simon

"Uncle Sam's Farm" (1850), E. P. Christy and Jesse Hutchinson

"Wave" (2001), Alejandro Escovedo

"When I First Came to This Land," DeCormier Singers (P. D.)

"Xich vs. the Migra Zombies" (1997), Concrete Blonde y Los Illegals

ENTIRE LPS

Mercy on the Arizona Trail, various artists

Thousands Are Sailing: Irish Songs of Immigration (1999), various artists

Tucson (AZ) Songwriters Response to the Human Crisis on the Mexican Border

APPENDIX B: REPRESENTATIVE LIST OF IMMIGRATION *CORRIDOS*

The following *corridos* are listed in alphabetical order by song title followed by recording date or issue date when available and the name of the artist (followed in parentheses by the name of the composer, if different).

"Adiós California" (1975), Los Troqueros (Chucho Nila)

"Ahí viene la migra" (1985), Ramón Ayala (Blanca Estela Limón)

"Al cruzar la frontera" (1966), Dueto Río Bravo (Eladio Velarde)

"Bajo el cielo de Morelia" (1980), Felipe Arriaga (Bulmaro Bermúdez)

"Canto del bracero" (1930s)

"Camisa mojada" (1985), Los Tigres del Norte (Enrique Valencia)

"Corrido de los mojados" (1977), Los Alegres de Terán (Luis Armenta)

"De bracero a petrolero" (1980), Felipe Arriaga (Melesio Díaz)

"De California te escribo" (1981), Ricardo Falcón (José Luz Alanís)

"Defensa de los norteños"

"De las tres que vienen ahí," Antonio Aguilar

"Deportados" (1930s)

"Desafiando la migra"

"Desde México de afuera," Las Hermanas Huerta (José Vaca Flores)

"Despedida de un norteño"

"El bracero" (1979), Dueto Frontera (Rafael Buendía)

"El chicano" (1976), Juan Zaizar

"El corrido de los mojados," Los Halcones de Salitrillo (D. A. R.)

"El corrido del Padre Toribio," Los Cristeros de Arandas (many *corridos* have been composed about this Catholic saint who is known as "El Patrono de Los Mojados" (Patron of the migrants)

"El deportado"

"El emigrado" (1979), Los Alegres de Terán (Eugenio Abrego)

"El emigrante" (1980), Vicky (Alfonso Dávila R.)

"El emigrante" (1981), Ricardo Falcón (Ramón Ortega)

"El gringo y el mexicano" (1985) Los Tigres del Norte (Adolfo Salas)

"El ilegal," Joan Sebastian

"El otro México," Los Tigres del Norte

"El mojado rico"

"El lavaplatos" (1920s), Los Broncos de Reynosa (1978) (Pedro Dávila)

"El mojado"

"El mojado remojado" (1980), Alfonso Arua (Guillermo de Anda)

"El muro" (2007), Los Tigres del Norte

"El niño de la calle" (2004). Los Tigres del Norte

"El petróleo (ahora sí)" (1980), Los Ases de Durango (Enrique Franco)

"El prieto lunares y el güero patillas" (1976), Dueto Frontera (Homero A. Villarreal and Rafael Buendía)

"El sin papeles" (1978), Los Salvajes de la Frontera (Tony Ponce)

"El santo de los mojados" (2004), Los Tigres del Norte

"En los Estados Unidos" (1980), Los Troqueros (Aurelio Díaz)

"Espaldas mojada" (1977), Lupe y Polo (Benjamín Sánchez Mota)

"Este mojado está seco"

"Frontera de Tijuana" (1977), Los Alegres de Terán (Gregorio Hernández)

"Jaula de oro" (1985), Los Tigres del Norte (Enrique Franco)

"Juana la mojada"

"Juan gringo" (1980), Los Troqueros (Arturo Solana)

"Juan Mojao" (1977), Lalo González "El Piporro"

 "La discriminación" (1977), Dueto América (Juan Manuel and Leobardo Pérez)

"La desgracia del mojado" (1984), Los Alegres de Terán (Margarito Estrada)

"La historia del mojado" (1976), Los Humildes (Rudy Flores)

"Lamento del mojado" (1980), Guillermo de Anda (Guillermo de Anda)

"La venganza del mojado" (1984), Lorenzo de Monteclaro (Máximo Escalante Mendoza)

"Línea divisoria" (1963), Los Dos Reales (Hermanos Orozco)

"Los alambrados" (1978), Los Bukis (Marco Antonio Solís)

"Los chicanos" (1974), Los Diablos (Melisio "Melo" Díaz)

"Los emigrantes"

"Los hijos de Hernández" (2004), Los Tigres del Norte (Enrique Franco)

"Los hijos que se van" (1980), Los Ases de Durango (D. A. R.)

"Los ilegales"

"Los mandados," Vicente Fernández (Jorge Lerma)

"Los mexicanos que hablan inglés"

"Los norteños"

"Los que Cruzan" (1983), Los Madrugadores del Valle (R. Ortega Contreras and F. Vaca Flores)

"Los que cruzaron, Los Dos Reales (Víctor Cordero)

"Los reenganchados a Kansas" (early 1940s)

"Me fui para el norte" (1965), Los Donneños (Arnulfo Barrera)

"Mil fronteras" (1968), La Hermanas Huerta (Fernando Z. Maldonado)

"Mis dos patrias" (2008), Los Tigres del Norte

"Mojado tres veces"

"Nostalgia del bracero" (1981), Los Luceritos de Michoacán (Miguel García)

"Natalio Reyes Colás"

"Paso del norte" (1977), Los Potros (Matías Valdés Leal-Rivera)

"Pedro y Pablo" (1985), Los Tigres del Norte (Enrique Franco)

"Pobre mojado" (1986), Los Hermanos Ortiz (Paco Camarena)

"Por ser pobre" (2006), Dueto Los Centenarios (Andrés Santana Tejeda)

"Pregúntale a las fronteras" (1975), Federico Villa (Bulmaro Bermúdez)

"Recordando a México" (1977), Dueto Frontera (Rafael Buendía)

"Residentes y mojados" (1987), Rafael Buendía

"Santo Toribio Romo" (2007), Originales de San Juan

"Sin Fortuna" (1965), Gerardo Reyes (Angel González)

"Sin pasaporte" (1989), Joan Sebastian

"Somos más Americanos" (2008), Los Tigres del Norte

"Supermán es illegal" (1987), Los Hermanos Ortiz (Jorge Lerma)

"Te vas a la frontera" (1981), Ricardo Falcón (José Luz Alanís)

"Tierras de California" (1978), Beatriz Adriana (Pascuala Paredes)

"Tres veces mojado" (1989), Los Tremendos Gavilanes

"Un mojado sin licencia"

"Uno más de los mojados" (1976), Antonio Aguilar (José Manuel Figueroa)

"Vivían los mojados" (2006), Los Tigres del Norte (Luis Armenta)

"Ya nos dieron permiso" (1978), Los Tigres del Norte (Jesús Armenta)

APPENDIX C: REPRESENTATIVE SAMPLE OF MIGRATION DEATH *CORRIDOS*

The following *corridos* are listed in alphabetical order by song of CD title followed by recording date or issue date when available and the name of the artist (followed in parentheses by the name of the composer, if different).

"Deportee (Plane Wreck at Los Gatos)" (1948), Woody Guthrie

"Desierto de Arizona" (1983), Luis Y Julián (Julián García)

"José Pérez León" (2004), Los Tigres del Norte

"La tumba del mojado" (1985), Los Tigres del Norte

"Lamento de un bracero" (1976), Antonio Aguilar (Paco Camacho)

Migra corridos (2006; CD of five *corridos* issued by Elevación, Ltd., for the U.S. Border Patrol).

"Peligro en el desierto" (2008), Guillermo Sáenz (Celestino Fernández)

"Un noble engaño" (1983), Los Huracanes del Norte (Nicolás Ochoa and Raúl Sandoval)

"Vendiste los bueyes" (1940s), Hermanas Padilla (Fernando Ocampo)

NOTES

1. Portes and Rumbaut 2006.
2. Massey 2010.
3. Maciel and Herrera-Sobek 1998.

4. Rubio-Goldsmith et al. 2006; Martínez this volume

5. Johnson 2003.

6. Massey 2010; Ngai 2004; Portes and Rumbaut 2006.

7. Fernández and Officer 1989.

8. Martínez 1935.

9. Griffith and Fernández 1988.

10. Simmons 1957.

11. Mendoza 1939.

12. Paredes 1958.

13. Mull 1987.

14. Fernández and Officer 1989.

15. Handlin 1952; Ainslie 1998.

16. Massey, Goldring, and Durand 1994.

17. Berg 2009.

18. De la Torre 2008.

19. Fernández 1989; Taylor 1953; Herrera-Sobek 1998.

20. Glaser and Strauss 1967.

21. See, e.g., LeBrón 2009 or Rozemberg 2009.

22. Rubio-Goldsmith et al. 2006; Martínez this volume.

23. Copyright Celestino Fernández. 2010. The original was composed in Spanish and translated into English, and thus, the rhyming pattern could not be maintained in the English-language version. "Música y voz: Guillermo Sáenz," YouTube, https://youtu.be/6sq1_xFZZHA.

24. McCombs 2009a, 2009b.

25. McCombs 2009a.

26. McCombs 2009b.

THE CULTURAL PRESENCE OF
DEATH ON THE ARIZONA-SONORA
BORDER AND BEYOND

JAMES S. GRIFFITH

DEATH AND THE BORDERLANDS are no strangers to each other. Let us start with border-crossing deaths firmly in mind. The main plaza of the town of Altar, Sonora, is a well-used jumping-off point for crossing attempts—a place where would-be *pollos* (migrants) go to be picked up by their coyotes (smugglers). (*Pollos*—literally "chickens" in Spanish, is a common slang term for would-be border crossers who have hired a professional people smuggler, or coyote, to see them safely into the United States. The implied relationship of victim and predator is intentional.) The local Catholic priest has at various times fed and advised these folks, and in the plaza in front of the church, in January 2001, there were three crosses inscribed with the numbers of deaths on the California border, in the Sonoran Desert, and along the Rio Bravo in Texas. In 2001, the figures were around 600, 166, and 667, respectively. As illustrated in various chapters in this book, those numbers have since risen considerably.

A traditional way of memorializing sudden death in Mexico is to erect a cross where such a death occurred, a reminder that the soul that parted from its body in this place may yet be helped on its way by the prayers of the living.[1] Such death markers may involve elaborate arrangements including a cross, a crucifix, memorial plaques, flowers, candles, rows of whitewashed stones, or even memorial chapels; or they may be simple crosses. They are most often found on roads and highways, commemorating fatal automobile accidents. A portion of

FIGURE 13.1. Crosses commemorating migrant deaths in the Altar,
Sonora, plaza, January 14, 2001. From the left, the crosses represent deaths
on the California, Sonoran Desert, and Texas regions. Francisco "Paco"
Manzo is seated on the bench; the people in the background are probably
would-be migrants waiting for their coyotes. Photo by James S. Griffith.

the fatal car—a reflector, perhaps, or an entire fender—is often included in the
memorial. Many such markers stand along the major roads leading to the border, but it is of course impossible to tell whether or not any given monument
actually has to do with an intended border crossing. On Highway 15, between
Santa Ana and the Hermosillo toll booth, a distance of 140 kilometers, there
are 143 crosses at 123 locations. All these people were heading toward or away
from the border, but that is all one can say about them.[2]

Border-crossing-related fatalities are not confined to one time, one language, or one ethnicity, as we learn from a grave marker in the Nogales, Arizona, cemetery that reads "Killed while transporting contraband. In what foreign land do you now fly, amigo?"

Death is present in Mexican traditional culture in other ways, some of
which, paradoxically, may be tied to life and healing. Catholicism is still the

FIGURE 13.2. Roadside death marker on Mexican Highway 2, west of Sonoyta, Sonora, near the international border. This marker, which commemorates an older, respected man (as shown by the use of the honorific "Don") is probably not the result of a border-crossing-related fatality. This stretch of the highway, however, runs close to and parallels the border fence. May 2, 1998. Photo by James S. Griffith.

predominant religion in Sonora, and all Catholic churches are equipped with at least one crucifix, representing the brutally painful political execution suffered by Jesus. In addition, many churches also possess a *santo entierro*, a statue of the entombed Christ. Since colonial times, such statues, often life-size, have featured in Good Friday evening processions, a custom introduced by missionaries as a way of dramatizing the Christian narratives for their indigenous charges. In the town of Bacerac, on the Río Bavispe, is a particularly famous santo entierro statue that is the subject of legend and the object of pilgrimages and requests for miraculous cures.[3] This image was popular enough that at some time in the past, an engraving was made of it and sold. Photocopies of this engraving are still occasionally available in Bacerac.

Some sixty miles south of the border at Nogales is the colonial mission town of Magdalena, Sonora. In a side chapel of the Magdalena church lies a reclining statue of San Francisco Javier (St. Francis Xavier), which represents the saint either on his death bed or as his incorrupt body lies in state in Goa, India.[4] The statue is the focus of a huge multinational pilgrimage every October, involving thousands from Sonora, Arizona, and the Yaqui and Tohono O'odham nations. A similar statue resides in the eighteenth century Franciscan mission church of San Xavier del Bac, just south of Tucson, Arizona. This statue, too, is the object of an active popular devotion. In both cases, a visit to the saint often involves an attempt to lift the statue's head off its pillow in the belief that the saint will communicate his pleasure or displeasure with the visitor by whether or not he allows his head to be raised up. Similar statues, with similar beliefs and customs attached, may be found in most churches and chapels in Sonora.

Depicting saints by representing them in the act of death or as corpses is not uncommon elsewhere in Mexico. I have seen statues of the Dormition of the Virgin Mary and the tomb of St. Peter in Guanajuato (home of the famous Guanajuato Mummies and also home of pulled candy in the shape of those mummies). I have noted statues of other, less-known saints shown as corpses in

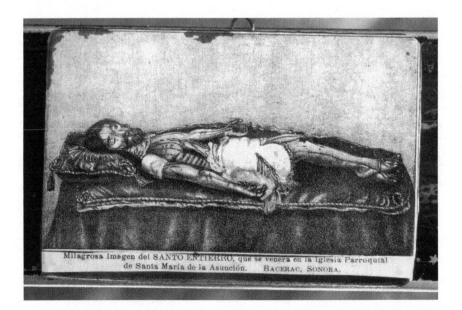

Milagrosa Imagen del SANTO ENTIERRO, que se venera en la Iglesia Parroquial de Santa María de la Asunción. BACERAC, SONORA.

FIGURE 13.3. Engraving depicting the *Santo Entierro* of Bacerac, Sonora. Although statues of the Entombed Christ are common in Mexico, only a relative few are used as the foci for petitions, as is this one. Photographed in a roadside shrine near Agua Prieta, Sonora, October 27, 2001. Photo by James S. Griffith.

FIGURE 13.4. Reclining statue of San Francisco Xavier, Magdalena, Sonora.
The original of this statue (destroyed during the Religious Persecution in 1935),
was probably brought to Magdalena by Father Eusebio Francisco Kino. The statue
represents San Francisco on his deathbed. Such representations, while extremely
rare in the Catholic world (I know of one other, which is in Bavaria), are ubiquitous
in Sonora and Southern Arizona. July 7, 1983. Photo by James S. Griffith.

churches in the city of Oaxaca. And in the church of San Francisco in Puebla,
one may visit the actual, incorrupt body of Blessed Sebastian Aparicio, protec-
tor of Mexican travelers and of immigrants.[5]

Representing a saint in death is in a way perfectly logical, for saints are by
definition dead. They are individuals who are considered by the Church to have
lived such exemplary Christian lives that upon death they were ushered immediately into heaven—that is, into the presence of God. From this vantage point
they can intercede for the living. This representational emphasis on death is
an important aspect of Catholic imagery and resonates strongly in Mexican
culture.

On the western end of the U.S.-Mexico border, in Tijuana's Panteón Jardín
Número Uno, rests all that is mortal of Juan Castillo Morales, better known as
Juan Soldado. Here is an outline of his story: On February 14, 1938, the body

of eight-year-old Olga Camacho was discovered near her home in Tijuana. She had been raped and murdered. Juan Castillo was arrested on circumstantial evidence and taken to the Tijuana jail. An angry lynch mob assembled, and both the *palacio municipal* and police headquarters were burned. At this point the army stepped in, put together a court, and had Castillo tried and executed. Public opinion underwent a change in later years, and Juan became for many powerless people a victim, a personage to be asked for assistance, especially with border-crossing-related problems.[6]

A small chapel stands by Juan Soldado's grave, another is on his execution site in the same cemetery, and vendors at the edge of the cemetery sell candles, printed prayers, and flowers to a steady stream of petitioners. Border crossing is seldom mentioned in the many ex-votos at his tomb, but from conversations at the site, it seems to be implied.

At almost the other end of the border, in Espinazo, Nuevo León, stands the hacienda where José Fidencio Constantino Síntora lived and effected cures from 1927 until his death in 1938. In his day he was possibly the most famous

FIGURE 13.5. Reclining San Francisco statue in the San Francisco chapel in Sonoyta, Sonora, just south of the international border. A photograph similar to this one appears on a locally sold T-shirt. June 5, 2004. Photo by James S. Griffith.

curandero (folk healer) in all Mexico, and his followers still tell of his curing President Calles of leprosy in exchange for a promise to make a truce between the Mexican government and the Catholic Church.

After Fidencio's death in 1930 (murdered by jealous doctors, some say), his devotees started channeling him. Mediums, called *materias* (or *cajones* if they are men—but the majority are women) go into altered states of being and assume the spirit of *el Niño Fidencio*. In other words, they become el Niño, dressed as he did in white robes and a red sash. Although the main sacred site of *fidencismo* is in the ex-hacienda of Espinazo, Nuevo León, *Fidencista materias* pursue their healing work all through the eastern borderlands. Working mostly in their homes, they enter into trances, take on the spirit and persona of their deceased leader, and effect their cures.[7]

El Niño Fidencio is not the only deceased figure who is regularly channeled along the border. Don Pedrito Jaramillo, the renowned healer of Los Olmos, Texas, is brought back to life in the same way, as is the Revolutionary figure Pancho Villa. The channeling of spirits of the dead has long been a standard procedure in some forms of *curanderismo* (folk healing). When I visited South Texas in the summer of 1998, I was told of a woman who traveled through the area channeling various saints.[8]

So the dead are remembered, prayed for, asked for help, and even encouraged to visit in Mexican border culture. So much for the dead. But what about Death herself?

She, too, is present along the border in the guise of La Santísima Muerte, a fast-growing devotion all over Mexico. Although her growing popularity seems to be a phenomenon of the past two decades, personifications of Death have been a part of the Mexican scene since before Conquest times. In her present guise, she is depicted as a robed skeleton, often carrying the world in one hand and a scythe in the other. Unlike the traditionally whimsical skeleton figures created for the Day of the Dead, La Santa Muerte is depicted as a grim, even menacing figure. I know of nine roadside *capillas* (mini chapels) in Sonora dedicated to her: five walk-in chapels and two small *nichos* clustered on Highway 15 just south of Nogales, one chapel a few miles farther south on the same road, and one just south of Agua Prieta. All are on roads leading directly to the border; all, for reasons unknown to this author, are on the west, or southbound, side of those roads. The devotion seems to be growing. When this paper was first written in March 2008, there were three chapels just south of Nogales; by late August of the same year, another chapel had been finished, a fifth was under construction, and the *nichos* were finished and occupied.

FIGURE 13.6. Life-size statue of La Santa Muerte with offerings. This is the interior of one of several chapels in a cluster on Mexican Highway 15, just south of Nogales, Sonora. As mentioned in the text, the number of these chapels is growing, as Holy Death gains in popularity. January 22, 2007. Photo by James S. Griffith.

In January 2009, it was reported that the statues in these chapels had been decapitated. When I visited them in March of the same year, one statue was missing entirely, one was headless, and the others had been given substitute heads of plaster or cement. This decapitation of powerful images, though rare, is not unheard-of in the Sonoran border country.[9] It may be a response to the failure of the sacred personage represented by the statue to perform a requested miracle. There is also the possibility of government action. In late March 2009 authorities in Nuevo Laredo, Tamaulipas, sent backhoe operators with a military escort to obliterate more than thirty shrines to La Santa Muerte in that city.[10] Among the reasons suggested for the action was the known devotion to La Santa Muerte on the part of *narcotraficantes* (narcotics smugglers).

La Santa Muerte is frequently accompanied by offerings, which may include fruit, money, liquor, beer, and cigarettes. The latter can be lit and stuck in the image's mouth. While the size and elaborate nature of some of the *capillas* may suggest the financial resources of the *narcotraficante* (narcotics smuggling) world, the devotion to La Santa Muerte is by no means limited to the *narcos* (drug smugglers), or even to those who travel on the far side of the law.

A friend in California told me the harrowing story of a family he knows who are her devotees and who never seem to be able to get ahead. When a child of theirs got very ill, they asked La Santisima Muerte for help. The child recovered, and two other children in the same family died. His gloss on the incident was that she'll give you what you ask for, but she'll always take something precious in exchange—often the thing you love most.

Everyone crossing or traveling along the border encounters these visual reminders of Death. How they are received and interpreted depends on the cultural background of the individual traveler. In this very incomplete set of vignettes, it seems that while many Anglo-Americans view Death as a separator, perhaps even a final one, Mexican culture permits viewing it as a part of a continuum. The dead must be memorialized, to be sure, but they may also be called on for help and even in some complicated way be brought back to life. And Death herself is always there in a two-edged, very ambiguous way.

NOTES

1. Griffith 2003.
2. Griffith 2005, 242.

3. Griffith and Manzo 2007, 67–68.

4. The story of the statue is a complex one and is treated at length in Griffith 1992, 31–66.

5. Saucedo Zarco 2002, 52–56.

6. Vanderwood 2004; Griffith 2003, 20–41.

7. Garza Quiroz 1991; Griffith 2003, 126–43.

8. Griffith 2003, 122–25.

9. Associated Press 2009.

10. Griffith 2006, 36–37.

THE LAST LORDS OF THE BORDER

A Hip-Hop Day of the Dead

JUAN FELIPE HERRERA

AN EXPERIMENTAL PERFORMANCE inspired by the border death conference "*¿No Vale Nada la Vida? La Vida No Vale Nada:* Political Intersections of Migration and Death in the U.S.-Mexico Border," held at the
University of Arizona, Tucson, in March 2008. For Maribel Alvarez, Claudio Lomnitz, Irasema Coronado, Will Power, and all border crossers, and the
coroner of Tucson, Arizona.

BACKDROP

DEATH AND ART

Unexpectedly, I was shattered.

Sitting on the left side of the conference space, scribbling notes, shooting pho-
tographs of the border death conference speakers and their charts and Power-
Point presentations, little by little, as I jotted phrases and numbers as fast as I
could, there came a moment when I fell apart. There were too many deaths of
undocumented workers and their families. Embroidered pillows that read "Siempre te amaré" (I will always love you), crumbled letters that noted "Quiero que
mi hijo nasca en los Estados Unidos" (I want my child to be born in the United
States), and layers of footprints baked on layers of more caked footprints on

the sand. My notes became wiry tangles and charred branches of ink. It is an odd thing to witness the death counts, death modes, and death passages of your own *familias* (families) and then to attempt to respond with art. What could assuage such horror? Nothing. Yet as a poet and a human being I had to attempt the impossible.

THREE FINDINGS

I took a breath. Assembled notes as best as possible. Then the impossible work began—a performance project that would have at its center only *three* out of a thousand facts and notions and findings and reflections and calls to action mentioned at the *conferencia* (conference). One was the concept of *animas solas* (lost souls) touching on research by the internationally known sociocultural anthropologist Dr. Claudio Lomnitz. The second piece was a number presented by Dr. Irasema Coronado—nine thousand children to date have been left wallowing in the streets of the United States after their parents were abruptly deported. The last item that struck me was a material fact. Because of the overwhelming number of deaths of migrants on the border desert during the month of July, the coroner of Tucson was pressed to purchase a new freezer in order to house the bloated and bulging stock of dead border bodies.

SOULS, TEENS, FREEZERS

With these three figures in hand, a new performance project and a possible new performance and spoken-word approach began to take shape called the *The Freezer*. At the centerpiece of this initial sketch, the unclaimed *animas* (souls) of the border dead emerge out of the coroner's new freezer. So begins their search for their homeland. Then I dismantled it.

AMERINDIAN SPACE

Around the same time of the border death conference, the last performance of *Salsalandia*, a musical I had written for the La Jolla Playhouse, was about to take place. And along with my piece, another play was closing at the same venue—playwright Will Power's *Seven*, a hip-hop remaking of Aeschylus's *Seven Against Thebes*. Tragedy, turf battle, a torn family, and music. Perfect, I said to myself. Is there something similar in Amerindian myth I can unearth—the continental space where these deaths occur? Just maybe. There was only one answer—the Popol Vuh. A new draft was born: *The Last Lords of the Border: A Hip-Hop Day of the Dead.*

The Popol Vuh seemed appropriate since it allowed for horrific episodes of bloodlettings and deaths and most of all for profound scales of transformation and transcendence. After fifteen drafts or so, the next step was to incorporate the freezer into the account. And to highlight the plight of youth, I chose to cast teens as the protagonists of the work. And of course, most important was to add on the larger tale of our contemporary ongoing experience of border death at the Arizona-Mexico border.

A DROP OF EUROPE

Finally, as a personal gem and a "drop of Europe," in the "open scenes" of the story I inserted the figure of serpents that tear away at some of the bodies in the freezer. This serpent-tearing-humans image is known as the *Laocoon*, a highly regarded sculpture group in art history. It was found in Michelangelo's day and, more importantly, was brought into play in James Joyce's groundbreaking *Portrait of the Artist as a Young Man* in the early twentieth century.

PERFORMANCE?

After having the story, the three conference findings that moved me, the Amerindian frame, and the outline of performance scenes in place, the next question was, what kind of performance is this—traditional theater, performance art, spoken word, *teatro* (theater), multimedia, dance? Having founded teatros (theaters), spoken word and multimedia ensembles in California for the last forty years, it occurred to me to take a hint from the actual core of the piece; that is, border crossing. So, I developed SPO-BOMO (Spoken Word Movement). In brief, SPO-BOMO is a crossing of the borders between traditional stand-up spoken word and hip-hop dance movement—*spo*ken word *bo*rder *mo*vement. Here, the spoken word artist suddenly crosses into movement, then crosses back to the word. *Cross-into-cross-back*, this is the major key to SPO-BOMO. There is no dance continuity, no choreo-continuum. The movement is based on an image being recited in the spoken word piece. There is no set style as in rap or traditional hip-hop. Once traditional forms emerge, SPO-BOMO cannot take place and the story cannot be told. The genre itself, like the border crosser, is always at peril.

THE STORY IN PERIL: OPEN SCENES

As in the desert border-crosser's journey, and perhaps from the blurred lens of an *anima sola* (lone soul), there is no map, no direction home; there are only open scenes of danger. What will be said, how it will be put into motion, what motivates the characters, who they are, the actual order of the scenes, the stories of the characters—all this and more will be detailed and changed by collective effort of those who wish to be involved in the experiment of the performance.

THE LAST LORDS OF THE BORDER: A HIP-HOP DAY OF THE DEAD

CAST (SIMULTANEOUS CASTING)

The First Two Lords of the Dead
The First Set of Twins—Uncle and Father
The Second Set of Twins—Son and Daughter
Young Mother
The Dancers of the Dead—First Set
Two Serpent Dancers
MC Machete
The Last Two Lords of the Dead
The Dancers of the Dead—Second Set—in The Freezer

OPEN SCENES

FIRST MOVEMENT

SCENE 1 Two migrant twins barely survive the ordeal of crossing the dark desert without moon or stars. They follow threads of clothes bits of the border dead. When they see a nightclub light ahead, they celebrate because they have crossed into North Country, their destination. They roll up the threads into a ball that if unraveled can lead them back home. They play with the ball and dance with delight as they amble toward the nightclub, farther into North Country. The club's name glows in the night, The Freezer.

SCENE 2 They make joyous noise as they dance and wake up the Lords of the Border. The Lords see them playing ball and dancing and challenge them to dance with them, since they are master dancers themselves. The two teens lose. The Lords rip most of the ball thread over the desert.

SCENE 3 Since they don't allow anyone from the South to cross into their territory, the Lords sacrifice them for more dance status. They throw one twin into their Club, The Freezer, and decapitate the other and hang his head on a nearby tree.

SCENE 4 A teen girl migrant catches up to the scene by following the last bits of thread, barely alive. She runs to the tree thinking it bears fruit. Instead of fruit, the tree has decapitated heads hanging on it. The still aching head of the slain twin can't speak but cries and drools and spits into her hands. The girl is thirsty and licks the spit.

SCENE 5 The teen girl becomes pregnant with twins.

SECOND MOVEMENT

SCENE 6 In time, the new twins become great dancers themselves, fabulous dancers. Better than their father who was thrown into The Freezer and uncle who was decapitated, they soon discover. They make vengeful noise and dance even harder—they plan to take action against the Lords. The Lords see them and hear their plan. Acting innocently, they summon them to a dance battle at their famous club, The Freezer, an underground dance cave, run and MCed by the lackey, MC Machete.

SCENE 7 The Freezer entrance has a face. The eyes and mouth serve as entrances. Once lured inside, the twins discover that all the dancers inside are the wandering spirits of the dead dreaming they are still alive somewhere in the North—(migrants that died in the scorching moonless desert). Many of them are missing limbs (from the Machete). They are the Dancers of the Border Dead. The twins beseech them to wake up, that they are dead and can never return home and have a proper burial since no one back home knows their whereabouts, so therefore they will be condemned to be wandering souls forever. The Lords argue and state that the Dead should be grateful, since they have given them a home—in The Freezer. Of course they must pay tribute to the Lords in exchange. However, the Lords promise the twins the return of the remnants of the ball so they can lead the souls out of The Freezer and back home, away from their (the Lords) turf, North Country, once and for all, never to return, *if they cooperate with the Lords and enter into a dance battle.* The twins are unsure and conflicted.

SCENE 8 In The Freezer, as an inducement for the twins to make up their minds, the Lords call on MC Machete to bring out the main act, The Dance of The Serpents. The Twin's uncle is hauled out—he is being pulled and torn in opposite directions by serpent dancers that have earned special privileges from MC Machete—the object of the dance it to split them apart—one half for the North, the other, for the South. The uncle tells the twins his plight and asks them to leave and not fall into the trap set by the Lords, as he and his twin brother did.

SCENE 9 The twins decide to fight and enter the dance battle. The Lords defeat them, grind down some of their bones, drag them to the river that divides the North/South border—and dump them.

SCENE 10 The twins are reborn as fish. They cannot talk; they are clumsy, slippery, and dumb. Other new arrival migrants hook them and fight for their flesh, rip them apart, and throw their bones back into the river.

SCENE 11 The twins are reborn again as a traveling troop of clown dancers and perform for dead migrant souls who escaped The Freezer. The clowns can only mime in mechanized, robotic dance moves; they can only see what is in front of them. The dead tell the twins of their plight. Most of all, since no one knows of their kin's whereabouts, the dead will never be buried properly and are doomed to wander forever. The twins tell them that they can get back home by following the ball of thread—that they soon will retrieve. The migrant souls proceed to tell them of The Freezer, how they escaped, and its location. The migrants give them their only food to eat—brilliant corn. After eating the corn, the clowns morph, become very agile, gain the ability to see in the night, and dance with power again.

SCENE 12 The twins and the dead find The Freezer. The twins are conflicted again, having lost the last battle. Maybe they just should return to the Southlands. They peek into The Freezer. They see their mother being hauled out with their uncle by MC Machete in a grand Serpent Dance, being torn apart by two opposing serpents.

SCENE 13 The twins quickly speak into each other's ears and conjure a plan. They enter The Freezer and perform amazing dance feats. In one of the dances, one of the twins beheads the other and then makes him whole again.

SCENE 14 The Lords are so delighted that they beg them to do the same dance to them so they can be sacrificed and be reborn again. If they do this, the twins can have the ball. The twins feign delight and oblige the Lords and dismember them. They take the ball. The Lords ask for rebirth and are denied.

THIRD MOVEMENT

SCENE 15 A celebration follows. The Dead in the Freezer are released, the young mother embraces the twins. While the twins celebrate, the Lords' various dismembered body parts slip into a crevice in the freezer floor. A chilling wind enters and freezes everyone. The floors of The Freezer collapse, and another cave of border dead opens: The Dome of Exiles. The dome opens filled with dead exiles of the world (Russia, Africa, Middle East, China). The exiles dance in icy servitude. Ruling over them are the Last Lords, fiercer, phosphorescent, beetle-like night creatures who can survive anything, dressed in diamonds. They herd the new migrants into their ice cages to work for them creating ice diamonds. The mother of the twins sings an old Mayan song as she works. The Dead Exiles dance old folk and tribal songs of their old countries. They dance into a trance. The Last Lords are attracted to these songs since all they can do is moan in the ice. The mother invites the Last Lords to climb up and go outside so they can learn the songs and dances at the Day of the Dead in their honor with their family, who has been searching for them, too, and where there exists a gem more precious than an ice diamond and larger than the cave itself. She explains that this is the reason why they must go outside by breaking through the Dome and The Freezer. The Last Lords agree, and all ascend and break out of The Freezer into the night. The twins throw the ball to the dancers. The ball goes round and round and back to the twins.

SCENE 16 The Twins throw the ball into the sky and ascend into the sky and become the sun and moon. The Last Lords are blinded and melt away.

SCENE 17 The migrant dead catch the ball remnants and hurl it into the sky, it explodes and they ascend into the sky and become stars. The rest on the ground become luminous. The Dead regain their limbs and unmask The Freezer and find that it is the Tucson coroner's freezer. They haul the Last Lords to the river and let them sprout back as a fish and a clown and run an ice cream vending stand outside the broken and empty coroner's freezer.

SCENE 18 The migrants head back home. Soon, other migrants appear, luminous, freely finding their way to North Country, once again.

CONCLUSION

AN AMEN

ARACELI MASTERSON-ALGAR AND
RAQUEL RUBIO-GOLDSMITH

Old English, from Late Latin amen, *from Ecclesiastical Greek* amen, *from Hebrew* amen *"truth," used adverbially as an expression of agreement (as in Deut. xxvii:26, I Kings i:36; compare Modern English verily,* surely, *absolutely in the same sense), from Semitic root* a-m-n *"to be trustworthy, confirm, support." Used in Old English only at the end of Gospels, otherwise translated as* Soðlic! *or* Swa hit ys, *or* Sy! *As an expression of concurrence after prayers, it is recorded from early 13c.*

—"AMEN," ONLINE ETYMOLOGY DICTIONARY

A LTHOUGH THE CONFERENCE took place in 2008, the issues of migration, and specifically migrant deaths along the U.S.-Mexico border, remain current, pressing, and unresolved. Fear of unauthorized, brown-skinned immigrants is fueled in conservative talk radio and fills the arks of the entertainment industry with programs such as National Geographic's *Border Wars*. Migrant stories are the subjects of novels, films, newscasts, and growing attention from scholars. Yet,

Death rates in our desert continue. History remains silent, and migration thereof is increasingly perceived as a matter of foreign policy and homeland security rather than part and parcel of U.S. history from the beginning and inseparable from the impunity surrounding the shootings and incarceration of black and brown bodies.

Death rates in our desert continue. The cultural dimensions (beliefs and ideologies about life, death, work, family, and life opportunities) that compel migrants to risk their lives even in the face of death-certain scenarios are severely misunderstood and blatantly manipulated to the benefit of a contradictory status quo. Border Patrol official policies since the 1990s deliberately "counted on" the harsh desert to serve as deterrence for would-be crossers—without addressing the underlining causes of migration that compel people to risk their lives attempting to cross the great Sonoran Desert.

Death rates in our desert continue. For at least fifteen years, Congress has rarely addressed the issue of immigration, and when it has, the possibilities for migration reform have been negotiated on commitments for the increasing militarization of the border, a bittersweet promise of improving the living conditions for some while taking the lives of others. This volume speaks *from* the borderlands and works against persistent efforts to present our home as "no-man's-land" and its dead bodies as "outsiders."

Death rates in our desert continue. As we started putting this volume together in the summer of 2014, record numbers of children from Mexico and Central America risked their lives to enter the United States while the U.S. government, and it follows the media and public opinion, failed to address the problem, simply moving children about, from Texas, for example, to Arizona. The absence of public awareness of the transnational dynamics fueling this process perpetuated the perception of these children as "outsiders," and "victims" at the hands of their "foreign" mothers and "far away" nations. As Alex Nava reminds us in his piece, "most of us North Americans have a profoundly short-term memory." *Amen.*

¿NO VALE NADA LA VIDA? LA VIDA NO VALE NADA (DOES LIFE HAVE NO WORTH? LIFE HAS NO WORTH)

This volume, its pilgrimage, is enunciated from the borderlands, from its memories, lived experiences, and hopes. Its title, also that of the conference in 2008, stems from the chorus of the well-known song, "Caminos de Guanajuato," by the great Mexican composer José Alfredo Jiménez (1926–1973), and we turn to it for our closure. The choice of this title is not exclusively based on the resonance of those two verses. "Caminos de Guanajuato" walks us through Jiménez's native Guanajuato, the home state of the third largest group of Mexican nationals residing in the United States. The song traces a journey in time and through space in an effort to question the meaning of life. That question, as does José Alfredo Jiménez's nostalgic tone—not unlike the melodies of much of U.S. country and folk traditions—transcends national boundaries.

Mostly, this popular song traces José Alfredo Jiménez's way back to Dolores Hidalgo (Guanajuato), the town of his birth and childhood, but only to find that one can never fully return to what one was or to its spaces. That is the reality that leads to the "lesson": *No vale nada la vida / comienza siempre llorando y así llorando se acaba / por eso es que en este mundo / la vida no vale nada* (Life has no value / it begins with a cry, and crying it ends / that is why in this world life has no value). José Alfredo's journey, as any question about the past, can only aspire to, in the words of Julio Ramos, "trazar la presencia de una ausencia" (trace the presence of an absence) in order to untangle the "espesor de la aporía" (the thick density of its aporias) (Ramos 2003, 435). This volume walks that same journey. Its pilgrimage relies heavily on that which remains in an effort to trace what is often silenced and absent from the archive.

Yet along with its symbolic value, "Caminos de Guanajuato" is grounded. It is a pilgrimage back to a place of birth and childhood—to the past—but it is as much metaphorical as it is steps and stones. The locations in the song invoke memories that are folded into the terrain. Jiménez takes us along the paths (*caminos*) of Guanajuato through mountain ranges (*sierras*) and hills (*lomas*). He makes stops in various towns, each a specific place in the landscape of Guanajuato and also in his personal life trajectory. Salamanca brings pain to his memory (*me hiere el recuerdo*), in León the bets on human lives are high, and near Santa Rosa, at El Cristo del Cerro del Cubilete, those who suffer find solace (*consuelo de los que sufren*). The song tills grounds shaped from human experiences and social practices. Similarly, each contribution to this volume walks the Sonora-Arizona desert and inquiries into the conversion of our space of dwelling into a *camposanto* (cemetery) and its *caminos* (paths) into venues of death.

In a poetic expression of the popular bumper sticker, "The meaning of life is to live it," José Alfredo's penmanship turns the most mundane—the act of crying (*llorando*)—into the very meaning of life. José Alfredo asks that, in order to trace the meaning of life, we turn to the most habitual—the cry of birth, and the tears of departure. In that sense, the song's questioning on the value of life is in fact drawing attention to the value it deserves: life simply *is*. In other words, it is not life that has no worth but rather, its value is such that the question should not be worth asking.

And yet, in response to the dead in the desert, this is the question that runs through this volume. It is the question we must ask when, returning to the opening by Claudio Lomnitz, "good deaths"—those "within the fold of religion, of family and community"—are replaced with "the track across the desert . . . so often predicated by an ideal of family unity and reproduction." Deaths in the desert, writes Lomnitz, are "shattered unity" and "the opposite of the ideal of the good death." Our question *¿No vale nada la vida?* (Does life have no value?) erupts only when life cannot complete its cycle, when it cannot come and go through those tears of which José Alfredo sings—when the cry *of* life is replaced with "cries *for* life."

As we write, migrants are crossing one of the deadliest deserts in the world. This does not make them criminals or saints. This volume affirms what should not need stating: They are people. It also asks a question that should not need formulating: ¿No vale nada la vida? Yet unlike us—the researchers, human right advocates, artists, and readers who make up this volume—the value of migrants' lives is overtly measured by the cost of their deaths, disappearance, and "deportability." *¿No Vale nada la vida? La vida no vale nada.*

REFERENCES

Abramsky, Sasha. 2003. "Incarceration, Inc." *Nation* 279 (3): 22–28.

Acuña, Rodolfo. 1988. *Occupied America: A History of Chicanos.* 3rd ed. New York: Harper and Row.

———. 2002. "A Tolerance of Violence on the Border." https://forchicanachicano studies.wikispaces.com/Rodolfo+f.+Acu%C3%B1a%2C+%E2%80%9CA +Tolerance+of+Violence.

Agamben, Giorgio. 1998. *Homo Sacer: Sovereign Power and Bare Life.* Stanford, CA: Stanford University Press.

———. 2005. *State of Exception.* Chicago: University of Chicago Press.

Aguilera, Michael B., and Douglas S. Massey. 2003. "Social Capital and the Wages of Mexican Migrants: New Hypotheses and Tests." *Social Forces* 82 (2): 671–701.

Ainslie, Ricardo C. 1998. "Cultural Mourning, Immigration, and Engagement: Vignettes from the Mexican Experience." In *Crossings: Mexican Immigration in Interdisciplinary Perspectives*, edited by Marcelo M. Suárez-Orozco, 285–300. Cambridge, MA: David Rockefeller Center for Latin American Studies, Harvard University.

———. 2002. "The Plasticity of Culture and Psychodynamic and Psychosocial Processes in Latino Immigrant Families." In *Latinas/os: Remaking of America*, edited by Marcelo M. Suarez-Orozco and Mariela M. Paez, 289–301. Berkeley: University of California Press.

Alanís-Enciso, Fernando S. 1999. *El primer programa bracero y el gobierno de México.* San Luis Potosi: El Colegio de San Luis.

Alarcón, Alicia. 2002. *La migra me hizo los mandados.* Houston: Arte Publico Press.

Alonso, Ana María. 1995. *Thread of Blood: Colonialism, Revolution, and Gender on Mexico's Northern Frontier.* Tucson: University of Arizona Press.

———. 2008. "Borders, Sovereignty, and Racialization." In *A Companion to Latin American Anthropology,* edited by Deborah Poole, 230–53. Malden, MA: Blackwell.

Alvarado, Jeanette E. 2004. "The Federal Consequences of Criminal Convictions: Illegal Reentry after Removal. Unpublished manuscript prepared for the State Bar of Arizona.

Anderson, Bruce E. 2008. "Identifying the Dead: Methods Utilized by the Pima County (Arizona) Office of the Medical Examiner for Undocumented Border Crossers: 2001–2006." *Journal of Forensic Sciences* 53 (1): 8–15.

Andreas, Peter. 1998. "The U.S. Immigration Control Offensive: Constructing an Image of Order on the Southwest Border." In *Crossings: Mexican Immigration in Interdisciplinary Perspectives,* edited by Marcelo M. Suarez-Orozco, 341–56. Cambridge, MA: Harvard University, David Rockefeller Center for Latin American Studies.

———. 1998/1999. "The Escalation of U.S. Immigration Control in the Post-NAFTA Era." *Political Science Quarterly* 113 (4): 591–615.

———. 2001. *Border Games.* Ithaca, NY: Cornell University Press.

———. 2003. "A Tale of Two Borders: The U.S.-Canada and U.S.-Mexico Lines after 9–11." In *The Rebordering of North America: Integration and Exclusion in a New Security Context,* edited by Peter Andreas and Thomas J. Biersteker, 1–23. New York: Routledge.

Anzaldo, Carlos, and Minerva Prado. 2005. *Indicies de marginación, 2005.* Mexico: Consejo Nacional de Población. http://www.conapo.gob.mx/work/models/CONAPO/indices_margina/margina2005/IM2005_principal.pdf.

Arditti, Rita. 1999. *Searching for Life: The Grandmothers of the Plaza De Mayo and the Disappeared Children of Argentina.* Berkeley: University of California Press.

Arendt, Hannah. 1998. *The Human Condition.* Chicago: University of Chicago Press.

Aretxaga, Begoña. 1999. "A Fictional Reality: Paramilitary Death Squads and the Construction of State Terror in Spain." In *Death Squad: The Anthropology of State Terror,* edited by Jeffrey Sluka, 46–69. Philadelphia: University of Pennsylvania Press.

Associated Press. 2008. "Human Smugglers' Money Trail Cuts Across Arizona Border" KTAR News, May 25.

———. 2009. "Mexico's Death Cult Protests Shrine Destruction." *Arizona Daily Star*, March 30. http://www.azstarnet.com/sn/fromcomments/286556.php.

Ballinas, Víctor. 2009. "Investiga la CNDH asesinato de tres migrantes en Chiapas." *La Jornada*, January 11. http://www.jornada.unam.mx/2009/01/13/index.php?section=estados&article=027n1est.

Ballinas, V., and A. Becerril. 2008. "ONU: desde hace décadas legisladores de México tienen una deuda con migrantes." *La Jornada*, March 12. http://www.jornada.unam.mx/2008/03/12/index.php?section=sociedad&article=049n1soc.

Basu, Rupa, Francesca Dominici, and Jonathan M Samet. 2005. "Temperature and Mortality Among the Elderly in the United States: A Comparison of Epidemiologic Methods." *Epidemiology* 16 (1): 58–66.

Beebe, James. 2001. *Rapid Assessment Process: An Introduction*. Walnut Creek, CA: AltaMira.

Benford, Robert, and David Snow. 2000. "Framing Processes and Social Movements: An Overview and Assessment." *Annual Review of Sociology* 26: 611–39.

Benjamin, Walter. 1969. *Illuminations: Essays and Reflections*. New York: Schocken.

Benton-Cohen, Katherine. 2009. *Borderline Americans: Racial Division and Labor War on the Arizona Borderlands*. Cambridge, MA: Harvard University Press.

Berg, Justin A. 2009. "White Public Opinion Toward Undocumented Immigrants: Threat and Interpersonal Environment." *Sociological Perspectives* 52: 39–58.

Bernard, Susan M., and Michael A. McGeehin. 2004. "Municipal Heat Wave Response Plans." *American Journal of Public Health* 94 (9): 1520–22.

Bernstein, Nina. 2009. "Target of Immigrant Raids Shifted." *New York Times*, February 3, U.S. sec. http://www.nytimes.com/2009/02/04/us/04raids.html.

Blackhawke, Ned. 2006. *Violence over the Land: Indians and Empires in the Early American West*. Cambridge, MA: Harvard University Press.

Blankstein, Andrew, and Pablo Kay. 2015. "LAPD Officer Arrested at US-Mexico Border for Alleged Human Smuggling." NBC News Los Angeles, March 16. http://www.nbclosangeles.com/news/local/LAPD-Officer-Arrested-at-US-Mexico-Border-for-Alleged-Smuggling-296401141.html.

Boss, Pauline. 2000. *Ambiguous Loss*. Cambridge, MA: Harvard University Press.

Bouchama, Abderrezak, and James P. Knochel. 2002. "Heat Stroke." *New England Journal of Medicine* 346 (25): 1978–88.

Butler, Judith. 2010. *Frames of War: When Is Life Grievable?* London: Verso.

Carruthers, Ian, and Robert Chambers. 1981. "Rapid Appraisal for Rural Development." *Agricultural Administration* 8: 407–22.

Cassia, Paul Sant. 2007. *Bodies of Evidence: Burial, Memory and the Recovery of Missing Persons in Cyprus.* New York: Berghahn.

Castro, Luque, Ana Lucía, Jaime Olea Miranda, and Blanca E. Zepeda Bracamonte.
2006. *Cruzando el desierto: Construcción de una tipología para el análisis de la migración en Sonora.* Hermosillo, Sonora: El Colegio de Sonora.

Cerruti, Marcela, and Douglas S. Massey. 2001. "On the Auspices of Female Migration from Mexico to the United States." *Demography* 38 (2): 187–201.

Clavelle, Karen. 2002. "Songs of Love and Longing: Songs of Migration." In *Canadian Migration Patterns: From Britain to North America*, edited by Barbara J.
Messamore, 263–94. Ottawa: University of Ottawa Press.

Clifford, James. 1994. "Diasporas." *Cultural Anthropology* 9 (3): 302–38.

Coe, John. 1993. "Time of Death and Changes After Death." In *Medicolegal Investigation of Death: Guidelines for the Application of Pathology to Crime Investigation*,
3rd ed. edited by Werner U. Spitz, 50–64. Springfield, IL: Charles C. Thomas.

Cole, Jennifer. 2004. "Painful Memories: Ritual and the Transformation of Community Trauma." *Culture, Medicine and Psychiatry* 28: 87–105.

Conover, Ted. 1987. *Coyotes: A Journey Through the Secret World of America's Illegal
Aliens* New York: Vintage.

Cornelius, Wayne A. 1989. "Impacts of the 1986 US Immigration Law on Emigra-
tion from Rural Mexican Sending Communities." *Population and Development
Review* 15 (4): 689–705.

———. 1998. "The Structural Embeddedness of Demand for Mexican Immigrant
Labor: New Evidence from California." In *Crossings: Mexican Immigration in
Interdisciplinary Perspectives*, edited by Marcelo M. Suarez-Orozco, 115–55. Cam-
bridge, MA: Harvard University Press.

———. 2001. "Death at the Border: Efficacy and Unintended Consequences of US
Immigration Control Policy." *Population and Development Review* 27 (4): 661–85.

———. 2004. *Controlling immigration.* 2nd ed. Stanford, CA: Stanford University
Press.

———. 2005. "Controlling 'Unwanted' Immigration: Lessons from the United States,
1993–2004." *Journal of Ethnic and Migration Studies* 31 (4): 775–94.

Cornelius, Wayne A., and Jessa M. Lewis. 2007. *Impacts of Border Enforcement on
Mexican Migration: The View from Sending Communities.* San Diego: Center for
Comparative Immigration Studies.

Cortés Larrinaga, Mario. 2004. *Riesgos asociados con el flujo migratorio mexicano y su relación con las políticas migratorias de México y Estados Unidos.* Doctoral thesis, Colegio de la Frontera Norte, Tijuana, México.

Coutin Susan B. 2000. *Legalizing Moves: Salvadoran Immigrants' Struggle for U.S. Residency.* Ann Arbor: University of Michigan Press, 2000.

Covarrubias, Miguel. 1947. *Mexico South: The Isthmus of Tehuantepec.* New York: Knopf.

Cunningham, Hilary, and Josiah Heyman. 2004. Introduction: Mobilities and Enclosures at Borders. *Identities: Global Studies in Culture and Power* 11: 289–302.

Custodio, Álvaro. 1975. *El Corrido Popular Mexicano.* Madrid: Ediciones Júcar.

Dávila, Alberto, José A. Pagán, and Gökçe Soydemir. 2002. "The Short-Term and Long-Term Deterrence Effects of INS Border and Interior Enforcement on Undocumented Immigration." *Journal of Economic Behavior and Organization* 49 (4): 459–72. doi:10.1016/S0167-2681(02)00010-0.

De Genova, Nicholas P. 2002. "Migrant 'Illegality' and Deportability in Everyday Life." *Annual Review of Anthropology* 31: 419–47.

———. 2005. *Working the Boundaries: Race, Space, and "Illegality" in Mexican Chicago.* Durham, NC: Duke University Press.

De la Torre, Renée. 2008. "La religiosidad peregrina de los jaliscienses: Vírgenes viajeras, apariciones en los no lugares y santos polleros." *E-Misferica* 5 (1).

de León, Antonio García. 1985. *Resistencia y utopia: memorial de agravios y cronicas de revueltas y profecias acaecidas en la Provincia de Chiapas durante los últimos quinientos años de su historia.* Mexico City: Ediciones Era de León.

———. 2002. *Fronteras interiores: Chiapas: Una modernidad particular.* México D.F.: Océano.

de Los Angeles Crummett, Maria. 1993. "Gender, Class, and Household: Migration Patterns in Aguascalientes, Mexico." In *Building with Our Hands: New Directions in Chicana Studies*, edited by Adela de la Torre and Beatríz M. Pesquera. Berkeley: University of California Press.

Dirdamal, Tim. 2005. *De nadie (Border Crossing).* Producciones Tranvía. Van Nuys, CA: Amigo Films.

Dixon, David, Julie Murray, and Julia Gelatt. 2006. *America's Immigrants: US Retirement Migration to Mexico and Panama.* Washington, DC: Migration Policy Institute.

Donato, Katherine M. 1993. "Current Trends and Patterns of Female Migration: Evidence from Mexico." *International Migration Review* 27 (4): 748–72.

———. 1994. "U.S. Policy and Mexican Migration to the United States, 1942–92." *Social Science Quarterly* 75 (4): 705–30.

Donato, Katherine M., and Evelyn Patterson. 2004. Women and Men on the Move: Undocumented Border Crossing. In *Crossing the Border: Research from the Mexican Migration Project*, edited by Jorge Durand and Douglas Massey, 111–30. New York: Russell Sage Foundation.

Donoghue, E. R., M. A. Graham, J. M. Jentzen, B. D. Lifschultz, J. L. Luke, and H. G. Mirchandani. 1997. "Criteria for the Diagnosis of Heat-Related Deaths: National Association of Medical Examiners. Position paper. National Association of Medical Examiners Ad Hoc Committee on the Definition of Heat-Related Fatalities." *American Journal of Forensic Medicine and Pathology* 18 (1): 11–14.

Dunn, Timothy J. 1995. *The Militarization of the U.S.-Mexico Border, 1978–1992: Low-Intensity Conflict Doctrine Comes Home*. Austin: University of Texas Press.

Durand, Jorge, and María Aysa-Lastra. 2015. "International Migration and Employment in Latin America: Uncertain Times and Changing Conditions." In *Immigrant Vulnerability and Resilience*, edited by María Aysa-Lastra and Lorenzo Cachon, 183–206. Cham, Switzerland: Springer International.

Durand, Jorge, and Douglas S. Massey. 2004. *Crossing the Border: Research from the Mexican Migration Project*. New York: Russell Sage Foundation.

Durkheim, Émile, John A. Spaulding, and George Simpson. 1979. *Suicide*. New York: Free Press.

Eckhart, Meister. 1981. *Meister Eckhart: The Essential Sermons, Commentaries, Treatises, and Defense*. Translated by Edmund Colledge and Bernard McGinn. New York: Paulist Press.

Edkins, Jenny. 2011. *Missing: Persons and Politics*. Ithaca, NY: Cornell University Press.

Egan, Timothy. 2004. "Border Desert Proves Deadly for Mexicans." *New York Times*, May 23, U.S. sec. http://www.nytimes.com/2004/05/23/us/border-desert-proves -deadly-for-mexicans.html?pagewanted=1.

El Imparcial. 2008. "Alertan sobre secuestros entre 'coyotes' in Arizona." *El Imparcial*, July 19, B5.

Eliot, T. S. 1943. "Little Gidding." In *Four Quartets*. New York: Harcourt, Brace.

Endres, Kirsten W. 2008. "Engaging the Spirits of the Dead: Soul-Calling Rituals and the Performative Construction of Efficacy." *Journal of the Royal Anthropological Institute* 14: 755–73.

Erfani, Julie A. Murphy. 2009. "Crime and Violence in the Arizona-Sonora Borderlands." In *Violence, Security, and Human Rights at the Border*, edited by K. Staudt, T. Payan, and Z. A. Kruszewski, 63–84. Tucson: University of Arizona Press.

Eschbach, Karl, Jacqueline Maria Hagan, and Nestor Rodriguez. 2001. *Causes and Trends in Migrant Deaths Along the U.S.-Mexico Border, 1985–1998.* Houston, TX: University of Houston Center for Immigration Research.

Eschbach, Karl, Jacqueline Hagan, Nestor Rodríguez, Rubén Hernández-León, and Stanley Bailey. 1999. "Death at the Border." *International Migration Review* 33 (2): 430–54.

Espenshade, Thomas J. 1995. "Unauthorized Immigration to the United States." *Annual Review of Sociology* 21: 195–216.

Farmer, Paul. 1997. "On Suffering and Structural Violence: A View from Below." In *Social Suffering*, edited by Veena Das, Arthur Kleinman, and Margaret Lock, 261–83. Berkeley: University of California Press.

———. 2004. "An Anthropology of Structural Violence." *Current Anthropology* 45 (3): 305–25.

———. 2005. *Pathologies of Power: Health, Human Rights, and the New War on the Poor.* Berkeley: University of California Press.

Felbab-Brown, Vanda. 2009. *The Violent Drug Market in Mexico and Lessons from Colombia.* Policy Paper, Brookings Institution, Foreign Policy Studies, no. 12. Washington, DC: Brookings Institution.

Fernández, Celestino. 1989. "Humor and Satire in Mexican Immigration Corridos." *Meta* 34: 91–101.

Fernández, Celestino, and James E. Officer. 1989. "The Lighter Side of Mexican Immigration: Humor and Satire in the Mexican Corrido." *Journal of the Southwest* 31 (4): 471–496.

Foucault, Michel. 1990. *The History of Sexuality.* Vol. 1, *An Introduction.* 5th ed. Translated by Robert Hurley. New York: Vintage.

Franco, Jean. 1985. "Killing Priests, Nuns, Women and Children." In *On Signs*, edited by Marshall Blonsky, 414–42. Baltimore: Johns Hopkins University Press.

Frost, Robert. 1936. "Desert Places." http://www.internal.org/Robert_Frost/Desert_Places

Fussell, Elizabeth. 2004. "Sources of Mexico's Migration Stream: Rural, Urban, and Border Migrants to the United States." *Social Forces* 82 (3): 937–67.

Galtung, Johan. 1969. "Violence, Peace, and Peace Research." *Journal of Peace Research* 6 (3): 167–91.

García Castro, Ismael. 2007. *Vidas compartidas: Formación de una red migratoria transnacional: Aguacaliente Grande, Sinaloa y Victor Valley California.* Mexico City: Plaza y Valdés.

García de León, Antonio 1985. *Resistencia y utopia: memorial de agravios y crónicas de revueltas y profecías acaecidas en la Provincia de Chiapas durante los últimos quinientos años de su historia.* Mexico City. Ediciones Era.

García Lorca, Federico. 1994. "Songs." In *Federico García Lorca: Selected Verse*, edited by Christopher Maurer, 121. New York: Farrar, Straus and Giroux.

García Márquez, Gabriel. 1982. "Nobel Lecture." Nobelprize.org, December 8. http://www.nobelprize.org/nobel_prizes/literature/laureates/1982/marquez -lecture-sp.html.

Garske, Monica. 2013. "Former Border Patrol Agents Sentenced to Decades in Prison." *NBC News San Diego*, June 22. http://www.nbcsandiego.com/news /local/Former-Border-Patrol-Agents-Raul-Villareal-Fidel-Villareal-Sentenced -to-Prison-212620711.html#ixzz3kKiJF3cM.

Garza Quirós, Fernando. 1991. *El Niño fidencio y el fidencismo.* (Quinta Edición). Monterrey, Mexico: Editorial Font, S.A.

Gathmann, Christina. 2008. Effects of Enforcement on Illegal Markets: Evidence from Migrant Smuggling Along the Southwestern Border. *Journal of Public Economics* 92 (10–11): 1926–41. doi:10.1016/j.jpubeco.2008.04.006.

Gilroy, Paul. 2005. *Postcolonial Melancholia.* New York: Columbia University Press.

Glaser, Barney G., and Anselm L. Strauss. 1967. *The Discovery of Grounded Theory: Strategies for Qualitative Research.* Chicago: Aldine.

González, Daniel. 2003. "Gangs Are Menacing 'Coyotes,' Immigrants: Assaults, Kidnappings are Rampant." *Arizona Republic*, April 17.

González y González, Luis. 1973. *Invitacion a la microhistoria.* Mexico City: Sep-Setentas 72.

González y González, Luis. 1989. *Todo es historia.* México D.F.: Cal y Arena.

González y González, Luis, and Álvaro Ochoa. 1994. *Pueblo en vilo: La fuerza de la costumbre: Homenaje a Luis González y González.* Guadalajara: El Colegio de Jalisco.

Goody, Jack. 1962. *Death, Property and the Ancestors: A Study of the Mortuary Customs of the LoDagaa of West Africa.* Stanford, CA: Stanford University Press.

Granberry, Phillip J., and Enrico A. Marcelli. 2007. "In the Hood and on the Job": Social Capital Accumulation Among Legal and Unauthorized Mexican Migrants." *Sociological Perspectives* 50 (4): 579–95.

Green, Linda B. 1999. *Fear as a Way of Life: Mayan Widows in Rural Guatemala.* New York: Columbia University Press.

———. 2011. "The Nobodies: Neoliberalism, Violence, and Migration." *Medical Anthropology* 30 (4): 366–85.

Griffith, James S. 1992. *Beliefs and Holy Places: A Spiritual Geography of the Pimería Alta*. Tucson: University of Arizona Press.

———. 2003. *Folk Saints of the Borderlands: Victims, Bandits and Healers*. Tucson, AZ: Rio Nuevo.

———. 2005. "Voices from Inside a Black Snake: Religious Monuments of Sonora's Highways." *Journal of the Southwest* 47 (2): 233–48.

———. 2006. "Voices from Inside a Black Snake, Part II: Sonoran Roadside Capillas." *Journal of the Southwest* 48 (3): 233–59.

Griffith, James S., and Celestino Fernández. 1988. "Mexican Horse Races and Cultural Values: The Case of Los Corridos del Merino." *Western Folklore* 47: 129–51.

Griffith, James S., and Francisco Javier Manzo Taylor. 2007. *The Face of Christ in Sonora / El rostro del Señor en Sonora*. Tucson, AZ: Rio Nuevo.

Guendelman, Sylvia, and Auristela Perez-Itriago. 1987. "Migration Tradeoffs: Men's Experiences with Seasonal Lifestyles." *International Migration Review* 21 (3): 709–27.

Guidotti-Hernández, Nicole Marie. 2011. *Unspeakable Violence: Remapping U.S. and Mexican National Imaginaries*. Durham, NC: Duke University Press.

Hadden, Gerry. 2003. "The Trail of Latino Migration: A Desert Crossing." National Public Radio, *Morning Edition*, October 1.

Handlin, Oscar. 1952. *The Uprooted*. Boston: Little, Brown.

Hall, Stuart. 1990. "Cultural Identity and Diaspora." In *Identity: Community, Culture, Difference*, edited by Jonathan Rutherford, 222–37. London: Lawrence and Wishart.

Harvey, David. 2007. *A Brief History of Neoliberalism*. Oxford: Oxford University Press.

Heckmann, Friedrich. 2007. "Towards a Better Understanding of Human Smuggling." IMISCOE Policy Brief, Institut an der Universität Bamberg. http://www.efms.uni-bamberg.de/pdf/Policy_brief_Human_smuggling.pdf.

Hendricks, Tyche. 2004. "Dangerous Border: Crossing into U.S. Has Increasingly Become a Matter of Life and Death." *San Francisco Chronicle*, May 30.

Henríquez, E. 2009. "Policías chiapanecos balean camión que llevaba migrantes: 3 muertos." *La Jornada*, January 9. http://www.jornada.unam.mx/2009/01/10/index.php?section=estados&article=024n1est.

Henríquez, E., and A. Mariscal. 2009. "Aún sin identificar, los cuerpos de 3 migrantes tiroteados en Chiapas." *La Jornada*, January 10. 2010. http://www.jornada.unam.mx/2009/01/11/index.php?section=estados&article=027n1est.

Hernández, Kristian. 2015. "Bond Set for Former McAllen Cop Accused of Human Smuggling. *Monitor*, June 18.

Herrera-Sobek, María. 1998. "The Corrido as Hypertext: Undocumented Mexican Immigrant Films and the Mexican/Chicano Ballad." In *Culture Across Borders: Mexican Immigration & Popular Culture*, edited by David R. Maciel and Maria Herrera-Sobek, 227–58. Tucson: University of Arizona Press.

Hertz, Robert. 1960. *Death and the Right Hand*. Glencoe, IL: Free Press.

Hondagneu-Sotelo, Pierrette. 1994. *Gendered Transitions: Mexican Experiences of Immigration*. Berkeley: University of California Press.

Huckelberry, C. H. 2005. *Pima County's Border Costs*. Memorandum to Pima County Board of Supervisors. Tucson, AZ, December 5.

Ibarra, Ignacio. 1999. "Death on the Border: Road Crashes, Exposure Claim Record Number of Migrants." *Arizona Daily Star*, October 3.

Inda, Jonathan. 2006. *Targeting Immigrants: Government, Technology and Ethics*. Malden, MA: Blackwell.

Izcara Palacios, Simón Pedro. 2014. "Coyotaje and Drugs: Two Different Businesses." *Bulletin of Latin American Research* 34 (3): 324–39.

Johnson, Kevin R. 1993. "Free Trade and Closed Borders: NAFTA and Mexican Immigration to the United States." *U.C. Davis Law Review* 27: 937.

———. 2003. *The Huddled Masses Myth: Immigration and Civil Rights*. Philadelphia: Temple University Press.

Kino Border Initiative. 2010. Presentation at Casa Nazaret shelter for women, August 21.

Kleinman, Arthur, and Joan Kleinman. 1996. "The Appeal of Experience: The Dismay of Images: Cultural Appropriations of Suffering in Our Times." *Daedalus* 125 (1): 1–23.

La Jornada. 2008. "Los indocumentados que sean detenidos en México ya no enfrentarán cargos penales." *La Jornada*, July 22. http://www.jornada.unam.mx/2008/07/22/index.php?section=politica&article=012n1pol.

Langford, Jean M. 2009. "Gifts Intercepted: Biopolitics and Spirit Debt." *Cultural Anthropology* 24 (4): 681–711.

Lakoff, George. 2002. *Moral Politics: How Liberals and Conservatives Think*. Chicago: University of Chicago Press.

LeBrón, Marisol. 2009. "'Migracorridos': Another Failed Anti-Immigration Campaign." North American Congress on Latin America (NACLA), March 27.

Lee, Jennifer. 2006. "Human Smuggling for a Hefty Fee." *New York Times*, May 28. http://www.nytimes.com/2006/05/28/weekinreview/28basic.html?_r=0.

Lomnitz, Claudio. 2005. *Death and the Idea of Mexico*. New York: Zone Books.

Lomnitz, L. A. 1994. "Supervivencia en una barriada en la ciudad de México." In *Redes Sociales, Cultura y Poder: Ensayos de Antropolgogía Latinoamericana*, 47–98. México D.F.: FLACSO.

Lyotard, Jean Francois. 1988. *The Differend: Phrases in Dispute*. Minneapolis: University of Minnesota Press.

Maciel, David R. and Maria Herrera-Sobek, eds. 1998. *Culture Across Borders: Mexican Immigration and Popular Culture*. Tucson: University of Arizona Press.

Magaña, Rocío. 2008. "Bodies on the Line: Life, Death, and Authority on the Arizona-Mexico Border." PhD diss., University of Chicago.

Mandelstam, Osip. 2010. "Epigram Against Stalin." Translated by Esther Allen from Jose Manuel Prieto's "Reading Mandelstam on Stalin." *New York Review of Books*, June 10.

Marcelli, Enrico A., and Wayne A. Cornelius. 2001. "The Changing Profile of Mexican Migrants to the United States: New Evidence from California and Mexico." *Latin American Research Review* 36 (3): 105–31.

Marchand, Marianne H., and Anne Sisson Runyan. 2000. "Introduction. Feminist Sightings of Global Restructuring: Conceptualizations and Reconceptualization." In *Gender and Global Restructuring: Sightings, Sites, and Resistances*, edited by Marianne H. Marchand and Ann Sisson Runyun, 1–22. London: Routledge.

Martínez, Daniel E., Robin C. Reineke, Raquel Rubio-Goldsmith, and Bruce O. Parks. 2014. "Structural Violence and Migrant Deaths in Southern Arizona: Data from the Pima County Office of the Medical Examiner, 1990–2013," *Journal on Migration and Human Security* 2 (4):257–86.

Martínez, Héctor Pérez. 1935. *Trayectoria del Corrido*. Mexico City.

Martínez, Oscar. 1996. *U.S.-Mexico Borderlands Historical and Contemporary Perspectives*. Wilmington, DE: Scholarly Resources.

Martínez, Ramiro, and Abel Valenzuela. 2006. *Immigration and Crime: Race, Ethnicity, and Violence*. New York: New York University Press.

Marx Ferree, Myra, et al. 2002. *Shaping Abortion Discourse: Democracy and the Public Sphere in Germany and the United States*. Cambridge: Cambridge University Press.

Massey, Douglas S. 1987. "Understanding Mexican Migration to the United States." *American Journal of Sociology* 92 (6): 1372–1403.

Massey, Douglas S., ed. 2010. *New Faces in New Places: The Changing Geography of American Immigration*. New York: Russell Sage Foundation.

Massey, Douglas S., Joaquín Arango, Graeme Hugo, Ali Kouaouci, Adela Pellegrino, and J. Edward Taylor. 1993. "Theories of International Migration: A Review and Appraisal." *Population and Development Review* 19 (3): 431–66.

Massey, Douglas S., Joaquín Arango, Graeme Hugo, Ali Kouaouci, Adela Pellegrino, and J. Edward Taylor. 2005. *Worlds in Motion: Understanding International Migration at the End of the Millennium.* New York: Oxford University Press.

Massey, Douglas S., Jorge Durand, and Nolan J. Malone. 2002. *Beyond Smoke and Mirrors: Mexican Immigration in an Era of Economic Integration.* New York: Russell Sage Foundation.

Massey, Douglas S., and Kristin E. Espinosa. 1997. "What's Driving Mexico-U.S. Migration? A Theoretical, Empirical, and Policy Analysis." *American Journal of Sociology* 102 (4): 939–99.

Massey, Douglas S., and Felipe García España. 1987. "The Social Process of International Migration." *Science*, n.s., 237 (4816): 733–38.

Massey, Douglas S., Luin P. Goldring, and Jorge Durand. 1994. "Continuities in Transnational Migration: An Analysis of Nineteen Mexican Communities." *American Journal of Sociology* 99: 1492–1533.

Mattingly, Cheryl. 2000. "Emergent Narratives." In *Narrative and the Cultural Construction of Illness and Healing,* edited by Cheryl Mattingly and Linda C. Garro, 181–211. Berkeley: University of California Press.

Mazzota, Giuseppe. 1979. *Dante, Poet of the Desert.* Princeton, NJ: Princeton University Press.

Mbembe, Achille. 2003. "Necropolitics." *Public Culture* 15 (1): 11–40.

McCombs, Brady. 2007. "Guard Numbers on Border to Be Halved." *Arizona Daily Star,* July 25, A2.

———. 2008. "BP Targeting 40 Illegal Crossers a Day in Tucson Sector." *Arizona Daily Star,* January 24 (accessed August 31, 2008; no longer posted). http://www.azstarnet.com/metro/221983.

———. 2009a. "Deadliest SW Border Stretch Is Getting 209 More Agents." *Arizona Daily Star,* August 4, A11.

———. 2009b. "Four Illegal Immigrants' Bodies Found Recently on O'odham Land." *Arizona Daily Star,* August 4, A13.

McGinn, Bernard. 1981. "The God Beyond God: Theology and Mysticism in the Thought of Meister Eckhart." *Journal of Religion* 61: 1–19.

———. 1994. "Ocean and Desert as Symbols of Mystical Absorption in the Christian Tradition." *Journal of Religion* 74: 155–81.

Mendoza, Cristóbal. 2006. Transnational Spaces Through Local Places: Mexican Immigrants in Albuquerque (New Mexico). *Journal of Anthropological Research* 62 (4): 539–61.

Mendoza, Vicente T. 1939. *El Romance Español y El Corrido Mexicano.* Mexico City: Universidad Nacional Autónoma de México.

Mendoza, Vicente T. 1954. *El Corrido Mexicano.* Mexico City: Fondo de Cultura Económica.

Michel-Rolph, Trouillot. 1997. *Silencing the Past: Power and the Production of History.* Boston: Beacon.

Monsiváis, Carlos. 2007. "Adónde vas que más valgas." *El Universal,* February 18. http://www.eluniversal.com.mx/editoriales/36807.html.

Monteverde García, Ana María. 2004. "Propuesta de campaña preventiva contra la violencia hacia la mujer inmigrante y operadora de la industria maquiladora en la ciudad de Nogales Sonora." Tesis profesional, Universidad de las Américas, Cholula, Puebla, Mexico. http://catarina.udlap.mx/u_dl_a/tales/documentos/lco /monteverde_g_am/.

Mrela, Christopher, and Will Humble. 2004. *Heat Related Deaths on the Rise in Arizona.* Prevention Bulletin: Arizona Department of Health Services Division of Public Health Services. Phoenix, AZ: Arizona Department of Health Services.

Mull, Dorothy S. 1987. "Contemporary Mexican Villains in Story and Song: The Popular Representation of Durazo and Caro Quintero." *Proceedings of the Pacific Coast Council on Latin-American Studies* 14 (2): 61–75.

Nagengast, Carole. 2002. "Inoculations of Evil in the U.S.-Mexican Border Region: Reflections on the Genocidal Potential of Symbolic Violence." In *Annihilating Difference: The Anthropology of Genocide,* edited by Alexander Hinton, 325–47. Berkeley: University of California Press.

Nance, Kimberly. 2006. *Can Literature Promote Justice? Trauma Narrative and Social Action in Latin American Testimonio.* Nashville, TN: Vanderbilt University Press.

National Commission on ICE Misconduct and Violations of 4th Amendment Rights. 2009. *Raids on Workers: Destroying Our Rights.* United Food and Commercial Workers International Union, June. http://www.ufcw.org/icemisconduct/.

Neruda, Pablo. 1982. *Pablo Neruda: The Poetics of Prophecy.* Ithaca, NY: Cornell University Press.

Nevins, Joseph. 2002. *Operation Gatekeeper: The Rise of the "Illegal Alien" and the Making of the U.S.-Mexico Boundary.* New York: Routledge.

———. 2003. "Thinking Out of Bounds: A Critical Analysis of Academic and Human Rights Writings on Migrant Deaths in the U.S.-Mexico Border Region." *Migraciones Internacionales* 2 (2): 171–90.

———. 2005. "A Beating Worse Than Death: Imagining and Contesting Violence in the U.S.-Mexico Borderlands." *AmeriQuests* 2 (1). http://ejournals.library.vanderbilt.edu/ojs/index.php/ameriquests/article/view/64.

Nevins, Joseph, and Mizue Aizeki. 2008. *Dying to Live: A Story of U.S. Immigration in an Age of Global Apartheid*. San Francisco: Open Media/City Lights Books.

New Oxford American Dictionary. 2010. 3rd ed. Oxford: Oxford University Press.

Ngai, Mae M. 2004. *Impossible Subjects: Illegal Aliens and the Making of America*. Princeton, NJ: Princeton University Press.

Ochoa Serrano, Álvaro. 1994. *Pueblo en vilo, la fuerza de la costumbre: homenaje a Luis González y González*. Edited by Alvaro Ochoa Serrano. Guadalajara: El Colegio de Jalisco.

O'Leary, Anna Ochoa. 2008. "Close Encounters of the Deadly Kind: Gender, Migration, and Border (In)Security." *Migration Letters* 15 (2): 111–22.

———. 2009a. "The ABCs of Unauthorized Border Crossing Costs: Assembling, Bajadores, and Coyotes." *Migration Letters* 6 (1): 27–36.

———. 2009b. "In the Footsteps of Spirits: Migrant Women's Testimonios in a Time of Heightened Border Enforcement." In *Violence, Security, and Human Rights at the Border*, edited by Kathleen Staudt, Tony Payan, and Z. Anthony Kruszewski, 91–112. Tucson: University of Arizona Press.

———. 2009c. "Mujeres en el Cruce: Remapping Border Security Through Migrant Mobility." *Journal of the Southwest* 51 (4): 523–42.

———. 2012. "Of Coyotes, Cooperation, and Capital: Social Capital and Women's Migration at the Margins of the State." In *Research in Economic Anthropology*. Vol. 32, *Political Economy, Neoliberalism, and the Prehistoric Economies of Latin America*, edited by D. C. Wood and T. Matejowsky, 133–60. Bingley, UK: Emerald Group.

Orrenius, Pia M. 2004. "The Effects of U.S. Border Enforcement on the Crossing Behavior of Mexican Migrants." In *Crossing the Border: Research from the Mexican Migration Project*, edited by Jorge Durand and Douglas S. Massey, 281–90. New York, Russell Sage Foundation.

Otto, Rudolph. 1950. *The Idea of the Holy*. Oxford: Oxford University.

Paredes, Américo. 1958. *With His Pistol in His Hand*. Austin: University of Texas Press.

Parsons, E. C. 1939. *Pueblo Indian Religion*. Chicago: University of Chicago Press.

Pascal, Blaise. 1995. *Pensees*. New York: Penguin Classics.

Passel, Jeffrey S. 2006. *The Size and Characteristics of the Unauthorized Migrant Population in the U.S.: Estimates Based on the March 2005 Current Population Survey*. Washington, DC: Pew Hispanic Center.

Passel, Jeffrey S., D'Vera Cohn, and Ana Gonzalez-Barrera. 2013. *Population Decline of Unauthorized Immigrants Stalls, May have Reversed*. Washington, DC: Pew Research Center.

Petros, Melanie. 2005. "The Costs of Human Smuggling and Trafficking." Migration Research Unit / Global Commission on International Migration (accessed February 1, 2009; no longer posted). www.gcim.org/attachements/GMP%20No%2031.pdf.

Pettigrew, Joyce. 1999. "Parents and Their Children in Situations of Terror: Disappearances and Special Police Activity in Punjab." In *Death Squad: The Anthropology of State Terror*, edited by Jeffrey Sluka, 204–25. Philadelphia: University of Pennsylvania Press.

Portes, Alejandro, and Rubén G. Rumbaut. 2006. *Immigrant America: A Report*. 3rd ed. Berkeley: University of California Press.

Portelli, Alessandro. 1981. "The Peculiarities of Oral History." *History Workshop Journal* 12 (1): 96–107.

———. 1991. *The Death of Luigi Trastulli, and Other Stories: Form and Meaning in Oral History*. Albany, NY: State University of New York Press.

———. 1997. *The Battle of Valle Giulia: Oral History and the Art of Dialogue*. Madison: University of Wisconsin Press.

Quesada, James, Laurie Kain Hart, and Philippe Bourgois. 2011. "Structural Vulnerability and Health: Latino Migrant Laborers in the United States." *Medical Anthropology* 30: 339–62.

Quinn, Dale, and Brady McCombs. 2007. "2 of 23 in Truck Killed," *Arizona Daily Star*, March 31.

Quinones, Sam. 2009. Phoenix, Kidnap-for-Ransom Capital. *Los Angeles Times*, February 12.

Ramos, Julio. 2003. *Desencuentros de la modernidad en América Latina: Literatura y política en el siglo XIX*. San Juan, PR: Editorial Cuarto Propio.

Rancière, Jacques. 2004. "Who is the Subject of the Rights of Man." *South Atlantic Quarterly* 103 (2/3): 297–310.

Record, Ian W. 2008. *Big Sycamore Stands Alone: The Western Apaches, Aravaipa, and the Struggle for Place*. Vol. 1. Norman: University of Oklahoma Press.

Rippy, J. Fred. 1921. *The Boundary of New Mexico and the Gadsden Treaty*. Hispanic American Historical Review 4(4): 715–42.

Robben, Antonius C. G. M. 1999. "State Terror in the Netherworld: Disappearance and Reburial in Argentina." In *Death Squad: The Anthropology of State Terror*, edited by Jeffrey Sluka, 378–88. Philadelphia: University of Pennsylvania Press.

Robinson, William I. 2003. *Transnational Conflicts: Central America, Social Change, and Globalization*. London: Verso.

Roman, Jose A. 2008. "Urge en México ley que proteja a migrantes extranjeros: NALACC." *La Jornada*, February 13. http://www.jornada.unam.mx/2008/02/13/index.php?section=politica&article=006n1pol.

Rosales, F. Arturo. 2000. *Testimonio: A Documentary History of the Mexican American Struggle for Civil Rights*. Houston, TX: Arte Público Press.

Rozemberg, Hernan. 2009. "Songs Teach Migration Danger." *San Antonio Express-News*, January 24.

Rubio-Goldsmith, Raquel, Melissa McCormick, Daniel Martinez, and Inez Magdalena Duarte. 2006. *The "Funnel Effect" and Recovered Bodies of Unauthorized Migrants Processed by the Pima County Office of the Medical Examiner, 1990–2005*. Report Submitted to the Pima County Board of Supervisors. Tucson, AZ: Binational Migration Institute.

————. 2007. *A Humanitarian Crisis at the Border: New Estimates of Deaths Among Unauthorized Immigrants*. Washington, DC: Immigration Policy Center, A Division of the American Immigration Law Foundation. http://www.immigrationpolicy.org/sites/default/files/docs/Crisis%20at%20the%20Border.pdf.

Ruiz Marrujo, Olivia T. 2009. Women, Migration, and Sexual Violence: Lessons from Mexico'a Borders. In *Human Rights Along the US Mexican Border*, edited by K. Staudt, T. Payan, and Z. A. Kruszewski, 31–47. Tucson: University of Arizona Press.

Sadasivam, Bharati. 1997. "The Impact of Structural Adjustment on Women." *Human Rights Quarterly* 19 (3): 630–65.

Said, Edward W. 1983. *The World, the Text, and the Critic*. Cambridge, MA: Harvard University Press

Samora, Julian. 1971. *Los mojados: The Wetback Story*. Notre Dame, IN: University of Notre Dame Press.

Sanchez, Gabriella E. 2014. *Human Smuggling and Border Crossings*. New York: Routledge.

Santa Ana, Otto. 1999. "'Like an Animal I Was Treated': Anti-immigrant Metaphor in U.S. Public Discourse." *Discourse and Society* 10 (2): 191–224.

———. 2002. *Brown Tide Rising: Metaphors of Latinos in Contemporary American Public Discourse*. Austin: University of Texas Press.

Sapkota, S., H. W. Kohl III, J. Gilchrist, J. McAuliffe, B. Parks, B. England, T. Flood et al. 2006. "Unauthorized Border Crossings and Migrants Deaths: Arizona, New Mexico, and El Paso, Texas, 2002–2003." *American Journal of Public Health*, 96 (7): 1282–87.

Saucedo Zarco, Carmen. 2002. *Historias de santos mexicanos*. México D.F.: Editorial Planeta.

Scarry, Elaine. 1985. *The Body in Pain: The Making and Unmaking of the World*. New York: Oxford University Press.

Scheper-Hughes, Nancy. 1993. *Death Without Weeping: The Violence of Everyday Life in Brazil*. Berkeley: University of California Press.

———. 2004. "Bodies, Death, and Silence." In *Violence in War and Peace*, edited by Nancy Scheper-Hughes and Philippe I. Bourgois, 175–85. Malden, MA: Wiley-Blackwell.

Scott, James C. 1985. *Weapons of the Weak: Everyday Forms of Peasant Resistance*. New Haven, CT: Yale University Press.

Shakespeare, William. (1606) 1993. *King Lear*. Folger Shakespeare Library Edition. New York: Washington Square Press.

Shepard-Durini, Suzana. 2008. *Mexico's Other Border: Issues Affecting Mexico's Dividing Line with Guatemala*. Council on Hemispheric Affairs, September. http://www.coha.org/mexicos-other-border-issues-affecting-mexico's-dividing-line-with-guatemala/.

Sheridan, Thomas E. 1986. *Los Tucsonenses: The Mexican Community in Tucson, 1854–1941*. Tucson: University of Arizona Press.

———. 1995. *Arizona: A History*. Tucson: University of Arizona Press.

Simmons, Merle E. 1957. *The Mexican Corrido as a Source for Interpretive Study of Modern Mexico (1870–1950)*. Bloomington: Indiana University Press.

Singer, Audrey, and Douglas S. Massey. 1998. "The Social Process of Undocumented Border Crossing Among Mexican Migrants." *International Migration Review* 32 (3): 561–92.

Slack, Jeremy, Daniel E. Martínez, Scott Whiteford, and Emily Peiffer. 2013. *In the Shadow of the Wall: Family Separation, Immigration Enforcement and Security*. Tucson, AZ: Center for Latin American Studies.

Sluka, Jeffrey A. 1999. "Introduction." In *Death Squad: The Anthropology of State Terror*, edited by Jeffrey A. Sluka, 1–45. Philadelphia: University of Pennsylvania Press.

Spener, David. 1999. "This Coyote's Life." *NACLA: Report on the Americas* 33 (3): 22–23.

Spicer, Edward H. 1981. *Cycles of Conquest: The Impact of Spain, Mexico, and the United States on the Indians of the Southwest, 1533–1960.* Tucson: University of Arizona Press.

Spivak, Gayatri C. 1999. *Toward a History of the Vanishing Present.* Cambridge, MA: Harvard University Press, 1999.

STPS (Secretaría del Trabajo y Previsión Social). 2002. *Encuesta sobre migración en la Frontera Norte de México (EMIF), 1999–2000.* Mexico City: Secretaría del Trabajo y Previsión Social, Coordinación General de Planeación y Política Sectorial.

Suárez-Orozco, Marcelo. 2004. "The Treatment of Children in the 'Dirty War': Ideology, State Terrorism, and the Abuse of Children in Argentina." In *Violence in War and Peace,* edited by Nancy Scheper-Hughes and Philippe I. Bourgois, 378–88. Malden,, MA: Wiley-Blackwell.

Tangeman, Anthony S. 2003. *ENDGAME Office of Detention and Removal Strategic Plan, 2003–2012: Detention and Removal Strategy for a Secure Homeland.* Washington, DC: U.S. Department of Homeland Security, Immigration and Customs Enforcement.

Taussig, Michael. 2004. "Culture of Terror—Space of Death: Robert Casement's Putumayo Report and the Explanation of Torture." In *Violence in War and Peace,* edited by Nancy Scheper-Hughes and Philippe Bourgois, 39–53. Malden, MA: Wiley-Blackwell.

Taylor, Paul S. 1953. "Songs of the Mexican Migration." In *Puro Mexicano,* edited by J. Frank Dobie, 221–45. Austin: Texas Folklore Society.

Tejeda, Armando. 2008. "En México se trata peor a los migrantes que en EU: Jorge A. Bustamante, relator de la ONU." *La Jornada,* March 16. http://migracion.jornada .com.mx/migracion/noticias/en-mexico-se-trata-peor-a-los-migrantes-que-en -eu-jorge-a-bustamante-relator-de-la-onu/.

Thompson, John. 2002. *Historias de Santos Mexicanos.* México: Editorial Planeta.

Topley, Marjorie. 1955. "Ghost Marriages Among the Singapore Chinese." *Man* 55: 29–30.

Trouillot, Michel-Rolph. 1997. *Silencing the Past: Power and the Production of History.* Boston: Beacon Press.

U.S. Border Patrol. 1994. *Border Patrol Strategic Plan 1994 and Beyond.* Washington, DC: Immigration and Naturalization Service.

U.S. Border Patrol. N.d. "Stats and Summaries." U.S. Customs and Border Protection. http://www.cbp.gov/newsroom/media-resources/stats?title=&page=1.

U.S. Citizenship and Immigration Services. 2003. "INS' Southwest Border Strategy." February 20 (no longer posted). http://uscis.gov/graphics/publicaffairs/fact sheets/BPOps.htm.

U.S. Citizenship and Immigration Services. 2010. *Freedom of Information Act.* https://www.uscis.gov/about-us/freedom-information-and-privacy-act-foia /uscis-freedom-information-act-and-privacy-act.

U.S. Department of Homeland Security. 2007. *2006 Yearbook of Immigration Statistics.* Washington, DC: U.S. Department of Homeland Security, Office of Immigration Statistics. https://www.dhs.gov/xlibrary/assets/statistics/yearbook/2006 /OIS_2006_Yearbook.pdf.

———. 2009. *2008 Yearbook of Immigration Statistics.* Washington, DC: U.S. Department of Homeland Security, Office of Policy, Office of Immigration Statistics.

U.S. Government Accountability Office. 2006. *Illegal Immigration: Border-Crossing Deaths Have Doubled Since 1995; Border Patrol's Efforts to Prevent Deaths Have Not Been Fully Evaluated.* Report to the Honorable Bill Frist, Majority Leader, U.S. Senate, August 16. Washington, DC: U.S. Government Accountability Office.

van der Geest, Sjaak. 2004. "Dying Peacefully: Considering Good Death and Bad Death in Kwahu-Tafo, Ghana." *Social Science and Medicine* 58 (5): 899–911.

Vanderwood, Paul J. 1998. "Santísima Muerte: On the Origin and Development of a Mexican Cult Image." *Journal of the Southwest* 40 (4): 405–36.

———. 2004. *Juan Soldado: Rapist, Murderer, Martyr, Saint.* Durham, NC: Duke University Press.

Warren, Kay B. 1999. "Death Squads and Wider Complicities: Dilemmas for the Anthropology of Violence." In *Death Squad: The Anthropology of State Terror*, edited by Jeffrey Sluka, 226–47. Philadelphia: University of Pennsylvania Press.

Weil, Simone. 1956. *The Notebooks.* Vol. 1. London: Routledge.

Williams, George H. 1962. *Wilderness and Paradise in Christian Thought: The Biblical Experience of the Desert in the History of Christianity.* New York: Harper and Row.

Wilson, Tamar Diana. 2000. "Anti-immigrant Sentiment and the Problem of Reproduction/Maintenance in Mexican Immigration to the United States." *Critique of Anthropology* 20 (2): 191–213.

World Bank. 2008. *Migration and Remittances: Factbook 2008.* Washington DC: World Bank.

Zizek, Slavoj. 2008. *Violence.* London: Verso.

Zlotnik, Hania. 2003. "The Global Dimensions of Female Migration." *Migration Information Source*, March 1. http://www.migrationpolicy.org/article/global -dimensions-female-migration.

CONTRIBUTORS

Bruce E. Anderson is the forensic anthropologist for the Pima County Office of the Medical Examiner (PCOME) in Tucson, Arizona. Dr. Anderson received his PhD degree in 1998 from the University of Arizona, where he is an adjunct assistant professor of anthropology. Before being hired by PCOME in 2000, he served as senior anthropologist for the U.S. Army's Central Identification Laboratory in Hawaii (CILHI) where his principal duties were the field recovery and laboratory analyses leading toward identification of human remains associated with past military conflicts. Dr. Anderson currently mentors anthropology students in the Forensic Anthropology Internship Program at PCOME and works with postdoctoral fellows as part of PCOME's Forensic Anthropology Fellowship Program. He is a fellow in the American Academy of Forensic Sciences (AAFS), is certified as a diplomate by the American Board of Forensic Anthropology (ABFA), is a founding member of the Scientific Working Group in Forensic Anthropology (SWGANTH), and served as a forensic anthropologist during the development and initial launch of the National Missing and Unidentified Persons System (NamUs).

Javier Durán, professor of Spanish and border studies, is a specialist in cultural and literary studies along the U.S.-Mexico border. He is a native of the Arizona-Sonora desert region. Dr. Durán, a three-time University of Arizona alumnus, received his PhD in Hispanic Literatures from Spanish and Portuguese, an MA in Latin American Studies, and a BS in Plant Sciences. Dr. Durán's areas of teaching and research include U.S.-Mexican border studies, Latin American women writers,

Mexican literature and culture, and Chicana/Chicano-Latina/Latino narrative. He has received several research grants from state and federal agencies to conduct research and implement institutional programs during his career and since 2010 he directs the Confluencenter for Creative Inquiry, an interdisciplinary research center in arts, humanities, and social sciences at the University of Arizona. He is the author of the book *José Revueltas: Una poética de la disidencia*, published by the Universidad Veracruzana in Mexico, coeditor of five books on cultural studies, and author of numerous articles on literary and cultural themes. He has been editorial collaborator and reviewer for many journals as well. He is one of the founding members of the MLA Discussion Group on Mexican Cultural and Literary Studies, and he is past president of the Association for Borderland Studies, the leading international organization in the study of border issues. He is also investigating and teaching the connections between globalization, transnational identities, and the Mexican and Latin American diasporas.

Ricardo Elford, C.Ss.R., is a Redemptorist priest who has worked as an activist in the borderlands of the Arizona-Sonora Desert since 1967. For the last sixteen years he has led the Thursday evening vigil convened by Coalición de Derechos Humanos at the shrine of El Tiradito (He who was thrown away) in Tucson. This weekly vigil remembers and honors those killed by deadly enforcement policies and practices. Fr. Ricardo helped found and continues to manage Clínica Amistad, a free health clinic in South Tucson. For more than twenty-five years he has participated in the Community of Christ of the Desert, which embraces some forty-five activists as they gather for liturgy, discussion, and potluck each Saturday evening.

Celestino Fernández served as professor of sociology at the University of Arizona for thirty-nine years until his retirement (July 2015). He has also has served in several administrative positions at the University of Arizona, including the university's first Vice President for Undergraduate Education and Vice President for Academic Outreach and International Affairs, and as the founding Executive Vice President and Provost of Arizona International College. Professor Fernández also served as a university-wide faculty fellow. He taught courses and conducted research on various topics and issues pertaining to culture (including happiness and Mexican music), immigration, ethnic diversity, and education. Professor Fernández has published approximately fifty articles and book chapters on these topics; he has composed about as many *corridos* and served on an equal number of accreditation teams throughout the world. Professor Fernández received both his MA and PhD in sociology from Stanford University. During the years 2000–2001, he served as an American Council on Education (ACE) Fellow at the University of Phoenix. Professor Fernández has received wide recognition for his work. For example, he was honored by the American Association for Higher Education for his "Distinguished Leadership in Higher Education" and by the governor of Arizona for his commitment to "quality and excellence." He also received the "Distinguished Alumni Award" from his undergraduate alma mater, Sonoma State University. Professor Fernández has been the subject of three songs and two book chapters. In 2007, Professor Fernández was named University Distinguished Outreach Professor in recognition of his "exceptional service to the community, state, and nation."

Jessie K. Finch is an assistant professor of sociology at Stockton University in Galloway, New Jersey. She specializes in the study of race and ethnicity, the criminalization of immigration, identity conflict, social psychology, and Latino/a health disparities. She also studies culture—specifically popular culture and media. She has a PhD (2015) and MA (2011) in sociology from the University of Arizona and a BA (2007) in sociology and music from the University of Tulsa. Jessie has published in peer-reviewed journals such as *Teaching Sociology* and *Sociological Spectrum* and has received grants from the National Science Foundation and other sources. She currently teaches courses on deviance, popular culture, and happiness.

James S. Griffith received all three of his degrees from the University of Arizona, including a PhD in cultural anthropology and art history in 1973. From 1979 until his retirement in 1998 he ran the university's Southwest Folklore Center. He is currently a research associate at the university's Southwest Center. With his wife, Loma, he started the annual Tucson Meet Yourself folklife festival. Although he retired as director of the festival in 1995, he is once again heavily involved in this project. From about 1985, he wrote and hosted "Southern Arizona Traditions," a weekly three-minute spot on KUAT-TV's *Arizona Illustrated* program. He curated eleven exhibitions of regional traditional arts, the most recent being *"La Cadena Que No Se Corta/*The Unbroken Chain: The Traditional Arts of Tucson's Mexican American Community," at the University of Arizona Museum of Art in the winter of 1996–1997. Griffith has written seven books and many articles on the folklore and folk arts of the Border region. His most recent book is *A Border Runs Through It: Journeys in Regional History and Folklore* (Rio Nuevo, 2011). James S. Griffith's professional commitment has always been to try to understand the cultures of this part of the border and to pass along that understanding, as respectfully and accurately as possible, to the general public. He is currently researching for a book on the religious art of Sonora.

Born in Fowler, California, **Juan Felipe Herrera** attended the University of California, Los Angeles, on an Equal Opportunity Grant and Stanford University majoring in social anthropology, and received his MFA in poetry from the University of Iowa. In the late sixties, he became involved with the exciting *Floricanto* poetry generation and Chicano *Teatro* civil rights movement—reading and performing at schools, prisons, farm worker camps, and in many college campuses across the nation. With twenty-nine books published in poetry, spoken word, novels for young adults, and collections for children, he continues to work for all audiences and in 2015 was named Poet Laureate of the United States. Juan Felipe's awards for his writing include the Guggenheim Fellowship, the National Book Critic's Circle Award, the Latino International Award, the PEN USA award, the PEN Beyond Margins award, and the Josephine Miles Pen/Oakland Award. He serves as a chancellor on the board of chancellors for the Academy of American Poetry. He is professor of creative writing at the University of California, Riverside. Juan Felipe says, "If you want to write for the people pour kindness inside every word."

Claudio Lomnitz works on culture and politics in Mexico and in the Americas. His books include *Evolución de una sociedad rural* (Fondo de Cultura Económica, 1982); *Exits from the Labyrinth: Culture and Ideology in Mexican National Space* (University of California Press, 1992); *Modernidad Indiana: Nación y mediación en México* (Planeta, 1999); *Deep Mexico, Silent Mexico: An Anthropology of Nationalism* (University of Minnesota Press, 2001); *Death and the Idea of Mexico* (Zone Books, 2005); and, most recently, *The Return of Comrade Ricardo Flores Magón* (Zone Books, 2014). The Spanish version of *Death and the Idea of Mexico* was awarded the García Cubas prize for the best scientific contribution to anthropology and history and the award of Mexico's Camara de la Industria Editorial (CANIERM) for the best sociological essay; *The Return of Comrade Ricardo Flores Magón* was awarded the Latin American Studies Association's prize for best book published on Mexico in the humanities. Lomnitz is also the author of a number of journalistic essays and of a historical drama that received Mexico's National Drama Award in 2010. He served a term as editor of the journal *Public Culture* and has an op-ed column in the Mexico City paper *La Jornada*. Claudio Lomnitz is the Campbell Family Professor of Anthropology and founding director of the Center for Mexican Studies at Columbia University.

Daniel E. Martínez, PhD, is an assistant professor in the Department of Sociology and inaugural director of the Cisneros Hispanic Leadership Institute at George Washington University. He is a coprincipal investigator of the Migrant Border Crossing Study, a Ford Foundation–funded research project that involves interviewing recently deported unauthorized migrants about their experiences crossing the U.S.-Mexico border and residing in the United States. Martínez also does extensive research on undocumented border-crosser deaths along the U.S.-Mexico border. He received his PhD from the School of Sociology at the University of Arizona, and he holds an MA in sociology and an MS in Mexican American studies, also from the University of Arizona. Martínez would like to dedicate his chapter in this volume to his mentor, teacher, elder, and friend, Steve Casanova, who lost his battle with cancer in 2009.

Araceli Masterson-Algar received her PhD in border studies from the University of Arizona. She is currently associate professor and coordinator of Latin/o American Studies at Augustana College in Rock Island, Illinois, and associate editor of the *Journal of Urban Cultural Studies*. She is the author of *Ecuadorians in Madrid: Migrants' Place in Urban History* (Palgrave-Macmillan 2015). She teaches courses on Latin/o America and border studies, often with a focus on the cultural expressions of human mobility in transnational urban contexts. In the Quad Cities (Illinois-Iowa), she is co-founder of the Palomares Social Justice Center, a grassroots organization that works with residents of Mexican origin in the area, most of them with ties to the state of Guanajuato.

Alex Nava received his PhD from the University of Chicago in Religious Studies and is currently associate professor of religious studies at the University of Arizona. His first book is a study of the French philosopher Simone Weil and the Peruvian theologian Gustavo Gutierrez titled *The Mystical and Prophetic Thought of Simone Weil and Gustavo Gutierrez*. He recently completed his second major book on the theme of religion and literature in Latin America titled *Wonder and Exile in the New World*.

Anna Ochoa O'Leary holds a doctorate in cultural anthropology from the University of Arizona. Her dissertation research, "Investment in Female Education as an Economic Strategy Among U.S.-Mexican Households in Nogales, Arizona," was supported by a National Science Foundation grant. She is currently associate professor and head of the Department of Mexican American Studies at the University of Arizona, where she also codirects the Binational Migration Institute. In 2006 she was awarded a Fulbright scholarship to research the project "Women at the Intersection: Immigration Enforcement and Transnational Migration on the U.S.-Mexico Border," in which migrant women's encounters with immigration enforcement agents was examined. She has published numerous research articles in both English and Spanish on migration and gender. She has also published a Chicano studies textbook, *Chicano Studies: The Discipline and the Journey* (Kendall Hunt, 2007), is coeditor (with Colin Deeds and Scott Whiteford) of *Unchartered Terrain: New Directions in Border Research Method and Ethics* (University of Arizona Press, 2013), and has edited a two-volume reference work, *Undocumented Immigrants in the United States Today: An Encyclopedia of Their Experiences* (ABC-CLIO/Greenwood Press, 2014).

Bruce O. Parks is a clinical professor of pathology at the University of Arizona Department of Pathology and former chief medical examiner of Pima County, Arizona (1991–2011). Following graduation from medical school, he completed a residency in anatomic and clinical pathology and then a fellowship in forensic pathology, all at the University of Arizona. Teaching responsibilities at the University of Arizona include pathology resident instruction and lectures to medical students. He is a fellow of the American Academy of Forensic Sciences and a member of the National Association of Medical Examiners. Research interests of Dr. Parks include heat-related death and traumatic injuries. He has published in scientific medical journals including the *Journal of Forensic Sciences* and the *American Journal of Forensic Medicine and Pathology*. In 2006, Dr. Parks coauthored "Unauthorized Border Crossings and Migrant Deaths: Arizona, New Mexico, and El Paso, Texas," which was published in the *American Journal of Public Health*. The Pima County medical examiner's office shares data on migrant deaths with multiple other researchers.

Eric Peters in an American Board of Pathology–certified forensic pathologist and has been practicing forensic pathology full time since 1997. He is the deputy chief medical examiner for Pima County, Arizona (Tucson) and is a clinical associate professor of pathology at the University of Arizona. He has performed nearly five thousand forensic autopsies and has testified at trial, deposition, and pretrial interviews more than two hundred times. He has consulted for the prosecution and defense in both criminal and civil cases at the county, state, and federal levels.

Cynthia Porterfield is a forensic pathologist working at the Pima County Office of the Medical Examiner. She earned her doctor of osteopathic medicine degree from the Chicago College of Osteopathic Medicine in 1989. She holds certifications from the American Board of Pathology in anatomic pathology (1996) and forensic pathology (1997). Her residency was at Michael Reese Hospital at the University of Illinois in anatomic and clinical pathology from 1989 to 1993. She also held a fellowship at the Cook County Office of the Medical Examiner focusing on forensic pathology from 1993 to 1994.

Robin Reineke is cofounder and executive director of the Colibri Center for Human Rights (www.colibricenter.org), a family advocacy organization working to end death and suffering on the U.S.-Mexico border by partnering with families of the dead and the missing. From Seattle, Washington, Reineke received a BA in anthropology from Bryn Mawr College and an MA in anthropology from the University of Arizona, where she is currently a doctoral candidate in the School of Anthropology completing her dissertation titled "Naming the Dead: Identification and Ambiguity Along the U.S.-Mexico Border." In 2014, she was awarded the Institute for Policy Studies' Letelier-Moffitt Human Rights Award and the Echoing Green Global Fellowship.

Raquel Rubio-Goldsmith, a native of Douglas, Arizona, earned her undergraduate and graduate degree in law and philosophy at the National Autonomous University of Mexico in Mexico, D.F. Founding faculty in history at Pima Community College (1969), she taught there until 1999, when she retired. While establishing history courses in the history of Mexican Americans, African Americans, Yaquis, and Tohono-O'odham nations, Rubio-Goldsmith focused her historical research on the history of Mexicana/Chicana on the U.S. Mexico border. Several scholarly articles presented at conferences were published both in the United States and in Mexico. Working in and with community partners has resulted in forty-five years of volunteer work in immigrant rights. A member of Manzo Area Council and later the Coalición de Derechos Humanos, she has developed numerous community-based research projects targeting the effects of U.S. immigration border enforcement on Mexicano and Latino communities. Joining other faculty, she has helped establish the Binational Migration Institute at the Department of Mexican American Studies at the University of Arizona. Through the institute, Rubio-Goldsmith conducts collaborative research with faculty, students, and the community that continues to result in numerous reports on migrant deaths on the border.

Prescott L. Vandervoet is an importer and distributor of fresh produce grown in Mexico and marketed in the United States and Canada. He is a strong proponent for building a more resilient local community and economy in his home of Nogales, Arizona. Using cross-border trade as a vehicle for a larger message, Prescott hopes to create a greater awareness of the effects of migration and trade policy on communities along the U.S.-Mexico border. He has previously been a research analyst at the Udall Center for Studies in Public Policy at the University of Arizona. His research interests include human-environment interactions along the U.S.-Mexico border, especially within the Sonoran Desert region. He holds bachelor and master degrees from the University of Arizona in ecology and evolutionary biology and Latin American studies, respectively. A lifelong resident of southern Arizona, Prescott has observed the evolving Arizona/Sonora borderlands for over twenty years.

David Winston is a forensic pathologist in Pima County, Arizona. He earned his undergraduate degree at Saint Louis University and completed his PhD and MD degrees at the Medical University of South Carolina. After his anatomic and clinical pathology residency, he completed his forensic pathology fellowship at the Office of the Medical Investigator in Albuquerque, New Mexico. He is board-certified in anatomic, clinical, and forensic pathology. He is a fellow of the National Association of Medical Examiners and the American Academy of Forensic Sciences. He has faculty appointments at the University of Arizona School of Medicine—which includes teaching medical students, pathology residents, and forensic pathology fellows—and Pima Community College, where he teaches a forensic pathology and death investigation course. He has published articles in the *American Journal of Forensic Pathology and Medicine*, *Journal of Forensic Sciences*, and *Academic Forensic Pathology*. In 2015 he co-authored "Management of Undocumented Border Crosser Remains," which was published in *Academic Forensic Pathology*. He has also co-authored an e-book, *Crossing the Line*—a fictional mystery based on the investigation of skeletal remains found in the Sonoran Desert—under the pseudonym A. L. Gomortis.

Jane Zavisca is an associate professor of sociology at the University of Arizona. She received her PhD in sociology from the University of California, Berkeley, in 2004. Her research focuses on the cultural underpinnings of political and economic institutions, in particular the legitimation of housing and mortgages markets. Her book *Housing the New Russia* (Cornell University Press, 2012), explores the sociological consequences of Russia's failed attempt to create a housing market modeled on the

American system. She is currently conducting survey research on the economic, demographic, and political consequences of housing status in several post-Soviet countries. She is also conducting research on the cultural foundations of mortgages in the United States. Professor Zavisca's teaching reflects these interests: she teaches courses on cultural sociology, the social meaning of money and credit, and research design.

INDEX

Note: Page numbers in *italics* indicate illustrations.